DRUG USE IN THE WORKPLACE

DRUG USE IN THE WORKPLACE

*Risk Factors for Disruptive
Substance Use Among Young Adults*

MICHAEL D. NEWCOMB
University of California, Los Angeles
University of Southern California

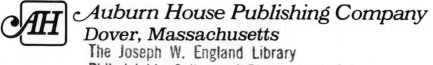
Auburn House Publishing Company
Dover, Massachusetts

Library of Congress Cataloging in Publication Data

Newcomb, Michael D.
   Drug use in the workplace: risk factors for disruptive substance use among young adults / Michael D. Newcomb.
      p.   cm.
   Bibliography: p.
   Includes index.
   ISBN 0-86569-182-7
   1. Drugs and employment—United States.   2. Young adults—United States—Drug use.   I. Title.
HF5549.5.D7N49   1988
658.3'82—dc19   87-34921
                                                           CIP
Printed in the United States of America

*To my father, Donald (Bud) Newcomb,
a man with a warm heart, much concern,
and many talents. Thank you, Dad.*

PREFACE

Substance use is a part of life and the lifestyle of many people in this country. This includes the ingestion of licit drugs such as alcohol, cigarettes, and over-the-counter medications as well as illicit substances such as marijuana and cocaine. An extreme use of any drug is devastating for the individual, for family and friends, and for society as a whole. When does use of a drug become abuse with the attendant adverse consequences?

Abuse can be defined in several ways, including amount consumed per occasion, negative consequences of use, physical or psychological addiction, and location or circumstances of use. This book focuses on the last definition for abuse; specifically, using drugs in work or school settings. Any use of psychoactive substances on the job or in school is not appropriate and can be considered abuse, since such behavior is antithetical to the function of that environment (i.e., working or learning). The only exceptions to this general principle are those jobs or classes that require drug use as an aspect of the task, such as whiskey taster or instructor in a wine-tasting class.

Currently, little is known about the extent of drug use in the workplace or in school. Even less is known about the type of person who engages in drug use on the job, determinants of such behavior, and the stability over time of using drugs in inappropriate settings. Using data from an ongoing longitudinal study of adolescents and young adults from the general community, I explore these issues and concerns in this book. The primary task of this volume is to describe the extent and nature of drug use on the job and in school for this group of people. Information regarding these patterns is vital for developing policy and techniques for prevention and intervention for dealing with drugs in the workplace.

This longitudinal study was originally begun by Dr. P. M. Bentler in the mid-1970s and he has maintained his involvement all along. He is a good friend and colleague and his support for this book is much appreciated. Several other people have worked on

vii

this project at various points and left their mark. These include Drs. Lisa Harlow, George Huba, Ebrahim Maddahian, and Joseph Wingard. Julie Speckart has handled all manuscript and figure preparation for this work, and her patience and meticulousness are fondly appreciated. Sandy Yu performed many of the analyses and all file preparations, for which she deserves my warm gratitude. Others who have helped with the preparation of this volume include Belinda Fong, Valerie Levine, Phuong Nguyen, and Doris Wong.

   This project exists because of the continuous funding provided by the National Institute on Drug Abuse in the form of program project grant DA 01070. We particularly appreciate the support, energy, and guidance offered by our current grant monitor, Dr. Beatrice Rouse, as well as her predecessors, Drs. Dan Lettieri and Louise Richards.

   This project also exists because of the cooperation and honesty of the participants. These young adults have contributed to this study for a substantial portion of their lives. Their dedication and willingness to advance these scientific efforts are vital to the success of this project. They have been asked many personal, private, and sensitive questions about their lives, and their candid and forthright responses guarantee an accurate, rich, and meaningful study of drug use in the workplace. To each of these young adults, I extend my heartfelt gratitude and appreciation for sharing their lives with us.

   Finally, but not at all the least, I want to thank Kathleen Andrews for her support and encouragement, both personally and professionally. She has been patient and tolerant, and I think she is glad this is finished.

MICHAEL D. NEWCOMB

CONTENTS

Chapter 1

INTRODUCTION

This book presents the first in-depth series of integrated analyses of drug use in the workplace from the perspective of the employee. Prior to developing and implementing effective education, prevention, policy, detection, and intervention procedures, we must have an accurate assessment and portrayal of the problem. Without much critical information, such procedures may be poorly gauged to the magnitude of the problem, ineffective because of unproven assumptions, misdirected because of an inadequate understanding of the nature of the problem, and not cost effective. The necessary detailed information has not yet appeared in the literature, and is the subject of this book.

Using data from a community sample of young adults, I explore the extent and patterns of drug use at work or school. Use of both licit and illicit drugs is examined, including alcohol, cannabis, and cocaine. Psychosocial factors such as personality, social integration, psychological functioning, deviant behaviors, attitudes, problems in life, and background characteristics are used to help understand individual propensities to use drugs on the job or in school. In addition, information gathered from these same people while in high school (including drug use in the classroom) is used to trace stability and change in using drugs in inappropriate settings over time. Psychosocial factors are examined to determine whether these can predict changes in drug use at work over the span of time from adolescence to young adulthood. Drug use at work or school is also related to other types of drug problems, such as selling drugs and driving while intoxicated. Finally, based on the results of these analyses, I present two indices of risk factors for predicting levels of use of drugs at work or school.

This book is designed for the experienced drug counselor and researcher who wants additional information and understanding about drug use in the workplace. It is also directed toward nondrug experts who have a vested interest in confronting drug use at work or in school, such as managers, supervisors, educators, policymakers, program designers, and employers.

There has been little research to date that has systematically examined issues and factors related to drug use in the workplace. There has been a great deal of speculation and armchair philosophizing, but little hard, data-based research. As a result, it is not possible to integrate the present findings into an extensive literature. In lieu of this, I provide reviews of the general drug use literature pertinent to particular issues related to drug use in the workplace. Although more general, this review at least provides the reader with an overview of a particular area and identifies specific questions that are addressed later in this book. These brief reviews should be particularly useful for the nondrug experts who are unfamiliar with the vast area of drug research (and who may not have the time to study it in depth) and how it applies to their particular problems in business, industry, and education.

Background

For a variety of complex reasons, drug use and abuse have again become top national and even international concerns. The dramatic increases in the incidence and prevalence of substance use, particularly among teenagers and young adults, have been characterized as epidemic increases (e.g., Robins, 1984). Drug use increased through the 1960s and 1970s, reached a peak in the early 1980s, and has remained generally stable since then (e.g., see Johnston, O'Malley, & Bachman, 1987 for a summary of yearly assessments of high school seniors; see Miller, Cisin, Gardner-Keaton, Harrell, Wirtz, Abelson, & Fishburne, 1983 and NIDA, 1986, 1987 for repeated national assessments of all age groups). One notable exception has been the continued rise in cocaine use, particularly among young adults in the western and eastern portions of the United States (e.g., Cohen, 1987; Kandel, Murphy, & Karus, 1985; Newcomb & Bentler, 1987a, 1988a). Of particular concern has been the increase in cocaine variants such as crack, free-basing, and coca paste. Because of the higher concentration of cocaine in these forms and therefore its more immediate access to the brain, these variants have resulted in increased deaths, hospital admissions, and likelihood of addiction (e.g., Estroff, 1987; Siegel, 1987; Wetli, 1987). These rather tragic and dramatic events have increased concern regarding the use of cocaine on the job (e.g., DuPont, 1987).

Even though the use of other drugs, both licit (alcohol, cigarettes, over-the-counter medications, prescribed drugs) and illicit (marijuana, stimulants, psychedelics, inhalants, hypnotics), has appeared to stabilize and even decline, the prevalence of use has leveled off at a point some people consider too high (e.g., Robins, 1984; Washton & Gold, 1987). Regular ingestion of drugs has become part of a lifestyle for many Americans (e.g., Castro, Newcomb, & Cadish, 1987) that goes beyond the benign use of substances in innocuous settings.

One major component of this national concern with drug abuse has been a focus on drug use in the workplace. For years employers have been plagued by the occasional alcoholic employee, who may be frequently absent or tardy and may in fact drink on the job. Recently, however, there has been a growing concern that this behavior is increasing and that the problem of drug use is no longer limited to the use of alcohol. All sorts of drugs are now creating havoc for employers, with increases especially in cocaine and marijuana use. Much of this concern is prompted by firsthand experience and accounts from managers and employers. Unfortunately, there are no large-scale surveys to substantiate these personal accounts and help managers understand this phenomenon in order to develop prevention and intervention programs. It is essential to understand the type of employee who is engaging in these behaviors and what motivates such behavior.

Many of these issues are addressed in this book, which focuses on the prevalence, patterns, and factors that are related to using drugs on the job. Drug use in the workplace is a type of substance abuse that is characterized by the location of occurrence. It is the ingestion of psychoactive substances in a setting not appropriate for being drunk, stoned, or high. As a result, this type of drug use is often, if not ultimately always if continued, disruptive and antithetical to the tasks of the environment. Thus, I have called drug use in the workplace disruptive drug use. If disruptive drug use is characterized by the setting of use, at least one other context is inappropriate for the ingestion of psychoactive substance; this is the classroom. In this book, I consider both types of disruptive substance use: that which occurs in school (high school and college) and that which occurs on the job.

There are many potential negative consequences from disruptive substance use, including the endangerment of self, other workers, and the public, loss of wages and productivity on the job, and academic failure, dropping out of school, and disturbance in class-room settings. Several of these losses are reviewed further below.

Unfortunately, few adequate or appropriate data exist to assess the magnitude, range, patterns, and predictors of disruptive drug use. Although alcohol is believed to be the most frequently used drug in the workplace (e.g., Cohen, 1986), comparison data on other drugs and their relationship to alcohol are not currently available. A few surveys have attempted to assess drug use in the worksite, and these typically gather estimates from management or union sources as opposed to the employee (e.g., Schreier, 1987; Steele, 1981). Such methods can elicit perceptions of the problem from knowledgeable observers who have hands-on experience with the problem. Nevertheless, these perceptions are undoubtedly influenced or distorted by a range of factors that threaten reliability. These influences may be the popular press or media. One distortion is that the typical employee may actively conceal his or her drug-using behaviors, particularly from managers and supervisors. From these types of data bases, Steele (1981) reported that 61 percent of union leaders and members felt that drug use in the workplace was a major problem. In the same survey, 76 percent reported that they felt there was an increase in drug use at work during the past five years and 54 percent believed that this increase would continue during the next five years. Clearly, these respondents considered drug use on the job to be a significant and growing problem.

Schreier (1987) has conducted four large surveys of employers regarding their experiences with drug problems in their businesses and the actions they have taken and plan to take regarding drug use on the job. These surveys have been taken every five years beginning in 1971. According to the most recent data, obtained in 1986, 95 percent of the employers had had a direct experience with handling a drug problem among their workers, and 98 percent felt that the problem was as bad or worse than it was five years ago. This corroborates the prediction from the earlier Steele (1981) survey that the drug problem in the workplace would increase during the coming five years. Over the several years of surveys, managerial concern has increased in two areas: cocaine and women. In the 1986 survey, 42 percent of the employers felt that women were abusing alcohol and other drugs more than in previous years. Similarly, 58 percent of the managers reported that cocaine was a problem in their company. The second figure is up from only 21 percent in 1981. On the other hand, more than half of those employers surveyed in 1986 felt that the problem of drug abuse at work would decline over the next five years. This was attributed to the increasing use of drug testing in the work environment and preemployment screenings. Although most managers favored prevention and education over harsher policies (fines, dismissal, lawsuits), fully 42 percent were testing their employees for drugs and 12 percent planned to initiate testing in the near future.

Despite the intriguing and informative aspects of these figures, little is known about the actual levels of drug use on the job, who is doing it, and what it is related to. In order to combat or prevent a problem it is essential to be fully informed about it. To gain an in-depth understanding of the problem, it is necessary to study the person who engages in disruptive drug use and contrast this person to those who do not.

In part because of a lack of knowledge regarding the extent, types, patterns, and correlates of drug use on the job, and in part because of the legitimate concerns for the livelihood, health, and safety of their employees and the survival of their businesses, many employers are grappling with the decision to institute drug testing of their workers (e.g., ADAMHA, 1987; Cohen, 1986; Hawks & Chiang, 1986). There are many practical and legal problems associated with drug testing in industry. Currently, the judicial system is confronting the question of the legality of such testing practices. There are also many problems with the actual testing procedures that affect the accuracy of the results. Nevertheless, nearly 30 percent of the Fortune 500 companies screen applicants for drug use and about 20 percent more are expected to begin testing in the near future (Castro, 1986).

Historical Perspective

Drug use has been a part of civilization since before recorded history. It is not a new problem, but one that receives cyclical attention on a national level. The heroic attempt and dramatic failure at Prohibition is well known. Similarly, the country grappled with cocaine in the early 1900s, "reefer madness" in the 1940s, and the drug cultures of the 1960s. Cocaine has again become a major problem along with the more exotic and difficult to detect "designer drugs."

A thorough review of the historical patterns and movements regarding drug use is beyond the scope of this book, and has been published elsewhere (e.g., Grinspoon & Bakalar, 1976 for cocaine). We can consider, however, a facet of the problem. An interesting history of drug use at work has been reviewed recently by Fillmore

(1984). She concludes that many of the changes in regard to the acceptability of drug use on the job have arisen as a result of the Industrial Revolution and the temperance movement. In fact, she points out that "prior to the industrial revolution, work and drinking appear to have been inseparable in the U.S. Although the drunken worker was disapproved, especially among the Puritans, drinking in the workplace was considered normal behavior. Drink was long associated with hard work" (p. 41). Thus, the condemnation of drug use in the workplace is a relatively recent development, arising largely out of the Industrial Revolution and the temperance movement. Even more recent is the growing awareness of the many "costs" of alcohol and drug abuse on the job (e.g., Quayle, 1983).

Costs of Disruptive Drug Use

The costs of drug and alcohol abuse are difficult to calculate for a variety of obvious and less than obvious reasons. Several attempts have been made to determine a "bottom line" monetary loss from drug use. These figures are always in the multibillions of dollars and have been increasing over the past twenty years. For instance, in 1971 the Institute of Alcohol Abuse and Alcoholism estimated that alcohol cost the country $25.4 billion, which rose to $32 billion in 1975 (cited in Belohlav & Popp, 1983). The Research Triangle Institute estimated that drug abuse cost the U.S. economy $47 billion in 1980, which increased to $60 billion in 1983 (cited in Bompey, 1986). More recently, the Metropolitan Life Insurance Company estimated that the direct cost of drug abuse to industry was $85 billion annually (cited in Cohen, 1984). Finally, the Alcohol, Drug Abuse, and Mental Health Administration estimated that business loses nearly $100 billion a year in lost productivity because of alcohol and drug abuse (Consensus Summary, 1986). These problems and costs are not limited to the United States. McDonnell and Maynard (1985) estimated that in England and Wales the social cost of alcohol misuse was in excess of £1.5 billion per year.

These figures are certainly staggeringly high. Partridge and Reed (1980) point out, however, that approximately 10 percent of the workforce have drug and alcohol problems, but cause management over 80 percent of their personnel problems. Included in these direct cost estimates are lost time, impaired productivity, injuries, absenteeism, and medical and insurance costs (Bompey, 1986; Burmaster, 1985; Cohen, 1984). Less tangible but not less devastating losses can result from the effects of disruptive drug use on social behavior, psychological functioning, and morale. Belohlav and Popp (1983) cite a partial list of additional problems related to drug abuse on the job that are not routinely included in the cost analyses. These include "faulty decision making, on- or off-the-job accidents, thefts, impaired morale of fellow workers, friction among workers, impaired consumer and public relations, early retirement, premature disability and death, personnel turnover, the loss of skilled or valued employees" (p. 31). Clearly, the list of problems and costs, both financial and psychological, from alcohol and drug abuse on the job is extensive and impressive.

Alcohol and drug abuse is considered one of the unresolved safety problems of industry (Lederer, 1985). For instance, Burmaster (1985) pointed out that "drug use at work affects perception, eye-hand coordination, and judgment. Injuries to the user and his fellow workers, damage to equipment, and the production of defective products are a common result. Loss of imagination, creativity, and decision-making capability can be costly to an enterprise and jeopardize the employment security of every employee" (p. 39). Cohen (1984) has identified several security and safety threats from drug and alcohol abuse on the job, including injury to self, injury to others, illness, absenteeism, breakage and rejected products, demoralization of the sober workforce, and theft. Cohen (1984) further pointed out that the reduced capacity resulting from alcohol and marijuana use persists beyond the period of intoxication, or feeling high. He gave an example related to airplane pilots that emphasized that the old adage of "12 hours from bottle to throttle" no longer applies. "The Federal Aviation Administration's requirement of an 8-hour alcohol-free interval before anyone can enter an airplane cockpit is much too brief to ensure full recovery from a binge or drug 'run' " (p. 4). Even the social drinkers have been defined as a liability to a company, since even though they "walk steadily and talk clearly, [they] are always somewhat mentally impaired, often for four to sixteen hours after lunch or a night out with the gang. Their poor judgment and ill-considered decisions could be running [the] company into the ground" (Beeman, 1985, p. 54).

Although we cannot deny the persisting aftereffects of drug use, we must maintain our perspective when confronting such an emotional and difficult issue as disruptive drug use. Certainly social drinking practices may affect employee behavior, but it is doubtful that they are "running your company into the ground," as Beeman (1985) would have us believe. Similar inflammatory and misleading (if not outright falsehoods) are being bantered about by both researchers and employers, and fueling the national hysteria over drug abuse. There is certainly a problem, but it is vital to keep it in perspective. For instance, Burmaster (1985) commented that "27 percent to 45 percent of their [academic institutions, commercial enterprises, government agencies, and industrial corporations] employed population is using illegal drugs to get through the day" (p. 39). This is inaccurate and misleading. The statement implies that over one-quarter of all employees are using illegal drugs (not counting alcohol) on a daily basis at work. This is simply not true and only serves to heighten the national and corporate hysteria. There is a problem and it must be addressed, but from a realistic and informed position, not from a misleading and uninformed bias.

Drug Use in the Military

Some of the best, though most problematic, data regarding the extent, correlates, and consequences of drug use on the job come from studies of the military (e.g., Cook, Walizer, & Mace, 1976). In one study, Beary, Mazzuchi, and Richie (1983) characterized drug use in the military as an adolescent misbehavior problem. They found that alcohol and cannabis were the most frequently used substances. Rates were highest for men, under twenty-five years of age, single, enlisted, and with little education. Newcomb and Bentler (1987a) found that alcohol and cigarette use increased upon joining the military, whereas use of illicit substances such as marijuana decreased. They interpreted these results as a reflection of the acceptance and prohibition of various types of drugs by the military, either implicitly or explicitly. Alcohol and cigarettes are tolerated substances (if not part of the mystique of military life), whereas illicit drugs provoke obvious and stringent sanctions. This finding supports an environmental demand factor in patterns of drug use (e.g., Burt, 1982).

Bray et al. (1986) reported on three anonymous surveys of drug use in the U.S. military that were taken in 1980, 1982, and 1985. They found that current illicit drug use (defined as use during the past thirty days) was at a high of 27 percent in 1980, decreased to 19 percent in 1982, and continued decreasing to 9 percent in 1985. The most commonly used illicit drug in 1985 was marijuana, with 7 percent reporting use during the past month. These substantial decreases in illicit drug use have been attributed in part to urine and breath testing for drug use instituted in the late 1970s. In fact, 23 percent of the respondents indicated that the urine-testing program kept them from trying some drugs. The reports on alcohol, however, are not as encouraging. In 1982, 14 percent reported heavy alcohol use (defined as five or more drinks on at least one occasion during the past week), which dropped slightly (but not statistically significantly) to 12 percent in 1985. Alcohol abuse appears to remain a substantial problem among the military. A 1983 survey of alcoholic soldiers receiving treatment indicated that more than three-quarters had used drugs other than alcohol (Hawkins, Kruzich, & Smith, 1985), emphasizing a problem of polydrug use at least among the heavy users.

These data are not directly applicable to determining the prevalence of disruptive or worksite drug use because they reflect general prevalence of drug use among military personnel, not specific use on the job. On-the-job use is difficult to define for military personnel, since the armed forces often constitute a "total environment" (e.g., Goffman, 1961) for its members. For example, Cohen (1984) points out that "in the military, where the individual is supposed to be available for duty at all times, even off-duty use can be considered culpable" (p. 5).

Corroborating the view that these drug use prevalence rates among the military may partially represent disruptive drug use are figures on lost productivity. In the same three surveys, Bray et al. (1986) found that lost productivity from reduced work performance, neglect of duty, intoxication at work, and tardiness resulting from drug use was over 20 percent in 1980. This figure decreased to 14 percent in 1982 and to 5 percent in 1985. Clearly, this decrease in lost productivity paralleled the decrease in illicit substance use. Allen and Mazzuchi (1985) examined the adverse consequences of alcohol and drug use in the 1980 and 1982 surveys for the four branches of the service and identified some interesting trends. Diminished work performance because of alcohol increased from 1980 (27 percent) to 1982 (34 percent), whereas diminished work performance from drug use decreased in the same period (as noted above). Diminished work performance because of alcohol was highest for the navy (42 percent in 1982) and lowest for the air force. Diminished work performance because of drug use was highest in the army (18 percent in 1982) and lowest again in the air force (7 percent). Drug and alcohol use in the military is not limited to the U.S. armed forces. In fact, substantial problems have been noted in the Canadian military and other armed forces (e.g., Lanphier & McCauley, 1985).

Certainly the military is not the only profession where drug use is a problem. Unfortunately, detailed data such as those cited above are not as readily available from other professions, particularly regarding lost productivity and drug use on the job. What is known about drug use and other occupations is summarized next.

Occupation and Drug Use

Particular occupations have long been associated with heavy drinking, as have certain countries. People in different types of jobs and in different countries certainly exhibit differences in drug usage, although the reasons behind these differences are not so clear. Most studies on these issues have focused on alcohol consumption and not other drugs.

For instance, based upon per capita consumption levels of alcohol, France, Italy, and Australia have the highest rates of alcohol use. The United States has the fifth highest (Hughes, 1975). These differences may reflect a national climate or attitude toward drug use, which in turn inhibits or allows drug use. It is not clear how such attitudes would affect levels of disruptive drug use, beyond creating a sociocultural context that may be conducive to or constraining on such behavior.

A variety of methods have been used to establish links between alcoholism and occupation. These have included surveys of alcohol treatment populations, agencies, and the general population and its drinking habits, as well as mortality studies, particularly of deaths from cirrhosis (e.g., Olkinuora, 1984; Plant, 1977). Results from these types of studies have identified occupations at high and low risk for alcohol problems. Those in the high-risk category are workers in entertainment and the liquor trade, caterers, seamen, executives, the military, service workers, laborers, doctors, lawyers, and medical students (e.g., Olkinuora, 1984; Plant, 1977, 1981; Slattery, Alderson, & Bryant, 1986). Jobs at low risk for alcohol treatment and mortality from cirrhosis include engineering foremen, jewelers, farmers, chemists, public drivers, construction employees, gardeners, and shopkeepers (Slattery et al., 1986). Workers in these low-risk occupations faced the threat of job loss for drunkenness; they were often "skilled craftsmen who underwent a lengthy period of apprenticeship or those who still work with their hands as well as their brains" (Slattery et al., 1986, p. 933).

The social dynamics of particular jobs or occupations that foster drinking are more easily identified than national characteristics that do the same, and may help account for the differential levels of drug use across occupations. Olkinuora (1984) and Plant (1981) identified several factors that were related to the connection between occupation and alcoholism. These included the availability of alcohol at work, social pressure to drink on the job, separation from normal social relationships, freedom from supervision, very high or very low income, collusion by colleagues, strains, stresses, and hazards, and preselection of high-risk people.

One question naturally arises is whether a person who is predisposed to alcohol problems is also attracted to specific professions, or whether certain professions contribute to the alcohol problems. In other words, a person may choose a particular job for the same reasons that propel his or her involvement with drugs. Thus, an association between drug or alcohol use and certain jobs may be accounted for by a third confounding factor located within the individual and not the work setting. Plant (1978, 1979) attempted to tease apart these differing hypotheses by comparing new recruits to the drink or brewery trade (a very high risk occupation) to those applying for jobs at low risk for alcohol problems. He found that those who applied to the liquor jobs had poorer employment records and were heavier drinkers prior to their employment in the alcohol production industry than were the applicants to lower-risk occupations. This supports the preselection hypothesis. Plant also found that those in the liquor industry increased their drinking behavior (including on the job) in conformity to perceived social norms. Thus, for at least this occupation self-selection and environmental pressure account for the higher rates of alcoholism.

Cosper (1979) and Cosper and Hughes (1982) challenged the notion that heavy drinking occupations actually reflect alcohol abuse or alcoholism. They suggest that the frequency, not the quantity of drinking, is higher in certain occupations and may not reflect problematic levels. They propose that conformity to norms of an occupation may generate these differences, and thus may not be indicative of deviance or low social conformity. Although this may be true in certain jobs (they studied naval officers and journalists), it does not account for the differential treatment rates or mortality differences.

Few of these studies consider the problem of drug use on the job (with the notable exception of the alcohol industry). It remains an untested assumption that those who drink or use drugs will also do so on the job or in other inappropriate settings. This may be the case, but it is certainly not established. These studies, therefore, provide some background for investigating disruptive drug use, but cannot truly inform us about this behavior. In addition, most of these occupational studies have focused solely on alcohol, leaving the role of other drugs unexamined.

Questions Addressed in This Book

This book examines in detail one particular style of drug use, that engaged in while at work or school. General levels of drug use in all contexts are occasionally included in the analyses to provide perspective and to distinguish drug use on the job from a general predilection to use drugs. A great deal of literature already exists on the etiological factors and correlates of using drugs in general. Virtually nothing similar has been undertaken with disruptive substance use. There may be similar factors associated with or predictive of both, or they may be quite different. This is an important question and it is addressed in the present analyses. Intuitively, I think that there is something quite different between getting drunk at home on one's own time and getting high at work. Thus, only tangentially do I examine general patterns of substance use. This does not mean that hangovers, absenteeism, and tardiness are not related to using drugs; only that these do not reflect the use of drugs in the workplace.

One of the critical concerns cutting through many of the analyses is whether disruptive substance use results from individual factors or whether it is generated by environmental conditions (either at work or elsewhere in the employee's life). Knowing the etiology should provide an essential starting point for prevention and intervention efforts.

Throughout this book I take the position that disruptive drug use is qualitatively different from drug use in appropriate settings, even though they may be quantitatively similar. Even a single instance of using drugs at work or school carries several implicit messages: it declares a reduced respect for the employer, for the job, and the safety and integrity of the workplace. If it represents a compulsion or addiction, it implies an inability of the worker to confront this problem. Because of these inherent differences between disruptive drug use and drug use in appropriate circumstances, I consider any amount of disruptive substance use to be abuse.

Using data from a community sample of young adults, I examine a range of issues concerning disruptive drug use. Chapter 2 provides a description of the sample as well as a summary of frequently used measures and types of analyses. Chapters 3 through 9 are cross-sectional examinations of these young adults and how disruptive drug use is related to or correlated with a wide range of demographic and psychosocial factors. Chapters 10 through 12 incorporate data from adolescence to predict changes in drug use in young adulthood. Chapter 13 presents a simple risk factor index for identifying those most vulnerable to disruptive drug use and examines other drug problems in relation to disruptive drug use. The final chapter (chapter 14) summarizes the series of empirical analyses and relates this information to theoretical and practical issues.

Below I summarize the basic concerns or issues addressed in each empirical chapter.

Chapter 2. What are the characteristics of the young adult sample and what types of measures were assessed and what analyses were used?

Chapter 3. How many people are engaged in disruptive drug use and what types of drugs are being used? The chapter examines the prevalence of disruptive substance use by sex and context. Nine licit and illicit drugs are considered. In addition, prevalence rates of general drug use (use in all contexts) are presented for the total sample and contrasted with national estimates of young adults gathered in 1982 and 1985.

Chapter 4. If one drug is used at work or school, are other drugs used in these contexts as well? The chapter examines whether those who use one type of drug disruptively also use other drugs in these environments. In other words, is disruptive substance use limited to a single drug for a particular person, or is disruptive drug use better characterized as polydrug use?

Chapter 5. What kind of people are engaged in disruptive drug use? This chapter considers various demographic and background variables and whether they can distinguish those who do and do not engage in disruptive drug use.

Chapter 6. How is using drugs at home related to disruptive drug use? In this chapter, rates of general drug use are contrasted with rates of disruptive drug use to determine the degree of similarity or difference. For instance, does using marijuana away from work guarantee that a person will also use it at work?

Chapter 7. How are work conditions related to disruptive drug use? This chapter examines the hypothesis that characteristics of the work environment contribute to using drugs on the job.

Chapter 8. Are personality, social connection, emotional distress, and life problems related to disruptive drug use? Several analyses are used to determine whether psychosocial factors are related to disruptive drug use. For instance, are those who are unhappy with their personal lives turning to drugs at work?

Chapter 9. Is using drugs at work just another symptom of a generally deviant or criminally inclined person? The chapter examines the association between a range of negative behaviors and disruptive drug use.

Chapter 10. Is disruptive drug use a tendency or predilection of the person that endures over time? Data from adolescence are used to explore the stability and change in using drugs in inappropriate settings over a four-year period. In addition, the chapter examines the question whether using alcohol at school as a teenager leads to using illicit drugs at work as a young adult.

Chapter 11. Does a student's perception of his or her life and self lead to an increase or decrease in or rejection of disruptive drug use later in life? Several psychosocial factors are used to predict changes in disruptive drug use from adolescence to young adulthood.

Chapter 12. Does an addictive personality lead to disruptive drug use? Several motivations for using alcohol and cannabis are examined as predictors of disruptive drug use, in contrast to general drug use.

Chapter 13. How is disruptive drug use related to other drug problems, and can disruptive drug use be understood by risk factors?

Within each chapter, a review of the relevant literature is provided to place the analyses in context. As mentioned above, these reviews are based on the general drug use literature, and only in rare instances are they based on studies of disruptive drug use.

Chapter 2

DESCRIPTION OF THE STUDY

This study began in 1976. It was originally designed to follow a group of adolescents through the teenage years to determine what etiological factors generated drug-taking behaviors. In year one of the study (1976), 1,634 students in the seventh, eighth, and ninth grades provided complete data. Informed consent was obtained from both the teenager and the parents. Participants were informed that their responses were protected legally by a grant of confidentiality from the U.S. Department of Justice. This grant of confidentiality has been maintained for the entire span of the study. Students were enrolled in eleven Los Angeles County schools and were roughly representative in their socioeconomic profile and ethnic background of the general student population in that county. At the initial testing, self-administered questionnaires were used to gather information about the students' drug use, personality, attitudes toward drugs, peer interaction, and perception of drug use by others.

Data were collected at four other occasions from the same participants during a period of eight years. These retestings occurred at years two, four, five, and nine of the study. At each testing the questionnaire was expanded and refined, so that by years five and nine an extensive assessment of many life areas was obtained. Years five and nine were the only occasions when use of drugs at work or school was assessed. Data for year five (1980) were collected when subjects were in late adolescence, either just completing high school or recently graduated. The young adult data were collected four years later (1984), when all participants were in their early twenties.

Over the years, the focus of the study has shifted from one of etiology to consequences of drug use. The etiological phase of the study resulted in many important findings regarding the initiation of drug use among teenagers (e.g., Huba & Bentler, 1982, 1983a, 1984; Huba, Wingard, & Bentler, 1981; Newcomb, Huba, & Bentler, 1983; Newcomb & Harlow, 1986; Newcomb, Maddahian, & Bentler, 1986). These analyses typically focused on the first five years of data. In the last follow-up year (year nine, in 1984), we assessed a wide range of possible outcomes, qualities, or events that might be influenced by earlier drug use. These data have been primarily used to illuminate the consequences of teenage drug use, and these results have been published in a book (Newcomb & Bentler, 1988a) and journal articles (e.g., Newcomb & Bentler, 1987b, 1988b).

In 1984, data were collected from 739 young adults from our original sample. Each young adult was paid $12.50 to complete the follow-up questionnaire. This number of subjects represents a 45 percent retention rate over the entire eight-year period of the study. This rate of subject loss is not unusual among real-world studies of this type. Various attrition analyses have been performed and are summarized below. The decline in the number of subjects between late adolescence (year five) and young adulthood (year nine) was not primarily because of voluntary withdrawal from the study (less than 5 percent actually refused to continue). This decline was primarily the result of the difficulty in recontacting the subjects during that very mobile and change-laden period in life from adolescence to young adulthood. In fact, participants were traced throughout the country and all over the world.

Sample Description

The characteristics of the 739 subjects at the young adult follow-up and the 654 subjects who provided data at both year five and year nine are listed in table 2.1. The 739 subjects are used for the descriptive cross-sectional analyses, and the 654 subjects are used in the longitudinal, prediction analyses. Seventy percent of the sample were women and 30 percent were men. This disparity between the number of women and men participants was also a feature of the sample at the beginning of the study, and does not represent differential attrition by sex. Current age ranged from 19 to 24 years, with a mean of 21.9. About 34 percent of the sample were from minority backgrounds (black, Hispanic, and Asian), 93 percent were high school graduates, average income was between $5,000 and $15,000, and most had not yet become parents. The most frequent current life pursuit was full-time employment,

Table 2.1 Description of Sample

Variable	Cross-sectional Young Adult Follow-up Sample	Longitudinal Sample
N	739	654
Sex		
Male	30%	29%
Female	70%	71%
Age		
Mean	21.93	21.90
Range	19–24	19–24
Ethnicity		
Black	15%	15%
Hispanic	10%	10%
White	66%	66%
Asian	9%	9%
High School Graduate		
Yes	93%	93%
Number of Children		
None	84%	85%
One	14%	14%
Two or more	2%	1%
Income for Past Year		
None	10%	9%
Under $5,000	33%	34%
$5,001 to $15,000	45%	45%
Over $15,001	12%	12%
Living Situation		
Alone	4%	4%
Parents	46%	48%
Spouse	10%	17%
Cohabitation	8%	9%
Dormitory	9%	6%
Roommates	5%	12%
Other	4%	4%
Current Life Activity		
Military	3%	3%
Junior college	12%	12%
Four-year college	21%	21%
Part-time job	14%	14%
Full-time job	50%	50%
Treatment History (past 4 years)		
Hospitalization for physical condition	10%	9%
Psychiatric hospitalization	1%	1%
Alcohol treatment program	1%	1%
Drug treatment program	0%	0%
Smoking cessation clinic	1%	1%

followed by attending a university, part-time job, and then junior college. The most typical living arrangement was staying with parents. The "other" living arrangement category was split between being single parents (living with a son or daughter) and living with other relatives who were not one's parents (e.g., sibling, cousin, or grandparents). About 10 percent of the sample had been hospitalized for a physical condition during the past four years, but only about 1 percent had been treated for emotional problems or substance abuse.

When these participant characteristics were compared to national surveys of young adults (e.g., Bachman, O'Malley, & Johnston, 1984; Glick & Lin, 1986; Miller et al., 1983) and other samples of young adults (e.g., Donovan, Jessor, & Jessor, 1983; Kandel, 1984), very similar patterns were noted. This group of young adults does not appear markedly different from young adults in general in their life activity or living arrangements. The main difference is that the current sample has a greater percentage of women than men, as it has had since the study began.

Although it may seem unusual to have such a large percentage of the sample living at home as young adults (52 percent of the men and 46 percent of the women), recent evidence indicates that this reflects a national trend in the United States. For instance, based on data from the U.S. Census Bureau, Glick and Lin (1986) found that 45 percent of young adults aged twenty to twenty-four were living with their parents in 1984. This percentage is quite similar to that obtained in our sample and emphasizes the representative nature of our sample.

Attrition Effects

In the first year of the study (1976), 64 percent of the sample were females and 36 percent were males, whereas in high school (1980) 68 percent were females and 32 percent were males. This indicates that the differential representation by sex in the young adult sample (1984) was also evident in the original sample and was not solely a result of differential attrition.

A series of analyses was run to determine whether the attrition in sample size from 1976 to 1984 (junior high school to young adulthood) was the result of a systematic influence. These extensive analyses, which have been reported elsewhere (Newcomb, 1986b; Newcomb & Bentler, 1988a), indicate that the loss of subjects between 1976 and 1984 was only slightly the result of a systematic selection or other influence based on personality, drug use, ethnicity, or sex.

Of the 739 current subjects, 654 had provided data in 1980, representing a 73 percent recapture rate from the previous data point. A series of analyses was run to determine whether the attrition in sample size from 1980 to 1984 was the result of a systematic influence. These extensive analyses indicate that the loss of subjects between 1980 and 1984 was not largely the result of a systematic selection or other influence based on personality, emotional distress, social support, or drug use (see Newcomb & Bentler, 1986c, 1988a for full details).

One constant concern in longitudinal drug studies is that the heavier drug users will drop out over time. This reduces the representativeness of the sample, decreases the variance on drug use items, and seriously weakens the results obtained.

One way to determine whether my sample has become unrepresentative of the general population because of loss of heavier drug-using subjects is to compare prevalence rates of drug use in my sample with carefully surveyed national samples. Such a comparison reveals that recent and lifetime prevalence rates between the two samples are similar. Details of these comparisons are reported in the next chapter as descriptive features of my community sample of young adults.

In general, comparisons with nationally representative samples indicate quite clearly that I have not lost large numbers of drug users, of either licit or illicit substances, from my sample. Thus, results based on my sample cannot be considered distorted because of losing the more deviant drug users. In fact, I have been fortunate to have retained many drug users in my sample, with many current and lifetime prevalence rates slightly higher than the national averages and equivalent to regional trends.

Changes in Drug Use

Frequency of use for twenty-six drug substances was assessed during adolescence (year five, 1980) and when the subjects were young adults (year nine, 1984). Comparing these reported levels of drug use, we found significant increases in the use of cigarettes, caffeine, beer, wine, liquor, amphetamines, non-LSD psychedelics, cocaine, and nonprescription cold medication. The largest increases were for caffeine, all alcoholic beverages, and cocaine. There were significant decreases in the use of marijuana, hashish, minor tranquilizers, barbiturates, sedatives, LSD, inhalants, and

PCP. The most dramatic change in illicit substance use was the increase in cocaine. As adolescents, 18 percent reported any use of cocaine in the past six months. As young adults, this proportion increased to about one-third of the sample. Interestingly, the significant increase in cigarette smoking did not reflect new people beginning use, but rather an increase of use among those already smoking, that is, becoming heavier and more committed (addicted?) users. Even though there was a significant decrease in cannabis use between adolescence and young adulthood, over 40 percent of the young adults reported marijuana use during the past six months. Thus, there appeared to be a greater reduction in the intensity of marijuana use (lowered frequency and quantity) than in actual numbers using the drug. Finally, about 80 percent of the adolescents reported using some alcoholic drink in the preceding six months, whereas about 90 percent of them as young adults reported doing so, with a concomitant increase in intensity.

Although these figures indicate that some important changes in drug use occurred between adolescence and young adulthood, it is also important to determine the stability of use over this period of time. Drug substances were averaged into five drug use categories: Cigarettes (one item), alcohol (three items), cannabis (two items), hard drugs (fifteen items), and nonprescription medication (four items). The stability correlation between adolescent cigarette use and young adult cigarette use was .63, whereas this correlation was .53 for alcohol, .60 for cannabis, .48 for hard drugs, and .33 for nonprescription medication. Since different types of drugs reflect a general factor of drug use or polydrug use, a latent construct of general adolescent drug use was used to predict a latent factor of general young adult drug use. General drug use at each point was assumed to be reflected by use of cigarettes, alcohol, cannabis, hard drugs, and nonprescription medications. Adolescent drug use accounted for 60 percent of the variation in young adult drug use. In other words, there was a moderate degree of stability as well as change in levels of substance use from adolescence to young adulthood. More details regarding patterns of stability and change in drug use over time in this sample are presented elsewhere (Newcomb & Bentler, 1986d, 1987a).

Assessment and Validity of Disruptive Drug Use

Nine items were used to assess the extent of drug use at work or school for the young adults. The specific question was, "About how many times in the last six months have you been drunk, stoned, or high on the following drugs while at work or school?" Responses were elicited for each of nine substances: beer, wine, hard liquor, marijuana, hashish, stimulants, hypnotics, cocaine, and heroin. Responses were given on coded rating scales that ranged from none (0) to more than thirty times (5). Thus, the frequency scores represent, not the number of times drugs were used at work or school, but a coding of the number of occurrences.

For some analyses, all nine individual items are used separately. For other analyses, the items are combined into scales representing the general type of substance. These included disruptive alcohol use (beer, wine, and liquor use at work), disruptive cannabis use (marijuana and hashish at work), cocaine (typically retained as a separate scale), and disruptive hard drug use (stimulant, hypnotic, and heroin use at work). In addition, there is a total score for all disruptive drug use, which combines all items into one scale.

In the longitudinal analyses that include data from adolescence, five items were used to assess disruptive drug use when the subjects were in late adolescence (year five of the study). The same question was posed for use of beer, wine, liquor, cannabis (marijuana and hashish), and other illicit drugs. The same response scale was used for the adolescent assessment as for the young adult assessment. These items were sometimes used as separate individual variables, sometimes the alcohol items were combined into one scale, and sometimes a total scale of all five items was used.

Two versions of these variables or scales are used: one that represents the frequency of use for the variable and another that represents the prevalence of use. The frequency variant captures the intensity of involvement in each type of disruptive drug use. The prevalence variant, on the other hand, indicates the use or nonuse of drugs at work or school during the past six months.

An important and essential concern about these variables is the validity of the responses. To what extent can responses to these items be accepted as truthful and accurate? Unfortunately, there is no objective or definitive way to evaluate the veracity of the responses. Nevertheless, several conditions that have been found to enhance truthfulness in responding were incorporated into the present design.

One condition is the confidentiality assured by the study. Each respondent was made aware of the grant of confidentiality provided by the U.S. Department of Justice, which legally protected all their responses from any private or governmental access. A copy of the legal document was made available to all subjects. In a review of the validity of self-report assessments of cigarette smoking among adolescents (an illegal behavior for that age group).

Pechacek, Fox, Murray, and Luepker (1984) found that reports were accurate, valid, and reliable when confidentiality could be assured.

Another condition of the present study that enhances the truthfulness of the respondents is that they have a history of providing data to my project. This was not the first time they had given responses to questions on illegal and criminal behavior. They have responded in the past with no repercussions, and thus should not anticipate any negative consequences from providing accurate information, even to admitting illegal behavior as young adults. In other words, they have formed an attachment to and trust in our research program, which should facilitate accurate responses (Harrell, 1985).

These two conditions address issues that might otherwise lead to concealment and underreporting by respondents in self-report data. As identified by Nurco (1985), these issues are assuring confidentiality and establishing rapport. He suggests another condition to improve the validity of self-reports: assessing recent events, which would involve less distortion of memory. The disruptive drug use items address the period of six months prior to the survey, which is a relatively short period of time and should promote accurate remembering. A monograph produced by the National Institute on Drug Abuse has been devoted to the validity of self-report methods of assessing drug use (Rouse, Kozel, & Richards, 1985). Many of the papers in this volume attest to the importance of the conditions cited above, and in fact provide data that demonstrate empirically the usefulness of such conditions for increasing the validity of self-report assessments of drug use (e.g., Gfroerer, 1985).

A final consideration are the data themselves. The distributions of the disruptive drug use items appear as expected. For instance, they are consistently lower than general drug use; only a very few report extremely high levels; the patterns of use tend to parallel general use; and the distributions are fairly smooth, although skewed. Thus, I conclude that even though certain threats to validity may remain, the responses are largely accurate, and do not represent gross distortions or biases from underreporting or overreporting.

Sex Differences

Many of the variables used in the analysis for this book may have different means or levels for men and women. Previous analyses have demonstrated that when this occurs, the differences are typically small in magnitude and do not lead to differences in the results (e.g., Newcomb & Bentler, 1986c, 1986d). Similarly, differential associations between drug use and other variables by sex have rarely been found (e.g., Newcomb, Maddahian, & Bentler, 1986).

Many of the analyses for this book were performed separately by sex, and the same conclusions were found for both men and women. As a result, most of the analyses presented are on the combined sample of men and women, without loss of detail and explanatory ability. In other words, even though there may be mean differences between men and women, the general processes (i.e., correlations) are quite similar for each sex (e.g., Stein, Newcomb, & Bentler, 1986a).

Nature of the Analyses

Since this book is an empirical investigation of disruptive drug use, a good deal of information is gathered via statistical analyses. Some of these are straightforward and familiar, whereas others may appear more complex, confusing, and unfamiliar.

To make effective use of this book, the reader need not understand or follow all of the statistical results. These are broadly interpreted in the final section of each chapter. The middle section of each chapter describes the measures or instruments used in the analyses and summarizes the statistical results. I have attempted to keep these sections brief and to the point. Unfortunately, in taking a middle road, I must present results that may be confusing to those unfamiliar with such analyses while providing insufficient detail for those sophisticated in such procedures.

I suggest that the general reader scan these sections, giving particular emphasis to the tables and figures. These contain the results and provide the information discussed briefly in the text. In the section below, I describe the various types of analyses made on the data.

Types of Analyses

I conduct various types of statistical analyses on the data in the subsequent empirical chapters. Many of these analyses are common and should be familiar to most researchers. Some, however, are new and may not be familiar to everyone. Understanding the substantive results of the analyses is not dependent upon always understanding all of the technical details.

Each empirical chapter has a Measures section, where I describe the specific variables used in the analyses for that particular chapter. This is followed by a Results section, where the technical details of the analyses are given, usually accompanied by tables and figures. If this section becomes too complicated for the reader, the substantive meaning and integration of the results are discussed in the last section of each chapter, the Interpretation section.

Below I provide brief definitions of the statistics used in the subsequent analyses. If further explanation is necessary, the reader is referred to any standard statistical text; for the latent-variable analyses, I provide specific references.

Significance Test. Many of the statistical analyses I present have significance tests associated with them. A significance test is reported in the form of a p-value (i.e., $p < .05$). A significance test indicates how likely the finding that was observed actually occurred by chance. The typical cutoff is $p < .05$, which indicates that in only one instance out of twenty would the observed result actually have arisen by chance. In the latent-variable models (described below), a nonsignificant p-value indicates that the model fits the data (i.e., cannot be rejected, a desirable outcome).

Prevalence Rate. A prevalence rate is the percentage of the sample (or subsample) with a particular characteristic. It is calculated by dividing the number of persons with the particular quality by the total number of people in the sample. Differences between prevalence rates are evaluated by a chi-squared test. If the chi-squared test is significant, the percentages are reliably different.

Means. A mean is an average. It is the amount of a particular variable (i.e., frequency of disruptive drug use) for the total sample (or specific subsamples). Means can be compared in analyses of variance (ANOVAs), where two or more groups can be compared, resulting in an F-statistic, or for two groups using the t-test or point-biserial correlation. For instance, if a point-biserial correlation is significant, the mean in one group is reliably different from the mean in a second group.

Correlation. A correlation represents the degree of correspondence or similarity between two continuous variables. It ranges from -1.00, indicating a perfectly negative association, to zero, indicating no association, to 1.00, indicating a perfectly positive association.

Multiple Regression Analysis. A multiple regression analysis is used to determine how well several variables (called independent or predictor variables) predict or account for a dependent or criterion variable. Results indicate which variables are independently related to the dependent variable. The important feature of this method is that it considers the extent of overlap or correlation among the independent variables when predicting the dependent variable. Several statistics emerge from this analysis: A beta weight, which reveals the magnitude of contribution of each independent variable to the predicted variable (with an associated significance test); an F-ratio, which indicates whether the predictor variables reliably predict the criterion variable (with an associated significance test); and a multiple R (correlation) and R^2 (the amount of variance accounted for in the dependent variable by the independent variables). The use of the term *predict* or *predictor* for this method is only descriptive and does not demonstrate a causal effect. Causal inferences can only be determined with appropriate longitudinal data.

Hazard Rate. A hazard rate is a statistic taken from medicine and represents the likelihood of a specific characteristic being present. For instance, Kandel and Logan (1984) have estimated that the hazard rate for initiating cocaine use continues to rise well into young adulthood. In other words, the peak age or most likely age for beginning cocaine use occurs, not during adolescence, but later in life. A conditional hazard rate indicates the likelihood of having a specific characteristic, given that another characteristic is also present. For instance, if I use illicit drugs at home, what is the hazard rate of also using drugs at work?

Latent-Variable Models. Latent-variable analyses are undoubtedly the most complicated method I use in this book. Structural equation modeling with latent variables is a relatively new analytic procedure that may not be familiar to many people (for reviews see Bentler, 1980, 1986a; Bentler & Newcomb, 1986; Loehlin, 1987). It is a method of simultaneously testing hypotheses in multivariate data. It can also include latent or unmeasured variables. A structural equation model can have two sections: a measurement model section and a structural or path model section.

The measurement model section operationalizes how various latent constructs are reflected in measured or observed variables. Results of this analysis include factor loadings of the observed variables on the latent factors, correlations among the latent constructs, and residual variances of the observed variables. The latent construct represents the common or shared portion of the association among the observed variables. Therefore, it is considered a more powerful indicator than the measured variables, since the measurement error has been removed. A second-order factor can be included to account for high correlations among first-order factors. When only correlations are permitted between latent constructs, this is called a confirmatory factor analysis model. A feature included in my analyses that is new, even to those familiar with this method, is nonstandard paths or correlations (see Bentler, 1987a; Bentler & Newcomb, in preparation; Newcomb & Bentler, 1988a). These are correlations between two variables, one of which is a residual variance of a measured variable or a latent factor. The residual variance represents the unique portion of a variable not attributed to the common or latent factor, plus measurement error. This method is important when studying behaviors such as disruptive drug use. For instance, it is important to study the relationships among all types of drugs at work or school, as well as only specific kinds of drugs at work or school (i.e., only cocaine use) with other relevant variables. Disruptive polydrug use is captured as a latent construct, and use of specific substances is captured in the residuals of the observed variables.

The structural or path portion of a structural equation model tests directional relationships between latent constructs, or with the residual variables using nonstandard paths. When appropriate longitudinal data are used, it is possible to draw some causal inferences from the results. This is like path analysis, but includes latent constructs.

The magnitude or importance of factor loadings, correlations, and paths is determined by significance levels. For a model to be interpreted it should reasonably fit the data; the hypothesized model should approximately reproduce the observed data. This is tested by the p-value associated with a chi-squared test, and various types of fit indices. For a model to fit, it should have a nonsignificant p-value (i.e., $p > .05$) and a normed fit index about .90 or higher. The normed fit index (NFI: Bentler & Bonett, 1980) varies from zero (no fit) to 1.00 (perfect fit) and indicates the proportion of the data covariation that is captured by the hypothesized model.

When many variables are used in large samples (as is the case in the present analyses), most models will not fit on the first attempt. Additions are typically made to the model on an empirical basis to improve the fit. In the present analyses, the Lagrangian multiplier test for adding parameters to a model is used (Bentler & Chou, 1986). Many of these added correlations or paths have substantive meaning and are presented as part of the results. The nonstandard effects included in the models are only available at present in the EQS computer program (Bentler, 1986b). These effects are not readily implemented in the LISREL program (Jöreskog & Sörbom, 1985).

Despite the apparent complexity of these analyses, this method provides the most parsimonious and elegant way currently available for studying a large number of variables at one time. This method, however, is not without critics (e.g., Baumrind, 1983; Freedman, 1987), but most of their concerns are based on the application of the method and not the procedure itself (Bentler, 1987b). Nevertheless, for those uncomfortable with this method, standard correlations and multiple regression results are also included.

Chapter 3

PREVALENCE RATES OF GENERAL AND DISRUPTIVE SUBSTANCE USE

In this chapter, the prevalence rates of general drug use (drug use in all contexts) reported by my sample are presented and contrasted with national estimates for a similarly aged sample. This information provides a base line against which to evaluate the extent of disruptive substance use reported by the persons in my sample. Following this, the prevalence of disruptive substance use is examined for each of the nine individual drugs that were assessed (beer, wine, liquor, marijuana, hashish, stimulants, hypnotics, cocaine, and heroin), as well as the three classes of substances they represent (alcohol, cannabis, and hard drugs) and a combined measure of any use of drugs in an inappropriate setting. These various estimates are given for the total sample, contrasted for men and women, and compared according to settings (military, junior college, university, part-time employment, and full-time employment).

A wide range of local and nationally representative data is available to determine the general prevalence of drug use and the degree of involvement for those who use drugs. Some of these data and trends over time were reported in chapter 1. Prevalence typically represents the percentage of those in a given sample who report any drug use (or any use of a specific substance) within a given period of time (e.g., past six months, past year, or lifetime). Degree of involvement is usually assessed by the frequency of using a particular substance or by the amount of that substance ingested on a typical occasion of use, or by both.

The most thorough assessment of this question is made every three years by the National Institute on Drug Abuse. The most recent estimates were gathered in 1982 (Miller et al., 1983) and 1985 (NIDA, 1986, 1987). These surveys determine the prevalence of use for ten different substances (cigarettes, alcohol, marijuana, hallucinogens, cocaine, heroin, stimulants, sedatives, tranquilizers, and analgesics) within three age groups (youth, ages 12–17; young adults, ages 18–25; and older adults, ages 26 and older).

Unfortunately, no similar data exist regarding the use of drugs on the job or in the classroom. Most articles and studies that address drug use in the workplace only cite general levels or prevalence of drug use, and infer that this rate of use also reflects drug use on the job. This may be true, but it is an assumption upon which no data have yet been brought to bear.

Most employers have been confronted with an employee who is using drugs at work, but this does not indicate that "everyone is doing it," as some of the more sensationalist articles in the popular press have suggested. Indeed, some personnel experts believe that the estimates of drugs on the job have been distorted or perhaps exaggerated by the media and other sources (e.g., Gordon, 1987). Certainly when some estimates of the prevalence of drug use at work appear, they are of a magnitude that cannot be taken lightly. For instance, Backer (1987) reports that "experts estimate that between 10% and 23% of all U.S. workers use dangerous drugs on the job." These estimates are based on "best guesses" and not on any systematic assessment of the general population's use of drugs on the job. These "guesses" are typically based upon two types of data: prevalence rates of addicted persons seeking treatment who admitted using drugs on the job and estimates of the prevalence of alcohol or drug problems of people in various occupations (not stipulating that the problematic use of drugs has occurred on the job). Although important and indirectly related to problems of drug use on the job, these data fail to establish the extent of workforce involvement with drugs, and in fact can be misleading (Alden, 1986).

We can more easily understand the discrepancies by examining estimates of drug use in the workplace established by studying those in treatment or seeking help for a drug problem. Washton and Gold (1987) found that 74 percent of the callers to a national cocaine hotline (called 800-COCAINE) had used drugs on the job, with cocaine being the most prevalent drug (83 percent), and 92 percent had performed their job while under the influence of a drug. These estimates are severely biased in two ways. Cocaine abusers are the ones most likely to call a cocaine hotline (as

opposed to abusers of other drugs), and those having problems
with drugs are most likely to call a hotline, in general. These
restrictions limit the applicability of the figures to only those who
admit to having a problem with cocaine and are willing to call a
hotline about it. Similarly, Levy (1973) found that 96 percent of a
group of 95 former addicts had used drugs on the job. This
approach is backward, and only tells us what a small group of
severe abusers or addicts seeking treatment have done on the job.

The second approach to estimating the prevalence of drug use
in the workplace is by determining the extent of drug use or abuse
among types of employees in various jobs. Although this provides
different information from that of the previous approach, the
precise extent of drug use on the job is not established. Of course,
going to work drunk or stoned, or missing work because of drug
problems, certainly influences health, safety, and productivity at
the worksite, and many employees from different occupations have
been studied for these incidents. Some occupations have been
studied independently such as nursing (e.g., Cronin-Stubbs &
Schaffner, 1985; Haack & Harford, 1984; Sullivan, 1986), dentistry
(e.g., Clarno, 1986), physicians (e.g., Brewster, 1986; Smith &
Seymour, 1985), police (e.g., Violanti, Marshall, & Howe, 1983),
managers (e.g., Shore, 1985), truckers (e.g., Guinn, 1983), pilots
(e.g., Palmer, 1983), teachers (e.g., Fimian, Zacherman, & Mc-
Hardy, 1985), migrant laborers (e.g., Watson, Mattera, Morales,
Kunitz, & Lynch, 1985), oil rig workers (e.g., Aiken & McCance,
1982), and the military (e.g., Allen & Mazzuchi, 1985; Burt, 1982;
Hawkins, Kruzich, & Smith, 1985); and some occupations have
been contrasted with others (e.g., Olkinuora, 1984; Plant, 1978).

There are some exceptions among the small studies to the
paucity of direct estimates of drug use on the job. For instance,
Guinn (1983) found that only 20 percent of a small sample of long-
distance truckers had never used drugs on the job and that 10
percent had used drugs regularly on the job.

In the analyses to follow, I present the prevalence of general
drug use among my subjects for ten different substances and
contrast this with the national estimates. Then I present the
frequency and prevalence of the nine drugs used on the job
assessed in my study, as well as the prevalence of drug use on the
job by general categories (alcohol, cannabis, hard drugs, any use).
These rates are compared for men and women and by type of
setting.

Prevalence of General Drug Use

Using the 1982 data provided by the NIDA-sponsored National
Household Survey of Drug Use (Miller et al., 1983) and the recent

1985 data from the same project (NIDA, 1986, 1987), I compare the lifetime prevalence and current prevalence of drug use between my young adult sample and the nationally representative stratified random samples (see tables 3.1 and 3.2).

The household surveys assessed ten classes of drugs that were used, without a physician's prescription, for nonmedical purposes. The ten categories of drugs included alcohol, cigarettes, marijuana, hallucinogens, cocaine, heroin, stimulants, tranquilizers, sedatives, and analgesics. An additional scale was created for any use of the last four drugs in the 1982 sample. Using the definitions provided in the National Household Survey (Miller et al., 1983) for each substance use category, I created similar categories from the drug use items included in the questionnaires given to my subjects.

I compared my sample and the National Household Survey sample on the lifetime prevalence of drug use in all categories (see table 3.1). Lifetime prevalence estimates in my sample are quite conservative. These were calculated on four waves of data over the eight-year period of the study. The first wave (1976) determined lifetime prevalence, whereas all other assessments were based on the previous six months. A subject was considered a user of a particular substance if the person acknowledged any use of the drug at any of the four assessments. Thus, it is extremely likely that a good deal of experimental use went undetected in this design because no assessments were made of drug use for a period of six and one half years during adolescence and young adulthood.

Point-biserial correlations were used to test for sex differences on these lifetime prevalence rates from the 1984 UCLA sample (see table 3.1). There were no significant differences between men and women on their lifetime prevalence rates for use of any of the ten substances.

I contrasted the lifetime prevalence rates from my young adults with those of the 1982 National Survey using confidence interval estimates provided in the National Survey. There were no significant differences in lifetime prevalence of drug use between our sample (indicated as UCLA) and the 1982 national sample for use of hallucinogens, heroin, sedatives, analgesics, and cigarettes. The UCLA sample reported significantly higher lifetime prevalence of use for marijuana, cocaine, stimulants, tranquilizers, alcohol, and any nonmedical drug use. On no drug did the national sample report a higher lifetime prevalence than my sample.

I next performed the same comparisons for the more recent 1985 national data (NIDA, 1986, 1987). Very similar results were found for the lifetime prevalence rates, with two exceptions: The

Table 3.1 Comparison of Lifetime Young Adult Drug Use Prevalence

Drug Category	1984 UCLA	r_{pb} Sex Difference[a]	Difference Test[b]	1982 National	Difference Test[b]	1985 National
Illicit Use of						
Marijuana	68.9	.03	>	64.1	>	60.5
Hallucinogens	22.9	-.05	=	21.1	>	11.5
Cocaine	40.3	.00	>	28.3	>	25.2
Heroin	2.1	.00	=	1.2	=	1.2
Nonmedical Use of						
Stimulants	30.3	.04	>	18.0	>	17.3
Tranquilizers	21.6	.04	>	15.1	>	12.2
Sedatives	17.1	.02	=	18.7	>	11.0
Analgesics	10.5	.02	=	12.1	=	11.4
Any nonmedical use	40.5	.03	>	28.4	NA	NA
Legal Use of						
Alcohol	96.9	-.04	>	94.6	>	92.8
Cigarettes	77.5	.00	=	76.9	=	76.1

[a]Point-biserial correlation mean sex difference tests on the 1984 UCLA lifetime prevalence rates (males = 1 and females = 2).

[b]Based on confidence interval estimates provided in the *National Survey*: > indicates that the UCLA sample had a significantly larger prevalence; = indicates that the prevalence rates were not significantly different; and < indicates that the national sample had a significantly larger prevalence.

UCLA sample reported significantly higher lifetime prevalence rates for hallucinogens and sedatives compared to the 1985 national survey.

I then looked at the current prevalence rates (see table 3.2). In this case the 1982 national sample was based on use during the past year, whereas my sample reported use during the past six months. Again, the results for my sample are conservative because of the different time periods. There were no significant differences between the 1982 national sample and the UCLA sample for current use of marijuana, hallucinogens, heroin, tranquilizers, and analgesics. The UCLA sample reported significantly higher current prevalence than the national sample for use of cocaine, stimulants, any nonmedical use, and alcohol. The national sample reported significantly higher current prevalence for use of sedatives and cigarettes. Only slight changes from these patterns were noted for the current prevalence rates in the 1985 survey: The UCLA sample reported significantly higher current use of marijuana and hallucinogens than the 1985 national sample, whereas no differences were found for the use of sedatives and alcohol.

It is possible that drug use was higher in the western United States, the area covered in my UCLA sample, than in the areas covered by the 1982 national sample. Regional breakdowns were provided for several drugs in the National Survey; these were then compared to my sample and were not significantly different.

Table 3.2   Comparison of Current Young Adult Drug Use Prevalence

Drug Category	UCLA (past 6 months)	Difference Test[a]	1982 National (past year)	Difference Test[a]	1985 National (past year)
Illicit Use of					
Marijuana	42.8	=	40.4	>	36.8
Hallucinogens	8.5	=	6.9	>	3.6
Cocaine	33.8	>	18.8	>	16.2
Heroin	0.4	=	0.5	=	1.0
Nonmedical Use of					
Stimulants	18.0	>	10.8	>	10.1
Tranquilizers	6.9	=	5.9	=	6.4
Sedatives	4.2	<	8.7	=	5.1
Analgesics	4.7	=	8.7	=	6.7
Any nonmedical use	22.1	>	16.1	NA	NA
Legal Use of					
Alcohol	90.0	>	83.4	=	87.2
Cigarettes	39.1	<	47.2	<	45.0

[a]Based on confidence interval estimates provided in the *National Survey:* > indicates that the UCLA sample had a significantly larger prevalence; = indicates that the prevalence rates were not significantly different; and < indicates that the national sample had a significantly larger prevalence.

Disruptive Drug Use for the Total Sample

I have summarized the responses given by all 739 subjects to each of the nine questions assessing the frequency of being high or stoned while at work or school during the past six months (see table 3.3). Six response categories were provided: never (coded 0), one to five times (1), six to ten times (2), eleven to twenty times (3), twenty-one to thirty times (4), and more than thirty times (5). In addition, the prevalence or any use of a specific substance is given, as well as the mean level of use for each drug. The means are based on the average of the category codes and do not represent the actual frequency of times used. Thus, the means are substantially smaller than the actual number of times the substance was used on the job.

No one reported any disruptive use of heroin. Because of this, heroin use is not included in any of the remaining analyses. The most prevalent and frequently used substance was marijuana: almost 17 percent of the sample reported using marijuana at work or school at least one to five times during the past six months. The second most frequently used substance was beer. Following marijuana and beer, cocaine and hard liquor were the most prevalently used substances in inappropriate settings. These were followed in order by wine, stimulants, hashish, and hypnotics. Almost 3 percent of the sample reported regular use of marijuana at work or school (more than thirty times during the past six months).

Fully 31 percent of the total sample reported using some drug in an inappropriate setting from one to five times during the past six months (see table 3.4, section [a]). Alcohol was the most prevalent class of drugs used in these contexts (18 percent),

Table 3.3 Summary of Responses to the Substance Use at Work or School Variables

	Times Used at Work or School Past 6 Months							
Substance	*Never*	*1–5*	*6–10*	*11–20*	*21–30*	*More than 30*	*Any Use*	*Mean*
Beer	87.0	10.6	1.4	0.5	0.3	0.2	13.0	.17
Wine	93.8	5.1	0.7	0.1	0.3	0.0	6.2	.08
Liquor	90.7	6.9	1.5	0.5	0.3	0.1	9.3	.13
Marijuana	83.4	9.1	1.8	1.8	1.1	2.9	16.6	.40
Hashish	98.8	1.1	0.1	0.0	0.0	0.0	1.2	.01
Stimulants	94.6	2.4	1.2	0.5	0.4	0.8	5.4	.13
Hypnotics	99.5	0.4	0.0	0.1	0.0	0.0	0.5	.01
Cocaine	90.7	6.6	1.4	0.7	0.4	0.2	9.3	.14
Heroin	100.0	0.0	0.0	0.0	0.0	0.0	0.0	0.0

Table 3.4 Class of Substance Used at Work or School by Context of Use and Gender

	(N)	Percentage of Sample			
		Alcohol	Cannabis	Hard Drugs	Any Use
(a) *Total Sample*	(739)	18.3	16.6	12.2	30.9
(b) *Gender*					
Male	(221)	28.5	22.2	13.1	39.4
Female	(518)	13.9	14.3	11.8	27.2
$\chi^2(1) =$		22.14***	6.94**	0.26	10.71***
(c) *Context of Use*		*Total Sample*			
Military	(23)	30.4	4.3	4.3	30.4
Junior college	(87)	21.8	19.5	12.6	33.3
University	(153)	13.7	6.5	4.6	18.3
Part-time job	(102)	15.7	19.6	11.8	30.4
Full-time job	(374)	19.3	20.1	15.8	35.6
$\chi^2(4) =$		5.84	18.08***	14.15**	15.45**
(d) *Gender × Context*					
$F(4,729)$		0.87	0.56	1.78	0.15
(e) *Context of Use*		*Men*			
Military	(20)	35.0	5.0	5.0	35.0
Junior college	(19)	42.1	26.3	31.6	52.6
University	(48)	18.8	8.3	2.1	22.9
Part-time job	(29)	27.6	31.0	10.3	34.5
Full-time job	(105)	29.5	28.6	17.1	46.7
$\chi^2(4) =$		4.45	12.75**	13.65***	9.64*
(f) *Context of Use*		*Women*			
Junior college	(68)	16.2	17.6	7.4	27.9
University	(105)	11.4	5.7	5.7	16.2
Part-time job	(73)	11.0	15.1	12.3	28.8
Full-time job	(272)	15.1	16.5	15.1	30.9
$\chi^2(3) =$		1.67	8.10*	7.86*	8.40*

*$p < .05$; **$p < .01$; ***$p < .001$.

followed by cannabis (16 percent), and hard drugs (12 percent). Contrasting these results with those discussed above, we can see that although marijuana is the most prevalently used individual substance, alcohol is the most prevalently used class of substances. Although the prevalence of any disruptive substance use during the past six months is high (nearly one-third of the sample), only a small percentage used drugs on the jobs or at school on a regular basis. Such committed use appears to be confined to marijuana.

Disruptive Substance Use by Gender

Thirty-nine percent of the men reported some disruptive substance use during the past six months, compared to 27 percent of the women (see table 3.4, section [b]). These differences were statistically significant ($p < .001$). In terms of general classes or categories of drug use, 28 percent of the men reported some disruptive alcohol use, 22 percent reported disruptive cannabis use, and 13 percent reported disruptive use of hard drugs. All prevalence rates for these three categories of drugs were lower for the women, and significantly less for alcohol and cannabis use at work or school (the rates of disruptive hard drug use did not differ significantly by gender).

The gender differences for the specific types of disruptive substance use corroborated and localized the differences among the three classes of drugs (see table 3.5, section [b]). Only the prevalence rates for disruptive beer use were significantly different for men and women (no reliable differences were found for disruptive wine or liquor use). Both cannabis substances (marijuana and hashish) had higher prevalence rates of disruptive use for men compared to women. Finally, there were no significant differences by gender on the prevalence of using any of the three hard drug substances (cocaine, stimulants, and hypnotics).

Context of Disruptive Substance Use

I compared the prevalence of disruptive substance use in the five inappropriate contexts of use: military, junior college, university, part-time job, and full-time job (see table 3.4, section [c], and table 3.5, section [c]).

There was no significant difference in the prevalence of disruptive alcohol use among the several contexts. Significant differences were found, however, for disruptive cannabis, hard drugs, and any use. Rates of disruptive substance use for these drug categories were highest for people in junior college, part-time jobs, and full-time jobs, and lowest for those in the military and university settings.

There were significant differences by context for disruptive use of beer, marijuana, and stimulants (see table 3.5, section [c]). Disruptive beer use was most prevalent among military personnel and least prevalent among university students. The differences on disruptive marijuana and stimulant use paralleled any use; specifically, there were higher prevalence rates for those in junior college, part-time jobs, and full-time jobs, compared to those in the military and in a university.

Two-way ANOVAs were used to determine whether there were any interactions between gender and context of disruptive substance use for the three general drug categories, any use (see table 3.4, section [d]), and the eight specific substances (see table 3.5, section [d]). No significant interactions were found on any of these tests.

Despite the lack of any significant interaction between gender and context for the prevalence of disruptive substance use, the reader may be interested in the breakdowns within contexts by sex. See table 3.4, sections (e) and (f), for the prevalence rates for the drug use categories, and table 3.6, sections (a) and (b), for the individual substances.

There were significant differences for the men on the prevalence of disruptive substance use by context for any use, cannabis, hard drugs, and marijuana. The pattern of these results is similar to that noted above for the total sample. The highest prevalence rate for disruptive use of any substance was for junior college males: over 50 percent (53 percent) reported using some drug from one to five times while attending school during the past six months (see table 3.4). This is an amazingly high figure, suggesting that drug use may have a substantial impact on the education of these young men. This appears to be a particularly critical finding, one that must be followed up with appropriate research and intervention.

There were significant differences for the women across contexts (only three women were in the military and thus these cases were combined with full-time job category) for the prevalence of disruptive use of any substance, cannabis, hard drugs, and marijuana. The pattern of these significant differences was similar to that noted for the total sample. Those in a full-time job were most likely to have used a drug at work at least one to five times during the past six months (31 percent). This was followed closely by those in part-time jobs (29 percent) and junior college (28 percent). Those women least at risk for disruptive drug use were those attending a four-year university.

Interpretation

The prevalence of disruptive drug use among this sample of young adults appears to be relatively high, as is their prevalence of general drug use (but not that much different from national and in particular regional estimates). Only a small percentage of the sample, however, uses drugs in work or school settings on a regular basis. Those who do so tend to use marijuana more than any of the other drugs. This does not mean that the occasional use of drugs in the workplace or at school should be minimized, since being

Table 3.5 Specific Substances Used at Work or School by Context of Use and Gender

	(n)	Beer	Wine	Liquor	Marijuana	Hashish	Stimu-lants	Hypno-tics	Cocaine
(a) Total sample	(739)	13.0	6.2	9.3	16.6	1.2	5.4	0.5	9.3
(b) Gender									
Male	(221)	27.1	6.8	10.0	22.2	3.2	6.3	0.5	9.5
Female	(518)	6.9	6.0	9.1	14.3	0.4	5.0	0.6	9.3
$\chi^2(1) =$		55.92***	0.17	0.14	6.94**	9.96**	0.52	0.05	0.01
(c) Context									
Military	(23)	30.4	4.3	21.7	4.3	0.0	0.0	0.0	4.3
Junior college	(87)	17.2	8.0	10.3	19.5	0.0	5.7	0.0	9.2
University	(153)	9.2	6.5	8.5	6.5	0.0	1.3	0.0	3.9
Part-time job	(102)	14.7	3.9	5.9	19.6	2.9	3.9	0.0	11.8
Full-time job	(374)	12.0	6.4	9.6	20.1	1.6	7.8	1.1	11.2
$\chi^2(4) =$		10.15*	1.61	5.89	18.08***	6.23	10.82*	3.93	8.27
(d) Gender × Context									
$F(3, 731) =$		1.23	0.15	1.44	0.65	2.01	1.49	0.00	1.43

*p < .05; **p < .01; ***p < .001.

Table 3.6 Specific Substances Used at Work or School by Context of Use for Men and Women

	(N)	Beer	Wine	Liquor	Marijuana	Hashish	Stimu-lants	Hypno-tics	Cocaine
(a)					*Men*				
All men	(221)	27.1	6.8	10.0	22.2	3.2	6.3	0.5	9.5
Context									
Military	(20)	35.0	5.0	25.0	5.0	0.0	0.0	0.0	5.0
Junior college	(19)	42.1	10.5	15.8	26.8	0.0	15.8	0.0	21.1
University	(48)	18.8	8.3	4.2	8.3	0.0	0.0	0.0	2.1
Part-time job	(29)	27.6	3.4	6.9	31.0	10.3	6.9	0.0	10.3
Full-time job	(105)	26.7	6.7	9.5	28.6	3.8	8.6	1.0	11.4
$\chi^2(4) =$		0.34	0.88	7.89	12.75**	7.86	8.36	1.11	6.97
(b)					*Women*				
All women	(518)	6.9	6.0	9.1	14.3	0.4	5.0	0.6	9.3
Context									
Junior college	(68)	10.3	7.4	8.8	17.6	0.0	2.9	0.0	5.9
University	(105)	4.8	5.7	10.5	5.7	0.0	1.9	0.0	4.8
Part-time job	(73)	9.6	4.1	5.5	15.1	0.0	2.7	0.0	12.3
Full-time job	(272)	6.3	6.3	9.6	16.5	0.7	7.4	1.1	11.0
$\chi^2(3) =$		2.95	0.73	1.48	8.10*	1.82	6.66	2.73	5.28

$*p < .05; **p < .01.$

high even once in a critical position may endanger the health and safety of the public or fellow workers. Males are certainly more likely to use drugs in inappropriate settings than are females. Finally, there appeared to be important differences in the context of use. For all other drugs except beer, the military environment had one of the lowest prevalences of disruptive substance use. But men in the military are particularly prone to use beer on the job compared to the other contexts. University students consistently had the lowest prevalence of disruptive substance use, whereas those in junior college (particularly men), part-time jobs, and full-time jobs had the highest rates of disruptive substance use. The primary drugs of abuse appear to be beer and marijuana; cocaine was the third most prevalently used drug in inappropriate settings.

Chapter 4

STRUCTURE OF DISRUPTIVE SUBSTANCE USE

A basic question of this investigation is whether someone who uses a particular drug in an inappropriate setting also uses other drugs in this context. This has several important and practical implications for both work and school settings. For instance, if a student or employee is caught using one drug, does this suggest that this person may be using other drugs as well in these contexts? Or on the other hand, does the discovery of one type of drug use define the extent of the problem? This chapter addresses the question whether disruptive substance use reflects polydrug abuse or abuse of a specific substance. In this chapter I begin using latent-variable analyses, which are incorporated in many of the remaining chapters. In this context, various technical issues are addressed because of the rather skewed nature of the data.

A great deal of previous research has indicated that use of drugs is not typically limited to a specific substance, but often involves a variety of substances. This is particularly true for teenagers and those who use illicit drugs (i.e., marijuana and cocaine). Clayton and Ritter (1985) reviewed a variety of large-scale studies of drug use and found that "more often than not, the persons who are using drugs frequently are multiple drug users" (p. 83). For instance, in other analyses of my data, we compared those who had and had not used cocaine as young adults and their use of other drugs (Newcomb & Bentler, 1986b). Cocaine users reported significantly higher prevalence rates for all other types of drugs considered, including cigarettes, alcohol, cannabis, over-the-counter medications, hypnotics, stimulants, psychedelics, inhalants, narcotics, and PCP. These large differences were found for

41

both men and women, and were also evident at younger ages (e.g., Newcomb & Bentler, 1986a).

The association between various types of drug use is so high that we have been able to identify a general construct or latent tendency toward polydrug use (Bentler & Newcomb, 1986). For instance, among our sample as adolescents (e.g., Newcomb & Bentler, 1987b), we found that alcohol use was correlated .72 with cannabis use and .52 with hard drug use. Cannabis and hard drug use were correlated .67. In fact, cigarette smoking was moderately correlated with each of these other types of drug use (ranging from .41 with hard drugs to .54 with cannabis). It must be emphasized, however, that these correlations, though high, do not approach unity, thus indicating that polydrug involvement does not capture everyone. There are those who stick with one drug, but at least for marijuana users this pattern has been decreasing over time (Clayton & Ritter, 1985). There is some evidence that as the adolescent matures to young adulthood, the tendency for polydrug involvement decreases slightly, and two clusters of drug users emerge: those who use alcohol (and perhaps cigarettes) and those who use illicit drugs (including marijuana) with alcohol secondary (e.g., Newcomb & Bentler, 1986d).

Another way to understand drug involvement has been the progression or stage theory. Kandel (1975; Kandel & Faust, 1975) was one of the first researchers to investigate this hypothesis. In general, she found that teenagers began, of course, with nonuse of any drugs, initiated use with beer or wine, progressed to cigarettes or hard liquor, or both, may then move to marijuana, and finally may progress to other illicit drugs (i.e., hard drugs). Of course, these shifts from a lower stage to a higher stage are not guaranteed, but are probabilistic, because only some of those at one stage will move to the next (e.g., O'Donnell & Clayton, 1982). This does suggest, however, that in general the sequence is invariant, that progressing in the opposite direction (i.e., hard drugs to alcohol) is unlikely and that stages in the sequence are rarely omitted (i.e., moving from alcohol to hard drugs without using cannabis).

This notion has been tested in a variety of samples with both cross-sectional and longitudinal data (e.g., Donovan & Jessor, 1983; Hays, Widaman, DiMatteo, & Stacy, 1987; Huba, Wingard, & Bentler, 1981; Kandel & Faust, 1975; Mills & Noyes, 1984; Newcomb & Bentler, 1986d). Results have generally confirmed the initial hypothesis with slight variations. For instance, Donovan and Jessor (1983) found that problem drinking occurred higher in the progression than general alcohol use. On the other hand, Newcomb and Bentler (1986d) found that several minisequences accounted for drug involvement from early adolescence to young adulthood, when the role of cigarettes and nonprescription medications were included.

These two conceptualizations, a tendency toward polydrug use and passing through stages, are not mutually exclusive, and may reflect different orders of abstraction (e.g,. Newcomb & Bentler, 1986d). For instance, even though there may be a sequence or progression of involvement with drugs, those who have tried the higher-level drugs may also be characterized by a general involvement with drugs. This seems particularly true when considering that the majority of high school seniors have tried an illicit drug at least once and most use alcohol (Johnston, O'Malley, & Bachman, 1987).

It is not clear, however, whether such patterns are also characteristic of disruptive substance use. No such studies have been presented. A more technical consideration is that much of the research on the structure of general drug use has relied on statistical methods that assume the data are normally distributed. Although use of alcoholic substances may be normally distributed in the general population, use of marijuana and other illicit and hard drugs is not (e.g., Huba & Bentler, 1983b). Some attempts have been made to determine the validity of the general findings using methods appropriate for nonnormal data. In general, these additional analyses have supported the previous conclusions (e.g., Huba & Bentler, 1983b; Huba & Harlow, 1983). Nevertheless, the distribution of disruptive substance use is even more skewed than general drug use, since the former is a much more infrequent behavior. Thus, it is important to verify that results based on standard methods of analysis (often with multivariate normality assumptions) are confirmed with more appropriate methods, such as those not feasible in large analyses.

In this chapter, I address, first, the general distribution of the eight items in disruptive substance use. Next, the associations between the individual items are examined with parametric and nonparametric tests. Following this, hazard rates are presented for using various pairs of substances or classes of drugs. Finally, I develop four latent-variable models to examine the simultaneous associations among the eight items of disruptive substance use. Two methods are used for these analyses: one makes normality assumptions and the other does not.

Results

Descriptive Statistics

According to the univariate statistics for the eight measures of disruptive substance use, none of the items is normally distributed (see table 4.1). Disruptive marijuana use came closest to a normal distribution with a skew of 3.62 and a kurtosis of 13.04. (Skew indicates the degree of right or left shift in the distribution, and kurtosis indicates the amount of peakedness of the distribution.) Hashish and hypnotics had the most extreme distributions. This confirms the suspicion mentioned above that disruptive substance use would probably be very poorly distributed. This necessitates testing the items in methods that do not require normal data. In addition, there is very little variance on disruptive use of hashish and hypnotics, which may distort analytic methods that have normality assumptions.

Item Correlations

The product-moment correlations among the eight items of disruptive substance use (above the diagonal) require normal data and thus may be distorted by the extreme skewness of these items. All pairs of substances were significantly correlated in a positive direction except one (stimulants with liquor) (see table 4.2). There were several moderately large correlations, particularly among the alcohol items. I have also presented rank-order correlations among the eight items (see table 4.2 [below the diagonal]). This is a nonparametric test that does not have normality assumptions. As can be seen, these correlations are similar in magnitude and direction to the product-moment correlations. All correlations that were large before were large here as well, and those that were small continued to be small.

Several conclusions can be drawn from these analyses. First, it appears that disruptive substance use is not limited to a single substance, but rather is associated with using other substances in inappropriate settings. The magnitude of the associations certainly

Table 4.1   Substance Used at Work or School

Substance	Any Use	Mean	Variance	Range	Skew	Kurtosis
Beer	13.0	.17	.30	0–5	4.95	33.93
Wine	6.2	.08	.13	0–4	6.22	50.08
Liquor	9.3	.13	.24	0–5	5.02	31.70
Marijuana	16.6	.40	1.35	0–5	3.62	13.04
Hashish	1.2	.01	.02	0–2	10.30	118.19
Stimulants	5.4	.13	.45	0–5	6.61	48.00
Hypnotics	0.5	.01	.02	0–3	19.51	425.43
Cocaine	9.3	.14	.31	0–5	5.50	37.88

varies among the substances. In general, the three alcohol substances were most highly correlated with each other, as were the two cannabis substances, and the three hard drug substances. There were significant associations between classes of substances as well. This indicates that disruptive polydrug use is not limited to a single class of drugs, but can involve alcohol, cannabis, and hard drugs used by the same person. Finally, the comparison between the two types of correlations shows that despite extreme nonnormality in the data, similar conclusions can be drawn with either analysis.

Hazard Rates

The conditional hazard rates for using drugs at work or school are given by individual substance (see table 4.3) and class of substance (see table 4.4). These hazard rates were calculated by dividing the conditional likelihood of use (probability of using one substance if the other were used in inappropriate settings) by the base rate of using the second substance (the percentage of people who have used that substance at work or school) and multiplying by 100. For example, of those who reported using beer at work or school, 27.1 percent also reported using wine at work or school. Thus, to arrive at the conditional hazard rate of using wine if one used beer, 27.1 is divided by 6.2 (prevalence of disruptive wine use), multiplied by 100, arriving at 437. This figure indicates that if someone used beer at work, that person was 4.37 times as likely to have used wine at work as well, compared to the general prevalence of disruptive wine use.

The use of one substance disruptively increased the likelihood of using another substance disruptively by many times. In addition, the any use category is included as both the first and second substance considered (of course, systematically excluding the specific substance compared). For instance, if someone used a substance at work other than cocaine, he or she was 2.84 times more likely to have used cocaine than the general prevalence rate of disruptive cocaine use. On the other hand, if someone used hard liquor at work, he or she was 2.77 times more likely to have used some other substance disruptively than the general prevalence rate for any disruptive substance use.

Conditional hazard rates for the general categories of alcohol, cannabis, hard drugs, and any use ranged from 168 to 335 (see table 4.4). For instance, if someone used cannabis at work, that person was 3.34 times more likely to have used a hard drug at

Table 4.2 Product-Moment (above the Diagonal) and Rank-Order (below the Diagonal) Correlations among the Eight Drug Use at Work or School Variables

Substance	Beer	Wine	Liquor	Marijuana	Hashish	Stimulants	Hypnotics	Cocaine
Beer	1.00	.48***	.52***	.23***	.08*	.09*	.13**	.13**
Wine	.35***	1.00	.52***	.12*	.10**	.16**	.30***	.14***
Liquor	.44***	.47***	1.00	.28***	.13***	.05	.18***	.17***
Marijuana	.30***	.15**	.25***	1.00	.36***	.26***	.18***	.40***
Hashish	.17**	.12*	.13*	.27***	1.00	.17***	.10*	.20***
Stimulants	.14**	.07	.07	.21***	.14*	1.00	.17***	.28***
Hypnotics	.03	.26***	.11*	.19**	.16*	.23*	1.00	.16***
Cocaine	.18***	.10*	.20***	.38***	.18**	.31***	.23**	1.00

*$p < .05$; **$p < .01$; ***$p < .001$.

Table 4.3 Conditional Hazard Rates of Using Specific Substances at Work or School

Substance Used	Hazard Rate of Also Using This Substance[a]								
	Beer	Wine	Liquor	Marijuana	Hashish	Stimulants	Hypnotics	Cocaine	Any Use[b]
Beer	13.0	437	448	270	525	250	200	246	250
Wine	435	6.2	655	236	542	202	440	211	274
Liquor	446	655	9.3	271	483	187	580	296	277
Marijuana	269	236	271	16.6	608	285	660	358	213
Hashish	513	537	477	602	1.2	617	2200	598	324
Stimulants	250	202	188	286	625	5.4	1500	511	235
Hypnotics	192	403	538	602	2083	1389	0.5	162	324
Cocaine	239	210	296	379	600	509	20000	9.3	267
Any use[a]	276	284	296	262	325	248	360	284	30.9

[a] The hazard rates were calculated by dividing the conditional likelihood of use by the base rate and multiplying by 100.
[b] Any use excludes the drug being compared (substance used).
Note: Numbers on the diagonal are prevalence of use.

Table 4.4 Conditional Hazard Rates of Using Classes of Substances at Work or School

| Class of Substance Used | Hazard Rate of Using This Class of Substance[a] | | | |
	Alcohol	Cannabis	Hard Drugs	Any Use[b]
Alcohol	18.3	254	237	168
Cannabis	253	16.6	334	213
Hard Drugs	237	335	12.2	227
Any Use	234	262	257	30.9

[a]Hazard rates were calculated by dividing the conditional likelihood of use by the base rate and multiplying by 100.

[b]Any use excludes the class of substance being compared.

Note: Numbers on the diagonal are prevalence of use.

work as well, when compared to the prevalence rate of disruptive hard drug use.

These analyses underscore the conclusion that if one substance is used at work or school, the likelihood of use of a different substance and even a different class of substances is several times the base rate or prevalence rate of using the other substance. Clearly, for this sample of young adults, disruptive substance use is not strictly limited to one substance or even one class of substances.

Latent-variable Analyses

Four latent-variable models were developed to examine the multivariate association among the eight measures of disruptive substance use. For each model, two different estimators are used: maximum likelihood (ML), which assumes normal data, and a distribution-free method that does not require this assumption (e.g., Bentler, 1983; Browne, 1984). Parameter estimates and fit statistics for each model are compared for each estimator.

For all models, three latent factors were hypothesized: Alcohol at Work, Cannabis at Work, and Hard Drugs at Work. Alcohol at Work was assumed to be reflected by beer at work, wine at work, and liquor at work. Cannabis at Work was assumed to be indicated by marijuana at work and hashish at work. Hard Drugs at Work was assumed to be indicated by stimulants at work, hypnotics at work, and cocaine at work (see table 4.5 for a summary of fit statistics for the four models).

Confirmatory Factor Analysis. The first model is a standard confirmatory factor analysis (CFA) model, which tests for the adequacy of the hypothesized latent constructs and provides the correlations among the latent factors (see table 4.5, model 1, and figure 4.1).

The model did not fit according to the ML estimator, but fit well with the more appropriate distribution-free estimator. The parameter estimates were similar for the two estimators. With both methods, the adequacy of the hypothesized factor structure was confirmed. All factor loadings were significant ($p < .001$). In addition, the three latent factors were substantially correlated in a positive direction. Hard Drugs at Work and Cannabis at Work were highly correlated, and Alcohol at Work was moderately correlated with each of these factors.

Second-order Factor. The latent factors in model 1 were correlated sufficiently high to suggest that a second-order factor might account for the association among the three first-order factors. This second-order factor model was tested next. The fit statistics were, of course, identical to the initial CFA model, since the three factor correlations were replaced by three factor loadings on the second-order factor (see figure 4.2 for the latent-factor portion of the model; the measured variables were not included in this figure, since the parameter estimates were essentially identical to those of figure 4.1).

Parameter estimates were similar for the ML and distribution-free estimators. In addition, Cannabis at Work and Hard Drugs at Work appeared to be excellent indicators of a general Drugs at Work factor, with Alcohol at Work contributing moderately to this higher-order factor.

Stage Model Tests. The final two models provide an initial, cross-sectional test of the stage theory of drug use applied to disruptive drug use. These analyses parallel those of other researchers on general drug use (e.g., Hays et al., 1987; Huba & Bentler, 1983a; Huba, Wingard, & Bentler, 1981). In the first model (model 3), Cannabis at Work was predicted from Alcohol at Work, and Hard Drugs at Work was predicted from both Alcohol at Work and Cannabis at Work. In this model the path from Alcohol at Work to Hard Drugs at Work was nonsignificant. A final model (model 4) was tested with this path deleted (see figure 4.3).

As with the other models, there were only slight differences between the ML and distribution-free estimates. This model implies that Alcohol at Work generated Cannabis at Work, which in turn generated Hard Drugs at Work. Cannabis at Work mediates the relationship between Alcohol at Work and Hard Drugs at Work.

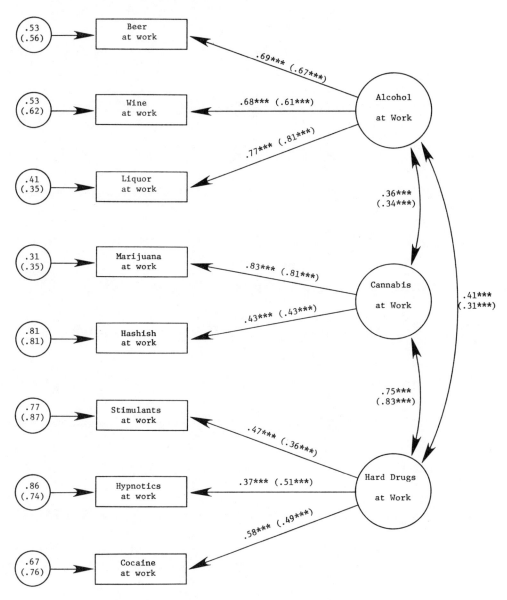

Figure 4.1 Confirmatory Factor Analysis Model of the Eight Disruptive Drug Use Items. The large circles are latent factors, the rectangles are measured variables, and the small circles are residuals. Parameter estimates are standardized, maximum likelihood estimates are listed first (distribution-free estimates are in parentheses), residual variables are variances, and significance levels were determined by critical ratios (*** $p < .001$).

Table 4.5 Summary of the Fit Indices for All Models

Model	Degrees of Freedom	Maximum Likelihood			Distribution Free		
		χ^2	p-Value	Normed Fit Index	χ^2	p-Value	Normed Fit Index
1. Confirmatory factor analysis	17	130.11	<.001	.88	11.49	.83	.98
2. Second-order factor	17	130.11	<.001	.88	11.49	.83	.98
3. Full simplex	17	130.11	<.001	.88	11.49	.83	.98
4. Strict simplex	16	134.57	<.00	.88	12.91	.80	.98
Model 3-2 difference	1	4.46	.03		1.42	.23	

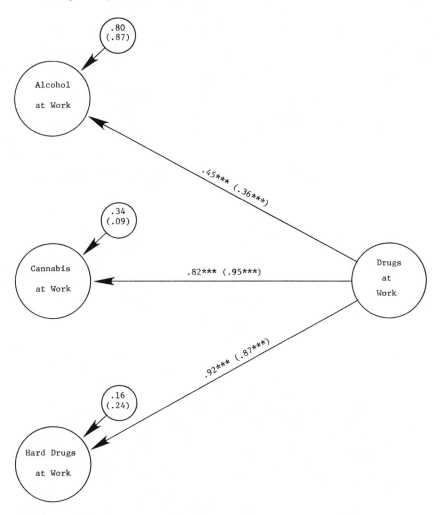

Figure 4.2 Final Stepwise Model of Disruptive Drug Use Latent Factors. The measurement portion of the model is not included in the figure. The large circles are latent factors and the small circles are residual or disturbance terms. Parameter estimates are standardized, maximum likelihood estimates are listed first (distribution-free estimates are in parentheses), residual variables are variances, and significance levels were determined by critical ratios (*** $p < .001$).

Interpretation

This series of analyses provides important answers to concerns about how use of one substance at work or school is related to use of other substances in these contexts. The overriding conclusion is that disruptive substance use is not a single-substance phenome-

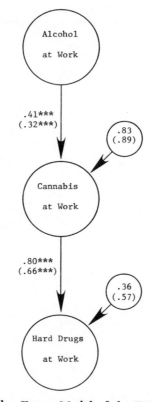

Figure 4.3 Second-Order Factor Model of the Disruptive Drug Use Latent Factors. The measurement portion of the model is not included in the figure. The large circles are latent factors and the small circles are residual or disturbance terms. Parameter estimates are standardized, maximum likelihood estimates are listed first (distribution-free estimates are in parentheses), residual variables are variances, and significance levels were determined by critical ratios (*** $p <$ .001).

non, but is highly related to similar types of substances as well as different classes of substances. Thus, if someone is caught using marijuana at work, it is quite likely that the person may be using hashish or alcohol or a hard drug on the job as well. In fact, the multivariate analyses suggest that disruptive substance use may best be characterized as disruptive polydrug abuse. Furthermore, there may be a general tendency to use drugs in inappropriate contexts and this is reflected in the use of a variety of substances at work or school.

Detailed information about specific conditional hazard rates for disruptive substance use confirmed the correlation analyses. Again, the use of one substance at work or school increased the likelihood of using other drugs in this context by several times.

From a methodological standpoint, the comparison of analyses with normality assumptions with analyses without such assumptions revealed greater similarity than differences. Since the use of the most appropriate, distribution-free methods is not possible in the larger models developed in subsequent chapters (based upon practical limitations of the method; see Bentler & Newcomb, 1986), necessary use of the ML estimator should not severely bias the results. In addition, both empirical (Harlow, 1985) and theoretical tests of ML (Satorra & Bentler, 1987) have demonstrated that ML is quite robust over normality violations.

Tests of the stage theory gave preliminary support to the extension of this hypothesis to disruptive substance use. It appears that disruptive alcohol use led to disruptive cannabis use, which in turn led to disruptive hard drug use. There was no direct path necessary between disruptive alcohol use and disruptive hard drug use; this relationship was mediated by disruptive cannabis use (e.g., Hays et al., 1987; Huba, Wingard, & Bentler, 1981). Longitudinal analyses, however, provide the most convincing and appropriate tests of this notion (see chapter 10).

For most of the remaining analyses, the eight disruptive substance use scales are used in combined forms. Since the latent-variable analyses confirmed the hypothesis that disruptive use of beer, wine, and liquor reflects a general tendency toward disruptive use of alcohol, these scales are combined to form the Disruptive Alcohol Use scale. Similarly, disruptive marijuana and hashish use are combined to form a Disruptive Cannabis Use scale. Although the three hard drugs all loaded well on the Hard Drugs at Work factor, cocaine use is kept separate because of the intense interest in this particular drug (e.g., Braham, 1986; Olson, 1986). As a result, the scales for the use of hypnotics and stimulants are combined, forming the Disruptive Hard Drug Use scale, and cocaine use appears as the Disruptive Cocaine Use scale. For latent-variable analyses, these four scales are used to reflect a general factor of Disruptive Drug Use as identified in the second-order factor analyses presented in this chapter. When the four scales are used separately, I have included a fifth scale that is the sum of all four scales and represents the frequency of disruptive drug use. The combined scales permit increased variance and improved psychometric properties of the scales, which enhance the reliability of the resultant statistics. This is particularly crucial with variables such as these, which are skewed and kurtose.

Chapter 5

DEMOGRAPHIC CORRELATES
OF DISRUPTIVE SUBSTANCE USE

To date, there has been very little, if any, research on demographic or background variables in relation to the use of drugs on the job or at school.

Here I examine demographic variables in relation to disruptive substance use, including sex of the respondent, ethnicity, age, education (high school graduate and educational plans), amount worked, income, cohabitation history, current marital status, and divorce history.

Most of the literature focuses on general drug use and therefore does not apply directly to disruptive substance use. In general, men use drugs more frequently and in greater quantities than women (e.g., Johnston, O'Malley, & Bachman, 1987; NIDA, 1987). Even so, not all studies support this conclusion (e.g., Clayton, Voss, Robbins, & Skinner, 1986). Three factors are important when considering these findings of greater use for men. First, society seems to be undergoing important change. In the past (twenty years ago or longer), drugs were used more by men than women. More recently, however, women's drug use has increased and now approaches the levels reported by men (e.g., Kalant, 1980). Second, the results may be related to the population under study. When the prevalence of drug use is estimated for general populations, rates appear to be fairly similar for men and women, especially more recently. But when special populations are studied, such as those in treatment or having trouble with drugs, more men than women appear in these groups. Thus, although women may be at only slightly less risk for using drugs than men, men are at substantially greater risk than women for developing problems with or abusing drugs. Third, more women may have been able to conceal drug use in the past. It may be easier to hide drug use when staying home as a housewife and mother (traditional women's roles) than when holding a job in the workforce (the contemporary role of many women). The additional stress of playing multiple roles (wife, mother, provider) may also result in increased drug use.

As reported in chapter 3, women engaged in disruptive substance use significantly less often than did men. In light of the discussion above, disruptive substance use may be considered more problematic and abusive than general use, which may help account for the greater prevalence of men engaging in such behaviors. If historical trends continue, however, women may increase their involvement in disruptive substance use, paralleling their increases in general drug use.

One particular difficulty in examining sex differences is determining what they really mean. Do we suppose that men are biologically or genetically more predisposed toward drug abuse than women? Or, more likely, does sex represent a factor that causes the different rates in drug use between men and women? It is possible that other demographic or background variables can explain the association between gender and disruptive substance use, which are confounded with sex. This is tested in the analyses in this chapter.

Differences in drug use have also been noted for various ethnic groups. Here, again, we find discrepancies based upon the population being studied. When abusing or treatment samples are considered, there are typically greater proportions of ethnic minorities such as blacks and Hispanics. On the other hand, when more general epidemiological samples are studied, whites and Native Americans tend to report the greatest use, followed by Hispanics, then blacks; Asians always tend to report the least use (e.g., Newcomb & Bentler, 1986f). Understanding these differences is yet another matter. Several attempts have been made to identify variables that explain these ethnic differences. For instance, Newcomb and Bentler (1986f) found that exposure to both adult and peer models of drug use explained some of the ethnic difference, although it could not explain all of the difference. Similarly, income and availability accounted for some degree of ethnic differences in drug use, but could not fully explain the differential rates of use (Maddahian, Newcomb, & Bentler, 1986). Rates of disruptive use by ethnicity are tested below and analyses are run to determine whether other demographic variables might explain whatever ethnic differences may emerge.

For adolescents, age is an important predictor of drug involvement. Young teenagers are usually not involved with drugs; the risk for using drugs increases up to late adolescence, when the greatest use of drugs is noticed (e.g., Kandel & Logan, 1984; Newcomb & Bentler, 1986d, 1987a). Changes continue into young adulthood, when both cocaine and alcohol use increase further in both prevalence and frequency, and use of cannabis and hard drugs tends to decline (e.g., Kandel, Murphy, & Karus, 1985; Newcomb & Bentler, 1987a). It is not clear, however, what, if any, changes occur during young adulthood. Although tapping only a narrow age range, such effects are examined as one demographic correlate of disruptive drug use.

An academic lifestyle has typically been found to be negatively associated with drug use. Those who do well in school and want to acquire a college education are less likely to be involved with drugs. It is possible that drug use may prevent a student from doing well at school or that those who do not do well in school may turn to drugs to relieve their frustration. Research into the causal direction between drug use and a lack of academic interest has found support for each position (e.g., Kandel, 1978; Newcomb & Bentler, 1986c; Newcomb, McCarthy, & Bentler, 1987). For the present, it is important to know that general drug use and academic and educational interests are inversely associated. I test whether a similar association is evident with disruptive substance use.

Two work-related characteristics are included as demographic variables: amount worked and income. Kandel (1984) and Bachman, O'Malley, and Johnston (1984) found that being unemployed was related to increased drug use. Thus, it could be argued that the more one worked (and assumed greater responsibility), the less one would use drugs. On the other hand, at least among teenagers, the amount of money earned has been found to be associated with more drug use (e.g., Mills & Noyes, 1984; Newcomb & Bentler, 1986a, 1988a). Interpreting some of their findings, Newcomb (1987) and Newcomb and Bentler (1988a) argue that early (teenage) involvement with a job and earning money are signs of deviance that are reflected in both higher earnings and greater drug use, compared to their peers who delayed entry into the workforce in favor of further education. Certain drugs such as cocaine are costly and may not be within reach of those with low incomes.

Marital and family variables have also been found to be related to drug use. Yamaguchi and Kandel (1985a, 1985b) have offered a role socialization theory to account for some of these associations.

They found that the use of marijuana created role strain in married couples, which was resolved by decreasing marijuana use (role socialization) or by divorcing (role transition). Thus, any role that requires greater family responsibility (e.g., being a spouse or parent) may be related to decreased drug use. Newcomb and Bentler (1985), however, found that those who used drugs in high school were more likely to get married or cohabit as a young adult than those who did not use drugs. They also found (as did Yamaguchi & Kandel, 1985b) that this high school drug use (and in particular cocaine use) also predicted divorce in these young marriages (Newcomb & Bentler, 1988a). Cohabitation (living together without being married) has also been found to be related to drug use (Newcomb, 1986a). Several indicators of family involvement are included as demographic variables in the analyses to follow. These include currently married, ever cohabited, number of children, and ever divorced.

Measures

Eleven demographic characteristics are examined in relation to disruptive substance use. These include ethnicity, sex, age, educational plans, high school graduate, amount worked, income, ever cohabited, number of children, ever divorced, and currently married. Four ethnic groups are considered based upon self-identification of the young adult (black, Hispanic, white, and Asian). Sex was coded for male (1) and females (2). Age was based on how old the respondent was when the person completed the young adult follow-up questionnaire in 1984. Ages ranged from nineteen to twenty-four years. Two variables were used to assess academic or educational orientation: educational plans and high school diploma. Educational plans were rated on six-point anchored rating scales that ranged from dropping out before completing high school (1) to doctoral degree (6). High school graduate recorded if the student had not completed high school by the time of the testing (1) or had completed it (2). Two variables were used to assess work involvement: income and amount worked. Income was indicated for the past year on an eight-point anchored scale that ranged from none (1) to more than $30,000 per year (8). Amount worked was rated for the past year on a six-point anchored rating scale that ranged from never (1) to more than nine months (6). Attending college was also considered work for this item. Four variables assessed marital or relationship history: ever cohabited, have children, ever divorced, and currently married. Each of these variables was answered in a yes (2) or no (1).

Results

Ethnic Differences

There were no significant differences among the four groups on disruptive alcohol use, but significant differences were found for all other substances (see table 5.1). Some small differences were apparent when isolating these effects between the means and prevalence rates, although the general patterns remained approximately the same.

In general, blacks reported using cannabis more prevalently and more frequently at work or school compared to the other ethnic groups. Asians reported the least disruptive cannabis use. Whites reported significantly more disruptive cocaine use than the other three ethnic groups. Whites and Hispanics reported the greatest disruptive use of hard drugs. Finally, blacks and whites reported the greatest use of any substance in a disruptive setting, Asians reported the least, and Hispanics fell between these two extremes.

Bivariate Correlations

Three dummy variables were created for ethnicity (black, white, and Asian were selected, since the greatest differences were noted

Table 5.1   Disruptive Substance Use by Ethnicity

Type of Substance	Black	Hispanic	White	Asian	F-ratio (3,735)
Alcohol					
Mean	.45	.32	.41	.26	.61
Prevalence	17%	15%	20%	13%	1.07
Cannabis					
Mean	.62ab	.28a	.44c	.06bc	3.98**
Prevalence	25%abc	15%ad	17%be	2%cde	6.44***
Cocaine					
Mean	.06a	.03b	.19abc	.08c	3.49*
Prevalence	4%a	3%b	13%abc	5%c	5.40***
Hard Drugs					
Mean	.00a	.13	.19ab	.02b	3.01*
Prevalence	.00ab	6%a	8%bc	1%c	4.62**
Any Use					
Mean	1.13a	.75b	1.23bc	.42ac	3.16*
Prevalence	29%a	25%b	35%c	14%abc	5.86***

$*p < .05; **p < .01; ***p < .001.$

Note: Having the same letters in a row indicates a significant difference.

on these above; one group had to be eliminated for the multiple regression analyses to follow).

Disruptive alcohol use was significantly correlated with being male, having cohabited, having no children, and not being currently married (see table 5.2). Disruptive cannabis use was significantly correlated with being male, having few educational plans, having cohabited, being black, and not being Asian. Disruptive cocaine use was significantly correlated with having few educational plans, high income, having cohabited, and being white. Disruptive hard drug use was significantly correlated with having few educational plans, high income, having cohabited, being white, and not being black. Finally, frequency of all disruptive substance use was significantly associated with being male, having few educational plans, higher income, having cohabited, not being currently married, being white, and not being Asian.

Multiple Regression Analyses

All thirteen demographic variables were next allowed to predict simultaneously each disruptive substance use scale. These analyses indicate which background variables are uniquely associated with disruptive drug use. If the gender or ethnic differences in disruptive substance use were accounted for by other demographic factors, the bivariate effects would be reduced or eliminated in these multivariate analyses (see table 5.2).

In general, these thirteen variables accounted for only a small amount of variance in the disruptive substance use measures. The amount of variance ranged from a low of 3 percent for disruptive alcohol use (although still significant) to a high of 9 percent on disruptive cannabis use and any disruptive drug use. All regression analyses were significant.

In most instances, the significant and independent predictors of disruptive substance use (indicated by beta weights) were similar to the significant bivariate correlations. This suggests that there may not be a great degree of overlap or intercorrelation among the thirteen demographic variables, challenging the demographic confound suggestion about the gender and ethnic differences. Comparing the bivariate to the multivariate results, I found no changes in the variables that were significantly associated with disruptive alcohol use. Disruptive cannabis use was significantly predicted from being male, having few educational plans, having cohabited, being black, and being white. Disruptive cocaine use was predicted from having few educational plans, high income, having cohabited, being a high school graduate, and being white. Disrup-

Table 5.2 Correlations and Multiple Regression Results of Demographic Variables with Disruptive Substance Use

Demographic Characteristics	Alcohol		Cannabis		Cocaine		Hard Drugs		Any Use	
	r	Beta	r	Beta	r	Beta	r	Beta	r	Beta
Sex	−.11***	−.09**	−.13***	−.13***	.01	.02	−.02	−.01	−.12**	−.11**
Age	.01	.00	.00	.02	−.03	.05	.03	−.06	.01	.00
Educational plans	−.01	−.04	−.15***	−.16***	−.14***	−.14***	−.12**	−.05	−.13***	−.15***
Amount worked	.02	−.01	.05	.03	.03	−.02	.05	.01	.05	.01
Income	.03	.01	.04	−.02	.11**	.08*	.12**	.07*	.08*	.03
Ever cohabited	.08*	.08*	.17***	.15***	.15***	.13***	.16***	.09**	.19***	.17***
High school graduate	.02	.02	−.05	−.02	.04	.06*	.02	−.01	−.01	−.01
Have children	−.08*	−.07*	−.01	−.05	−.01	−.02	−.04	−.03	−.06	−.07*
Ever divorced	−.01	−.01	−.01	−.02	−.01	−.02	.00	.00	−.01	−.02
Currently married	−.10**	−.07*	−.05	−.06	−.02	−.05	−.05	−.07*	−.09*	−.09*
Black	.02	.06	.07*	.14**	−.06	.03	−.08*	−.04	.01	.09*
White	.02	.04	.04	.08*	.12**	.13**	.10**	.04	.08*	.10*
Asian	−.03	.00	−.09*	−.01	−.03	.05	−.05	−.02	−.08*	.00
Multiple Regression Summary										
F-ratio (13,725) =	1.84*		5.20***		3.81***		2.14**		5.31***	
R	.18		.29		.25		.19		.29	
R²	.03		.09		.06		.04		.09	

*p < .05; **p < .01; ***p < .001.

tive use of hard drugs was independently associated with high income, having cohabited, and currently not being married. Any type of disruptive substance use was related to being male, having few educational plans, having cohabited, having no children, currently not being married, being black, and being white.

Interpretation

Results from the analyses presented above revealed that there are some consistent demographic correlates of disruptive substance use, that some demographic variables were differentially related to certain kinds of disruptive drug use, and that certain demographic characteristics were consistently unrelated to any type of disruptive substance use. In general, it seems just as difficult to predict disruptive substance use from demographic variables as it is to predict general substance use in any context. Similar sets of variables have been able to account for roughly the same percentage of variance in general drug use, compared to the rather small (but significant) portion of the variance accounted for in disruptive substance use found here (e.g., Mills & Noyes, 1984). In other words, background and demographic variables do not appear to be the best predictors for the variations in disruptive substance use. Nonetheless, some interesting patterns did emerge.

Gender was a significant predictor of all types of disruptive substance use, except for cocaine and hard drugs. Sex remained a significant predictor in the multivariate analyses, indicating that other interpretations of the sex differences cannot be found in the demographic variables included in the analyses. Interestingly, the sex differences in disruptive substance use appear to be more prominent than sex differences in general substance use in this sample (see chapter 3). Even though these young adult women have equivalent rates of general drug use, men are substantially more likely to use drugs at work or school than women. This may indicate that men may be more vulnerable or at risk for abuse of drugs than women, as considered at the beginning of this chapter. As a result, being male must be considered a risk factor for disruptive substance use in this sample of young adults.

Consistent effects were also noted for ethnicity, which could not be totally accounted for by the other demographic variables included in the multivariate analyses. There was no differential vulnerability to disruptive alcohol use by ethnic group. Blacks, however, were at the greatest risk for disruptive use of cannabis, and whites were at the greatest risk for disruptive cocaine and hard drug use. Asians were at the least risk for any disruptive substance use compared to the other ethnic groups. Hispanics reported moderate levels of disruptive substance use. These findings are generally in accord with the epidemiological studies of ethnic differences in drug use, and not the treatment or abuse studies. The exception to this is the high rate of disruptive cannabis use among blacks, who must be considered at high risk for use of marijuana or hashish in inappropriate settings. Thus, being black or white must be considered risk factors for disruptive substance use.

There were no significant effects for the age variable on any of the disruptive substance use scales. This is not particularly surprising, given the rather narrow age range included in the sample. This does point out, however, that the substantial changes in drug use prevalence during adolescence (e.g., Kandel, 1980; Kandel & Logan, 1984) does not continue into young adulthood. If changes occur in patterns of drug use from young adulthood on, they will generally happen over a greater span of years. This implies that drug use may be well established by the young adult years.

Among the work-related variables, only income was associated with disruptive substance use, and this only for cocaine and hard drugs. This suggests that those earning higher wages may be at greater risk for using cocaine or hard drugs at work or school than those with lower incomes. No such differences were found for disruptive alcohol or cannabis use, perhaps indicating that those with higher incomes may have a greater choice in the selection of drugs, but it does not stop them from using the more common drugs of alcohol and marijuana. Amount worked was unrelated to any type of disruptive drug use.

Among the educational or academic orientation variables, educational plans, but not high school graduation, were consistently associated with disruptive substance use of all types. This may indicate that a positive attitude toward education is a critical deterrent from using drugs in inappropriate settings, as opposed to one's actual success in the school system (i.e., graduating from high school). Having plans for further education may reflect an ability to plan long-term goals and an ability to delay gratification. These cognitive coping skills may reduce or help prevent disruptive substance use (e.g., Newcomb, McCarthy, & Bentler, 1987). As a result, having few educational plans must be considered a risk factor for disruptive substance use.

Finally, there were some consistent and surprising results in regard to the family and relationship background variables. As expected, having cohabited sometime in one's life (not necessarily currently) was significantly associated with all types of disruptive substance use. Living together without being married may indicate a lack of traditionalism or conventionalism that may predispose a person to perform other deviant acts, such as using drugs at work or school. Being married and having children (suggesting increased family responsibilities) were inversely related to disruptive substance use. This substantiates the findings of Yamaguchi and Kandel (1985b) and suggests that family-role responsibility is associated with work-role responsibility (not using drugs on the job). Contrary to the general literature on drug use (e.g., Kandel, 1980), however, those who had divorced were at no greater risk for disruptive substance use than those who had not divorced. Based on these results, being single, not having children, and having ever cohabited must be considered risk factors for disruptive substance use.

In conclusion, I have been able to identify several background or demographic variables that were significantly related to disruptive substance use. Nevertheless, it must be emphasized that even the largest of these differences was quite small in terms of accountable variance. As a result, we must turn to other factors to explain a greater portion of disruptive substance use.

Chapter 6

RELATIONSHIP BETWEEN GENERAL DRUG USE AND DISRUPTIVE DRUG USE

In this chapter, I examine the association between general and disruptive drug use. General drug use is the frequency of using drugs during the past six months in any context. Thus, the time frames for measuring the two types of drug use (general and disruptive) are identical; the context of use is directly specified for disruptive drug use (at work or school), but not for general drug use.

Based on these operationalizations, we would expect that general and disruptive drug use would be highly related. This is conceptualized in figure 6.1. The larger circle indicates general substance use and the smaller circle indicates disruptive substance use. The difference in sizes reflects what we have already discovered: specifically, that general substance use is substantially more prevalent than disruptive substance use. Section A of the figure represents the portion of general substance use that is unrelated to disruptive substance use. Another way of saying this is that section A accounts for the group of people who may use drugs regularly, but do not do so at work or school. Section B reflects the amount of general substance use that is related to or predictive of disruptive substance use. This overlap is the focus of this chapter. Finally, section C of the figure represents the portion of disruptive substance use that is not related to general substance use. It would be expected that this section would be relatively small, since it denotes those people who use drugs at work or school but do not do so outside these contexts.

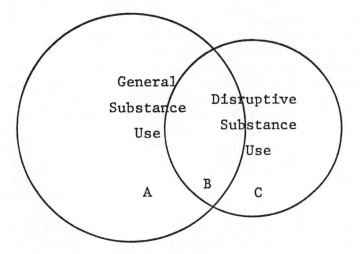

Figure 6.1 Abstract Depiction of General Drug Use and Disruptive Drug Use.   Sections A and C are specific to the two types of drug use and section B is the overlap.

There is no literature that addresses the issues posed in this chapter. Researchers have not yet confronted the degree of correspondence between one's general proclivity to use drugs and actually using drugs on the job. There seems to be an unspoken assumption, nevertheless, that the association is quite high, if not perfect. For instance, virtually all discussions of drug use on the job cite statistics of general drug use of various populations to argue that disruptive drug use must be rampant (e.g., Backer, 1987). This may not be a reasonable assumption, since even heavy users of drugs may have internal prohibitions against using them on the job or at school. A more reasonable assumption may be that at least some general drug use must precede disruptive drug use for most people. Further, it is important to determine what other factors account for disruptive drug use beyond a general tendency to use drugs. But before confronting this issue, which is the subject of the remainder of this book, it is vital to determine the extent of overlap between general drug use and disruptive drug use.

Some tangential evidence on this issue is available from studies that examine the association between consumption of drugs and problems with drugs. Although disruptive drug use can be conceptually understood as a problem with drugs, these researchers have not typically incorporated such measures in their investigations. For instance, Sadava and Secord (1984) found that consumption of alcohol and other drugs was relatively unrelated to problems with alcohol. In their review of the literature, they report that other research has typically found associations between drug consumption and drug problems to be correlated in the .3 range. In another study, Sadava (1985) found that among adults, consumption of alcohol was largely independent of problems with alcohol. He argued that alcohol consumption and alcohol problems must be more clearly separated, implying that one is certainly not a good proxy for the other. In one of our studies, we found that developmental predictors of general drug use differed from those for problematic drug use (Stein, Newcomb, & Bentler, 1987a). Despite the conceptual similarity between disruptive drug use and problems with drugs, it is not clear whether the findings noted above can be considered reliable for disruptive substance use as well.

Some preliminary analyses of my data have already been done on this issue. Stein, Newcomb, and Bentler (submitted) examined the association between latent factors of drug use frequency, drug use quantity, subjective problems with drugs, objective problems with drugs, and disruptive substance use. Disruptive substance use was correlated .55 with drug use frequency, .52 with drug use quantity, and .68 with subjective problems with drugs, after controlling for use of specific drugs. Several additional higher-order factor models were tested. Although disruptive drug use was a significant factor in all of these, it tended to be the smallest contributor, with between 59 percent and 83 percent of its variance not explained by the other drug use and problematic drug use factors. Thus, even though there were moderately large associations between disruptive drug use and a variety of other, more general drug-related measures, there was a far from perfect association with these. In fact, in no instance was even more than half the variance of disruptive substance use accounted for in these models.

Several analyses are presented in this chapter to examine in greater detail the relationship between general drug use and disruptive drug use. First, correlations between general drug use and disruptive drug use scales are examined. Multiple regression analyses are then used to determine the best combination of predictors for various types of disruptive drug use. In these analyses, greater specificity is given to the types of general hard drug use, breaking it down into scales for stimulants, hypnotics, inhalants, PCP, cocaine, psychedelics, and narcotics. In addition, cigarettes and nonprescription medications are examined. Next, the likelihood of using various types of drugs at work or school is compared for general users and nonusers of drugs in general. Following this, Guttman scaling analyses are used to determine where disruptive drug use falls in a sequence of general drug involvement or increasing progression of general drug use. Finally, several latent-variable models are used to capture the multivariate associations between general substance use and disruptive substance use.

Measures

The eight disruptive drug use items were averaged into four scales and a total score for all use. Disruptive alcohol use included disruptive use of beer, wine, and liquor. Disruptive cannabis use included disruptive use of marijuana and hashish. Disruptive cocaine use was a single item. Disruptive hard drug use included disruptive use of stimulants and hypnotics. The disruptive use of all drugs was the average of all eight items. Similar scales were generated for the general frequency of use items. In addition, one item assessed the general frequency of cigarette use, and four items were averaged to reflect nonprescription medication use (this included medications for sleep, stimulation, colds, and coughs).

Results

Correlations between General and Disruptive Drug Use

The seven general drug use measures were correlated with the five disruptive drug use scales (see table 6.1). All correlations were

Table 6.1 Correlations between General Substance Use Scales and Disruptive Substance Use Scales

General Substance Use	Disruptive Substance Use				
	Alcohol	*Cannabis*	*Cocaine*	*Hard Drugs*	*All Use*
Cigarettes	.10**	.23***	.15***	.12**	.23***
Nonprescription medication	.07*	− .01	.07*	.12**	.08*
Alcohol	.26***	.13***	.18***	.13***	.26***
Cannabis	.15***	.63***	.28***	.26***	.52***
Cocaine	.14***	.33***	.50***	.30***	.43***
Hard drugs	.16***	.36***	.28***	.56***	.48***
All use	.24***	.40***	.33***	.37***	.49***

*$p < .05$; **$p < .01$; ***$p < .001$.

significant except between nonprescription medication use and disruptive cannabis use. The magnitude of the correlations, however, varied tremendously. In general, use of nonprescription medications was least correlated with disruptive substance use. Cigarette use and general use of alcohol were moderately correlated with disruptive substance use. On the other hand, general use of cannabis, cocaine, and hard drugs was moderately to highly correlated with all disruptive drug use, with the exception of disruptive alcohol use.

One important pattern is also evident. General use of a particular substance was most highly correlated with the disruptive use of the same substance. For instance, general cannabis use was most highly correlated with disruptive cannabis use. Again, general use of all substances was most highly correlated with disruptive use of all substances. Together, these two patterns indicate that the general use of all types of drugs is moderately associated with disruptive use of all types of drugs (general polydrug use associated with disruptive polydrug use), as well as indicating strong correlations between general and disruptive use of specific substances. Nevertheless, even the largest of these associations (between general cannabis use and disruptive cannabis use) accounted for no more than 40 percent of the variance between these two styles of drug use. Thus, even though many are highly correlated, one cannot be used as a proxy for the other.

Multiple Regression Analyses

The next set of analyses used the general drug use scales to predict simultaneously each of the disruptive substance use scales. Since general hard drug use combines a variety of illicit substances, this scale was broken down into six scales. This was done in order to provide a more precise description of hard drug involvement, one that may differentially influence disruptive substance use. As a result, each disruptive drug use scale is predicted from use of eleven types of substances (see table 6.2). With only a few exceptions, primarily for inhalants, PCP, and nonprescription medications, all of the general drug use measures were significantly correlated with each of the disruptive drug use scales.

The scale for disruptive alcohol use was significantly predicted from more general alcohol use and narcotics use. Although significant, this equation accounted for only 8 percent of the variance of disruptive alcohol use, leaving 92 percent of the variance unexplained. Disruptive cannabis use was uniquely predicted from more general cannabis use, psychedelic use, less PCP use, and less use of nonprescription medications. This equation accounted for the greatest amount of variance among the disruptive drug use scales, but still left 57 percent of the variance unexplained. Disruptive cocaine use was predicted from more general cocaine, stimulant, psychedelic, and inhalant use. Disruptive hard drug use was uniquely predicted from more general use of stimulants, inhalants, and narcotics. Finally, all use of disruptive substances was predicted from more general use of cannabis, cocaine, hypnotics, stimulants, psychedelics, inhalants, and narcotics.

These results corroborate the bivariate analyses and underscore the conclusion that general use of a specific substance is the best predictor of disruptive use of the same substance. General alcohol use contributed only to the prediction of disruptive alcohol use and not to any of the other disruptive use scales.

Prevalence of Use Comparisons

The general use or nonuse of particular classes of drugs was compared to the use or nonuse of drugs in inappropriate settings; chi-square tests were used for statistical comparison (see table 6.3). Ninety percent of the sample reported some general use of alcohol during the past six months. Of the 10 percent who did not use any alcohol, none of these people used drugs at work or school. Thus, one necessary condition for disruptive drug use is some use of alcohol. Use of nonprescription medications was unrelated to use of drugs at work or school. Forty-three percent of the sample had used a cannabis substance at least once (in general) during the past six months. This group was several times more likely than nonusers of cannabis to have used drugs at work or school. Similar results were found for general prevalence of hard drug use, cocaine use, and, interestingly, cigarette use. Thus, general use of an illicit substance, and cigarettes to a lesser extent, increased the likelihood of disruptive substance use by several times, depending on the specific substance. On the other hand, being a general alcohol or nonprescription medication user did not appreciably raise the chances of disruptive substance use, but nonuse of alcohol appeared to preclude any disruptive substance use.

Guttman Scaling Analyses

As discussed in chapter 4, drug use is assumed to be acquired in a series of stages or steps. It is unclear, however, at which step the choice to engage in disruptive drug use is made. To explore this issue, Guttman scaling analyses were used on the general use or

Table 6.2 Bivariate and Multiple Regression Analyses between General Substance Use and Disruptive Substance Use

General Drug Use	Disruptive Substance Use									
	Alcohol		Cannabis		Cocaine		Hard Drugs		All Use	
	r	Beta	r	Beta	r	Beta	r	Beta	r	Beta
Cigarettes	.10**	.00	.23***	.02	.15***	−.03	.12**	−.06	.23***	−.01
Alcohol	.26***	.23***	.13***	.03	.18***	−.05	.13***	−.05	.26***	.05
Cannabis	.15***	.05	.63***	.63***	.28***	−.02	.26***	.00	.52***	.33***
Cocaine	.14***	.00	.33***	−.05	.50***	.48***	.30***	.04	.43***	.09*
Hypnotics	.11**	.02	.29***	.10	.16***	−.01	.28***	.01	.31***	.06*
Stimulants	.10**	−.04	.27***	.01	.30***	.08*	.60***	.54***	.42***	.17***
Psychedelics	.13***	.05	.30***	.08*	.28***	.12**	.19***	−.07	.33***	.06*
Inhalants	.07*	.03	.06	.02	.14***	.06*	.26***	.10**	.17***	.06*
Narcotics	.15***	.08*	.18***	−.04	.07*	−.05	.35***	.19***	.27***	.06*
PCP	.01	−.02	−.02	−.07*	.02	−.05	.10**	.05	.03	−.05
Nonprescription medication	.07*	.01	−.01	−.08**	.07*	−.03	.12**	−.03	.08*	−.05
Multiple Regression Summary										
F-ratio (11,727)	6.05***		49.13***		24.83***		45.06***		35.59***	
R	.29		.65		.52		.64		.59	
R²	.08		.43		.27		.41		.35	

*p < .05; **p < .01; ***p < .001.

nonuse of alcohol, cannabis, cocaine, and hard drugs. Use or nonuse of any drug at work or school was included with the four general drug use variables. Analyses were run for the total sample, and separately for men and women (see table 6.4).

The standard indices of scalability are listed at the bottom of the table and all indicate acceptable scales (e.g., Donovan & Jessor, 1983; Mills & Noyes, 1984). For all subjects, the order of progression went from nonuse, to alcohol, to cannabis, to cocaine, to using drugs at work, and finally to hard drugs. An identical sequence was noted for the women (not surprising, since women represent 70 percent of the total sample). A slightly different order of sequence was noted for the men; drugs at work occurred just after cannabis use and before cocaine use. Thus, disruptive substance use appeared earlier in the sequence of drug involvement for men compared to women, and may help explain the prevalence differences in disruptive substance use by sex. Nevertheless, these findings indicate that in general, someone who uses drugs at work is at least moderately involved with drug use away from work, at least to the extent of using an illicit drug (cannabis or cocaine).

Latent-variable Analyses

Since we know that the four disruptive substance use scales and the general drug use scales are intercorrelated (reflecting polydrug use in general or disruptively), it makes sense to examine all of these variables simultaneously. Two latent-variable models were developed. In each of these models there were two latent factors: one for General Substance Use, with indicators for alcohol frequency, cannabis frequency, cocaine frequency, and hard drug frequency, and the other for Disruptive Substance Use, with indicators of alcohol at work, cannabis at work, cocaine at work, and hard drugs at work. In order to capture the associations, noted in the previous analyses, between general use of a specific substance and disruptive use of the same substance, four paths were added to the models. For instance, alcohol at work was predicted from the residual variance of alcohol frequency. Similar paths were included for cannabis, cocaine, and hard drugs.

Direct Association.   Disruptive Substance Use was directly predicted from General Substance Use (see figure 6.2). With two unanticipated additions, this model adequately fit the data, χ^2 (12, $n = 739$) = 15.15, $p = .23$, NFI = .99. Results indicate that 38 percent of the variance in Disruptive Substance Use was accounted for by General Substance Use. All specific effects from the general substance residuals to the specific disruptive drug use variables

Table 6.3 Prevalence of Disruptive Substance Use by Prevalence of General Drug Use

Prevalence of General Substance Use	General Prevalence	Prevalence of Disruptive Substance Use				
		Alcohol	Cannabis	Cocaine	Hard Drugs	Any Use
General Prevalence		18.3	16.6	9.3	5.5	30.9
Cigarettes						
Use	39.1	26.6	28.4	15.9	10.0	50.2
Nonuse	60.9	12.9	9.1	5.1	2.7	18.4
$X^2(1) =$		22.38***	47.70***	24.27***	18.23***	83.04***
Nonprescription medication[a]						
Use	68.3	18.6	17.4	10.7	6.3	32.9
Nonuse	31.7	17.5	15.0	6.4	3.8	26.5
$X^2(1) =$		0.13	0.70	3.47	1.89	3.05
Alcohol						
Use	90.0	20.3	18.5	10.4	6.2	34.3
Nonuse	10.0	0.0	0.0	0.0	0.0	0.0
$X^2(1) =$		18.38***	16.42	8.47**	4.83*	36.69***

Cannabis						
Use	42.8	26.3	38.6	18.4	9.8	52.5
Nonuse	57.2	12.3	0.0	2.6	2.4	14.7
$\chi^2(1) =$		23.65***	191.95***	53.03***	19.14***	121.62***
Cocaine						
Use	33.8	28.0	36.8	27.6	15.2	58.8
Nonuse	66.2	13.3	6.3	0.0	0.6	16.6
$\chi^2(1) =$		23.97***	110.63***	148.86***	67.17***	138.32***
Hard Drugs						
Use	24.6	33.0	38.5	24.7	22.5	63.7
Nonuse	75.4	13.5	9.5	4.3	0.0	20.1
$\chi^2(1) =$		34.94***	82.85***	67.55***	132.85***	122.39***
Any Use						
Use	90.9	20.1	18.3	10.3	6.1	33.9
Nonuse	9.1	0.0	0.0	0.0	0.0	0.0
$\chi^2(1) =$		16.47***	14.71***	7.59**	4.33*	32.88***

$*p < .05; **p < .01; ***p < .001.$
[a]Not included in the any use total.

Table 6.4   Guttman Scaling Analyses of General Drug Use Scale and Any Disruptive Drug Use

All Subjects	Males Only	Females Only
Order of Progression		
Nonuse	Nonuse	Nonuse
Alcohol	Alcohol	Alcohol
Cannabis	Cannabis	Cannabis
Cocaine	Drugs at Work	Cocaine
Drugs at Work	Cocaine	Drugs at Work
Hard Drugs	Hard Drugs	Hard Drugs
Scalability		
.62	.65	.61
Coefficient of Reproducibility		
.89	.89	.89
Minimal Marginal Reproducibility		
.72	.70	.72

were significant as hypothesized. Two additional effects were needed in the model that were not hypothesized. First, General Substance Use had a direct effect on disruptive hard drug use. Second, hard drug frequency had a direct impact on Disruptive Substance Use.

Second-order Factor.   The previous model indicated that General Substance Use and Disruptive Substance Use were highly related, although not identical. In the next model, a general second-order factor of All Polydrug Use was hypothesized to account for the association between these two first-order latent factors. For the model to be identified, this second-order factor must have three indicators. Based upon modification indices, hard drugs at work was used as the third indicator of the second-order factor. As a result of including this extra factor loading, the already small loading of hard drugs at work on Disruptive Substance Use became nonsignificant and was deleted (see figure 6.3). Three small correlated errors were needed to fit the model, but are not interpreted. This model fit the data well, χ^2 (11, n = 739) = 14.82, p = .19, NFI = .99. The second-order factor of All Polydrug Use accounted for 61 percent of the variance in General Substance Use and 67 percent of the variance in Disruptive Substance Use. The remaining variance of Disruptive Substance Use can be interpreted as the amount of drug use at work or school that is not a part of a general drug-using lifestyle, but a specific feature of the work or school context.

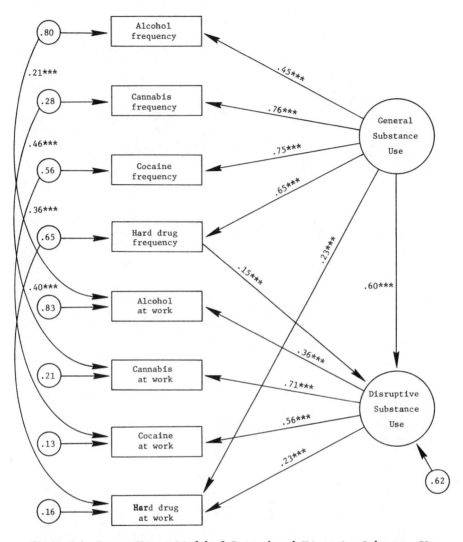

Figure 6.2 Latent Factor Model of General and Disruptive Substance Use That Assumes that General Use Precedes Disruptive Use. The large circles are latent factors, the rectangles are measured variables, and the small circles are residuals. Parameter estimates are standardized, residual variables are variances, and significance levels were determined by critical ratios (*** $p < .001$).

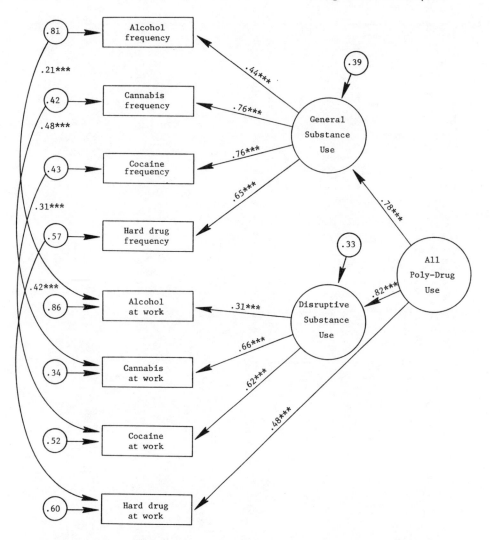

Figure 6.3   Second-Order Factor Model of General Substance Use and Disruptive Substance Use. The large circles are latent factors, the rectangles are measured variables, and the small circles are residuals. Parameter estimates are standardized, residual variables or disturbance terms are variances, and significance levels were determined by critical ratios (*** *p* < .001).

Interpretation

Results of the analyses lead to several conclusions on the association between general drug use (in all contexts) and disruptive drug use (at work or school). First, as expected, disruptive drug use and general drug use are highly related. They are not perfectly related (i.e., high general use of drugs does not guarantee disruptive drug use), however, and in most cases the extent of general drug use can only predict less than 50 percent of the variance in disruptive drug use. Thus, those researchers, journalists, and politicians who refer to prevalence rates of general drug use to characterize the extent of disruptive drug use are in error, since there is certainly not a one-to-one association. Nevertheless, it is possible that a person's general practice of substance use may be the best predictor of disruptive substance use, despite its decidedly less than full explanatory ability.

On the other hand, the prevalence patterns of disruptive drug use parallel those of general drug use, though the latter are substantially lower in magnitude. Even though the rank order of prevalence rates is identical for general and disruptive drug use (in descending order are alcohol, cannabis, cocaine, and hard drugs), they are not proportionally equivalent. For instance, the prevalence rates for general drug use during the past six months for alcohol and cannabis were 90 percent and 43 percent, respectively. Clearly the prevalence of general alcohol use was more than twice that of general cannabis use. In contrast, the rates for disruptive alcohol and cannabis use were 18 percent and 17 percent, respectively. From this we can conclude that disruptive drug use more often involves an illicit substance than the prevalence of general drug use would imply.

Corroboration of this point is found in the Guttman scaling analyses. Here it was found that drug use at work occurred subsequent to both alcohol and cannabis use for men and subsequent to these and cocaine use for women. This indicates that using drugs at work or school implies a level of drug involvement somewhere between cannabis and cocaine use on the low end, and hard drug use on the upper end. The different scaling results for men and women suggest that using drugs at work occurs sooner in a sequence of drug involvement for men than for women. This may help explain the large sex differences noted for most types of disruptive substance use. Men are more vulnerable to using drugs at work or school than women at the same level of general drug involvement.

The present analyses support the earlier suggestions by Sadava (1985; Sadava & Secord, 1984) that general drug consumption and problems from such use are not identical. Although disruptive substance use may not technically be a problematic use of drugs, it does reflect drug use in a problematic manner, identified specifically as use in an inappropriate location or context, and thus a problem. The present analyses have demonstrated that even though these two patterns of use are moderately related, one cannot be inferred perfectly from the other.

The conditional prevalence rates of disruptive drug use by general use or nonuse of substances were also quite informative. The 10 percent of the sample who did not use alcohol in general also did not use drugs at work or school (including drugs other than alcohol). In other words, knowing that someone had not used alcohol in any context during the past six months practically guaranteed that he or she had not used any other type of drug at work or school. The converse of this was not true. Knowing someone had used alcohol during the past six months provided no information about whether or not that person had engaged in disruptive drug use. On the other hand, knowing that someone had used cigarettes or an illicit drug during the past six months (cannabis, cocaine, or hard drugs) substantially increased the likelihood that he or she was also involved in disruptive substance use. In fact, of those who had used a hard drug at least once during the past six months, 64 percent had also used at least one type of drug on at least one occasion at work or school. The comparable prevalence rate for cocaine users was 59 percent, for cannabis users it was 53 percent, and for cigarette smokers it was 50 percent. In other words, if someone used cigarettes or an illicit drug during the past six months in any context, there was a better than fifty-fifty chance that the person had also engaged in disruptive substance use at least once during the same period.

Overall the patterns of use seem fairly clear. Heavy use of a particular substance increased the chances that the same substance was also used at work or school (particularly for illicit drugs). General polydrug use (use of a variety of drugs in any context) was highly associated with disruptive polydrug use. Both of these conclusions were most apparent in the latent-variable analyses. Nearly 40 percent of the variance in Disruptive Substance Use was accounted for by General Substance Use. Each of the specific types of disruptive substance use was significantly predicted from the residuals (specific, unique, or nonfactor determined portion) of their respective types of general substance use. In addition, it was found that high levels of General Substance Use (polydrug involvement) significantly increased hard drug use at work or school. In a complementary fashion, high involvement with hard drug use in general increased involvement with Disruptive Substance Use (use of all types of drugs at work or school). Thus, there appears to be a synergistic influence between polydrug involvement, use of hard drugs, and disruptive drug use of all types.

The final latent-variable analyses revealed that both General

Substance Use and Disruptive Substance Use could be partly accounted for by a higher-order construct or tendency toward All Polydrug Use. There remained 33 percent of the variance of Disruptive Substance Use not captured by this general construct that must be considered a unique variance attributable to only using drugs on the job (after the tendency toward polydrug involvement was controlled). Many analyses in the remaining chapters attempt to explain this variance. Since a sizable portion of the variance of Disruptive Substance Use is shared with General Substance Use, however, this would not be captured in the remaining 33 percent. As a result, I will explain the correlates and predictors of disruptive substance use in more than one way, in order to provide the most complete picture possible with the existing data.

First, I present the correlations and multiple regression analyses between types of disruptive drug use and the variables of substantive concern to the particular chapter. Next, I present latent-variable analyses that examine the associations between both disruptive drug use and general drug use and a variety of other psychosocial measures. Finally, I use a model similar to that of figure 6.3 to look again at these associations, but this time in terms of the All Polydrug Use factor, as well as the specific portions of variance (residuals) left from Disruptive Substance Use and General Substance Use. In addition, I test whether specific types of disruptive substance use (alcohol, cannabis, cocaine, or hard drugs) are also associated with these psychosocial factors. Thus, I am able to determine the variables related to disruptive drug use (including the component of general drug use), those related specifically to using drugs at work or school, and those associated with the specific types of disruptive drug use.

Chapter 7

DISRUPTIVE DRUG USE AND WORK-RELATED FACTORS

One of the most common concerns regarding drug use in the workplace is whether or not such behavior results at least in part from the work environment itself (e.g., Gupta & Jenkins, 1984; Jenkins, 1984; Seeman & Anderson, 1983). In this chapter I address this issue in regard to several work-related variables and sources of income. In particular, I present analyses that relate various types of disruptive drug use to measures of job instability, perceptions of problems at work, degree of work involvement, earned income, income from public assistance, perceived amount of emotional support for work-related problems, anticipated satisfaction with support for work-related problems, involvement with vandalism at the worksite, and seeking personal advice for work-related problems. Further analyses attempt to separate the associations among these variables related to general drug use (drug use in any context), specific drug use at work or school, and an overall tendency for all drug use (the overlap between general and disruptive drug use).

Herold and Conlon (1981) reviewed the available literature on the relationship between job-based variables and alcoholism, and found no conclusive evidence that a person's work environment contributed substantially to the emergence of alcohol abuse. In order to organize a perspective on these issues, they hypothesized three pathways that could account for a relationship between occupation and alcoholism. These pathways included a requirement of the job (i.e., a whisky taster), social influences, and response to the job. Olkinuora (1984) suggested four risk factors related to an occupation that could generate alcoholism in an employee. These included the availability of alcohol at work, social pressures to drink on the job, separation from normal social relationships, and freedom from supervision. These factors do not include work stress, which has been considered an important motivation for drug or alcohol abuse. Gupta and Jenkins (1984) hypothesized three antecedents to alcohol and drug abuse as an employee's response to the work environment. These included distancing forces that tend to separate a person from the work organization, attractions or distractions (dissatisfaction with the job), and constraints on employee behavior (emanating from the person, organization, or environment, such as cultural, legal, and economic).

These theories suggest that drug and alcohol abuse (in general or on the job) may be related to various characteristics of the work environment. Most of these theories assume that some type of job stress can result in drug or alcohol abuse. Gupta and Beehr (1979) have identified four types of job stress. Job stress can result from role ambiguity, role overload, underutilization of skills, and inadequacy of resources. It has been documented that various types of job stress are related to job dissatisfaction and unhappiness (e.g., Hackman & Lawler, 1971; Lyons, 1971, 1972). Job dissatisfaction, in turn, can lead to various forms of withdrawal by the employee (absenteeism and turnover) and drug or alcohol abuse (e.g., Gupta & Beehr, 1979). Similarly, Milbourn (1984) assumes that drug and alcohol abuse is a response to work-related pressures and stress. He suggests that there are two types of job stress: organizational frustration (institutional blocks to achieving goals) and job stress (job ambiguity and job conflict).

Although positing somewhat different types of job stress, these theories share the hypothesis that job stress affects job satisfaction, which then can generate drug or alcohol abuse, either in general or on the job (e.g., Gupta & Jenkins, 1984). Although this makes intuitive sense, the empirical literature does not always support this hypothesis, and in fact often challenges it.

In most studies, work-related variables are examined in relation to drug or alcohol abuse in the employee, but not necessarily on the job. At least two studies are an exception to this tendency and present data regarding job satisfaction and drug use on the job. In a sample of long-distance truckers, Guinn (1983) investigated the relation of drug use while trucking to a variety of other counterproductive behaviors, such as doing poor work on purpose, theft of cargo, failing to report damage to property, and spreading malicious rumors, as well as job satisfaction. Correlations were examined in two subgroups: those with fifteen years of experience or less and those with more than fifteen years of experience. He found that there was no significant association between drug use on the job and any of the counterproductive behaviors and job satisfaction for the most experienced truckers. On the other hand, drug use while trucking was significantly correlated with performing work badly on purpose and theft of cargo, but not with job satisfaction for the less experienced truckers. On-the-job drug use was not significantly associated with job satisfaction, vandalism, or spreading rumors in either group. In the second study, Mangione and Quinn (1975) used a national sample of wage and salaried workers to examine correlations between job satisfaction and various counterproductive behaviors at work (most of which were the same as those included in the previous study), including the use of "drugs or chemicals (except vitamins and aspirin) to help get through the work day." Correlations were examined in four groups: men and women under thirty years of age and men and women thirty years of age or older. In general, job satisfaction was significantly associated with most counterproductive behaviors including drug use on the job only for men over thirty years of age. Most correlations in all other groups were nonsignificant. In other words, there was no significant correlation between job satisfaction and drug use on the job for men or women under thirty years of age, the group most like the present sample.

Other studies have examined the associations between job stress, job dissatisfaction, and other job-related characteristics, and general use of drugs and alcohol. For instance, Markowitz (1984) examined the associations between a measure of covert alcoholism and several indices of perceived job characteristics including organization power, responsibility, autonomy, and participation in the organization. He found that a lack of responsibility and a lack of autonomy were significantly correlated with alcoholism tendencies. Powerlessness was marginally related to alcohol misuse, and participation was unrelated to alcoholism. Conway, Ward, Vickers, and Rahe (1981) found that occupational stress was related to increased cigarette and coffee consumption, but not related to changes in alcohol use. No other drugs were examined. Thus, despite the well-founded theories that job stress and dissatisfaction lead to alcohol and drug abuse, such associations have not been consistently identified in empirical studies.

In this chapter, job satisfaction is examined in relation to drug use on the job, as well as a range of other job-related variables that may be associated with disruptive drug use. These variables include job instability, degree of work involvement, amount of earned income, income from public assistance, amount of and satisfaction with support for work problems, extent of vandalism at work, and frequency of seeking advice for work-related difficulties. I have included a range of support factors on the hypothesis that availability and satisfaction with personal and organizational support to handle work problems may prevent drug use on the job. This is the employee assistance program notion: If resources are available to help an employee cope with work-related distress (or other types), this will diminish the chances that the employee will engage in alcohol or drug abuse to reduce this discomfort. The social support literature has emphasized the need to assess different dimensions of support such as family, friends, and organizations (Newcomb & Chou, 1987; B. R. Sarason, Shearin, Pierce, & Sarason, 1987).

Measures

The composite disruptive substance use measures used in the previous chapters are used here again. These include disruptive alcohol use, cannabis use, cocaine use, and hard drug use. For some analyses, a total score combining all four of these measures is used to reflect all disruptive drug use. In the latent-variable analyses, four frequency-of-use measures are used to reflect general drug use: frequency of alcohol use, cannabis use, cocaine use, and hard-drug use.

Three measures of job instability are used to reflect a latent factor: times fired past four years, times lost job past four years, and lost job past six months. The first two variables assess the number of years in the past four that the subject has been fired from a job or had lost a job. The last measure is a dichotomous assessment of whether the subject had lost a job during the previous six months.

Two variables were used to assess job dissatisfaction (and a latent factor for the same construct): unhappy with job and trouble with job. The variable of unhappy with job asked the respondent to indicate the degree of unhappiness or dissatisfaction with work on a seven-point scale, with responses ranging from delighted to terrible. The variable of trouble with job asked the young adult to indicate the difficulty experienced with a work problem during the past three months on a five-point scale with responses that ranged from no difficulty to great difficulty.

Two variables were used to represent amount of work involvement and to reflect a latent factor of this construct. These included amount worked and full-time job. Amount worked was indicated for the past year on a six-point scale that ranged from none to nine or ten months (about all of the time). Full-time job represented the number of years in the past four when the subject was employed full time.

Three variables were used to assess earned income during the past year during three random months (these are also used to reflect a latent construct of earned income). These variables are listed as income—August, income—October, and income—December. Gross income before taxes during August, October, and December was indicated on eight-point scales ranging from none to more than $2,500.

Two variables were used to reflect the extent of involvement with public assistance (and to reflect a latent factor of this construct): collected welfare past four years and collected food stamps past four years. These variables reflected the number of years during the past four that the respondent had received each type of public support.

Three variables were used to measure the amount of support for work problems (and used to reflect a latent factor): amount of family support for work, amount of friends' support for work, and amount of organizational support for work. These items asked the respondent to indicate the number of family members, friends, or community agencies they could turn to with a work problem. Responses were noted on a ten-point scale ranging from none to nine or more.

Three variables were chosen to assess the amount of satisfaction expected from support regarding a work problem (and were also used to identify a latent factor): satisfaction with family support for work, satisfaction with friends' support for work, and satisfaction with organizational support for work. For each of these items the young adult indicated the degree of satisfaction for support from each of these sources, on a five-point scale with responses that ranged from very dissatisfied to very satisfied.

Two variables were used to represent the amount of support or advice sought for work problems (and were also used to reflect a latent factor): sought advice from friends about work and sought advice from family about work. These two items asked the respondents to indicate the number of times during the past three months they had sought advice from these two sources regarding a work problem. Responses were given on a nine-point scale that ranged from none to nine or more times.

One item assessed the frequency of vandalism at work during the past six months (this variable was used as a single-indicator factor in the latent-variable analyses). The respondents indicated the number of times they had damaged property at work on purpose on a seven-point scale that ranged from none to six or more times.

Results

Because these variables are strictly related to the working environment, and thus are not relevant for school or college situations, only subjects who were employed in a full-time job or the military during the past year are included in the analyses. As a result, the analyses in this chapter are based on 468 young adults.

Bivariate Correlations

Product-moment correlations were calculated between each disruptive drug use scale and the twenty-one work-related variables (see table 7.1).

Disruptive alcohol use was significantly correlated with only four work-related variables: losing one's job during the past six months, increased vandalism at work, and frequency of seeking advice from family and friends about a work problem. Disruptive cannabis use was significantly correlated with the number of times a person lost a job during the past four years, losing a job in the past six months, having less support from family about work, and increased vandalism at work. Disruptive cocaine use was significantly related only with increased trouble with job and times lost job past four years. Disruptive hard drug use was significantly correlated with increased trouble with job, reduced satisfaction with organizational support for work problems, increased vandalism, and increased solicitation of advice from family and friends regarding a work problem. Finally, disruptive use of all drugs was significantly correlated with more times one lost a job during past four years, losing a job in the past six months, increased trouble with job, increased vandalism at work, and increased seeking of support and advice from family and friends for a work problem.

Multiple Regression Analyses

Multiple regression analyses were used to predict each of the disruptive drug use scales simultaneously from the twenty-one work-related variables (see table 7.1).

The equation for predicting disruptive alcohol use was marginally nonsignificant ($p < .1$) and accounted for only 6 percent of the

Table 7.1 Correlations and Multiple Regression Results of Disruptive Drug Use with Work-related Variables

Variables	Alcohol		Cannabis		Cocaine		Hard Drugs		All Use	
	r	*Beta*	*r*	*Beta*	*r*	*Beta*	*r*	*Beta*	*r*	*Beta*
Times fired past 4 years	.01	.03	.07	−.02	.05	−.10	.04	−.10	.07	−.06
Times lost job past 4 years	.01	−.06	.15***	.26***	.09*	.16*	.08	.15*	.13**	.20**
Lost job past 6 months	.09*	.10*	.20***	.17***	.07	.04	.01	−.04	.16***	.12**
Unhappy with job	−.02	.05	.06	.01	−.01	−.03	.05	.00	.04	.02
Trouble with job	.03	.01	.08	.02	.09*	.07	.12*	.07	.11*	.05
Amount worked	.03	.03	.04	.02	.04	.02	.03	−.04	.06	.02
Full-time job	.00	.00	.06	.07	.01	−.01	.08	.10	.06	.06
Income—August	−.01	−.06	−.03	−.06	.07	.01	.04	−.06	.01	−.07
Income—October	.00	−.01	−.02	.03	.08	.14	.06	.13	.02	.09
Income—December	.01	.04	−.02	−.01	.06	−.07	.05	−.02	.02	−.01
Collected welfare past 4 years	−.05	−.07	−.01	−.02	.00	.01	.01	.05	−.02	−.02
Collected food stamps past 4 years	−.02	.03	.01	.02	.01	.03	−.03	−.02	−.01	.02
Amount of family support for work	−.01	−.03	−.09*	−.09	−.04	−.07	−.03	−.04	−.07	−.09
Satisfaction with family support for work	−.02	.02	−.07	−.01	−.04	.00	−.08	−.06	−.08	−.02

Amount of friends' support for work	.08	.15**	−.05	.00	.02	.04	.02	.02	.02	.07
Satisfaction with friends' support for work	−.01	−.07	−.08	.00	−.04	−.04	−.03	.08	−.06	−.01
Amount of organizational support for work	−.08	−.18**	.00	.05	.03	.05	.02	.09	−.02	.00
Satisfaction with organizational support for work	.00	.09	−.07	−.05	−.02	−.03	−.11*	−.16**	−.08	−.05
Vandalism at work	.12**	.12**	.12**	.09*	−.05	−.07	.19***	.17***	.16**	.13**
Sought advice from family about work	.09*	.05	.04	−.03	.05	.01	.09*	.04	.09*	.02
Sought advice from friends about work	.09*	.05	.05	.06	.08	.05	.09*	.02	.11*	.07
Multiple Regression Summary										
R		.25		.30		.20		.30		.30
R²		.06		.09		.04		.09		.09
F-factor		1.43		2.15		.94		2.11		2.09
p-value		.10		<.01		>.50		<.01		<.01

*p < .05; **p < .01; ***p < .001.

variance. The significant predictors of disruptive alcohol use were losing a job in the past six months, having many friends supportive of a work problem, having few organizational supports for a work problem, and engaging in vandalism at work. The equation to predict disruptive cannabis use was significant ($p < .01$) and accounted for 9 percent of the variance. Disruptive cannabis use was predicted from frequent loss of jobs during the past four years, losing a job in the past six months, and increased vandalism. Disruptive cocaine use could not be reliably predicted from the twenty-one variables, with only one variable being significant: disruptive cocaine use was significantly associated with increased trouble at work. The equation for disruptive hard drug use was significant ($p < .01$) and accounted for 9 percent of the variance. Disruptive hard drug use was predicted from frequently losing jobs during the past four years, dissatisfaction with organizational support for a work problem, and increased vandalism at work. Finally, the equation for predicting disruptive drug use of all kinds was significant ($p < .01$) and accounted for 9 percent of the variance. All use of disruptive substances was predicted from frequent loss of jobs during the past four years, loss of job in the past six months, and increased vandalism at work.

Latent-variable Analyses

Two slightly different latent-variable models were developed for these data. Each model also included a construct of General Drug Use that had indicators of alcohol frequency, cannabis frequency, cocaine frequency, and hard drug frequency, in addition to a Disruptive Drug Use latent factor. All factors were identified as outlined above. The first model is a standard confirmatory factor analysis model (see chapter 2). In the second model, a second-order factor represents the two first-order drug use factors: General Drug Use and Disruptive Drug Use.

Confirmatory Factor Analysis Model. I tested an initial confirmatory factor analysis (CFA) model that included eleven latent factors (or single-indicator factors that are treated as constructs). These included General Drug Use, Disruptive Drug Use, Job Instability, Job Dissatisfaction, Work Involvement, Earned Income, Public Assistance, Amount of Support for Work, Satisfaction with Support for Work, Vandalism at Work, and Sought Advice about Work. This initial CFA model did not adequately reflect all of the data ($p < .001$), although the normed fit index (NFI) revealed that many of the features of the model were accurate (NFI = .90). All hypothesized factor loadings were significant.

Correlated errors were added to the model until an acceptable fit was achieved (p = .66, NFI = .95). All hypothesized factor loadings are significant and confirm the proposed factor structure (see table 7.2; the latent factors are identified by measured variables).

Among latent-factor intercorrelations, General Drug Use was significantly correlated with increased Disruptive Drug Use, increased Job Instability, increased Job Dissatisfaction, reduced Amount of Support for Work, reduced Satisfaction with Support for Work, and increased Vandalism at Work (see table 7.3). Disruptive Drug Use was significantly correlated with increased Job Instability, increased Job Dissatisfaction, increased Vandalism at Work, and increased Seeking of Advice about Work. See table 7.3 for other factor intercorrelations among the work-related constructs.

Second-order Factor Model. The final model for these work-related variables incorporated a second-order factor to represent the high association between General Drug Use and Disruptive Drug Use. In this way, work-related correlates can be examined for All Drug Use (the second-order factor) and then for the residuals of General Drug Use and the specific drugs (drug use that does not occur at work or school) and the residuals of Disruptive Drug Use and the specific drugs (drug use that specifically occurs at work or school). Nonstandard correlations were added to capture the full associations between various types of drug use and the work-related variables and factors (see table 7.4).

The final second-order factor model fit the data quite well (p = .99, NFI = .96). (See table 7.4 for a summary of all correlations that involve any drug variable or factor; latent factors are capitalized and measured variables are in lower case.) The second-order factor of All Drug Use was significantly correlated with increased Job Instability, increased Job Dissatisfaction, increased Earned Income, reduced Satisfaction with Support for Work, increased Vandalism at Work, increased Sought Advice about Work, and less amount of family support for work.

The residual of General Drug Use was significantly correlated with full-time job, high income in October, and reduced satisfaction with organizational support for work. General alcohol frequency was significantly correlated with amount worked and amount of friends' support for work. Cannabis frequency was significantly associated with losing a job in the past six months, increased unhappiness with job, reduced amount of friends' support for work, less satisfaction with friends' support for work, and reduced Sought Advice about Work. Cocaine frequency was correlated with losing a job in the past six months and reduced

Table 7.2 Factor Loadings in the Final Confirmatory Factor Analysis Model

Factor/Variable	Factor Loading	Factor/Variable	Factor Loading
General Drug Use		*Earned Income*	
alcohol frequency	.66	income—August	.85
cannabis frequency	1.00[a]	income—October	.99
cocaine frequency	.66	income—December	.88
hard drug frequency	.49	*Public Assistance*	
Disruptive Drug Use		collected welfare past 4 years	.77
alcohol at work	.34	collected food stamps past 4 years	.76
cannabis at work	.96	*Amount of Support for Work*	
cocaine at work	.44	amount of family support for work	.62
hard drugs at work	.38	amount of friends' support for work	.75
Job Instability		amount of organizational support for work	.47
times fired past 4 years	.91	*Satisfaction with Support for Work*	
times lost job past 4 years	.93	satisfaction with family support for work	.54
lost job past 6 months	.45	satisfaction with friends' support for work	.92
Job Dissatisfaction		satisfaction with organizational support for work	.42
unhappy with job	.37	*Vandalism at Work*	[b]
trouble with job	.98	*Sought Advice about Work*	
Work Involvement		sought advice from friends about work	.60
amount worked	.88	sought advice from family about work	.72
full-time job	.53		

All factor loadings are significant ($p < .001$).

[a] Residual constrained at zero to prevent it from being estimated as negative.

[b] A single-indicator factor.

collection of food stamps in past four years. Hard drug frequency was significantly correlated with increased Vandalism at Work and more Job Dissatisfaction.

Finally, there were no significant correlations with the residual of the Disruptive Drug Use factor, although there were several significant correlations with specific types of disruptive substance use. Alcohol at work (or disruptive alcohol use) was significantly correlated with loss of job during the past six months and reduced amount of organizational support for work problems. Cannabis use at work was independently correlated with loss of job during the past six months and less Earned Income. Cocaine use at work was correlated with reduced Vandalism at Work. Hard drug use at work was correlated with reduced satisfaction with organizational support for work problems, increased Vandalism at Work, and less satisfaction with friends' support for work.

Interpretation

The overall conclusion from the majority of these analyses is that disruptive drug use is only modestly related to a few of the work-related variables. All of the variables could not account for more than 10 percent of the variance in disruptive drug use. This does not mean that there were not significant relationships, only that among those that were found, the magnitude was only small to moderate.

Variables related to amount of work involvement and public assistance were only related to general drug use that was not associated with disruptive drug use. Receiving money from public assistance and the degree of work involvement were strictly not related to disruptive drug use.

Earned Income was significantly related to increased All Drug Use as a second-order factor and negatively with use of cannabis at work. This pattern represents an interesting differential effect with income. On the one hand, those with higher earnings are more likely to use a wide range of drugs in all contexts. This supports the precocious development theory (Newcomb, 1987; Newcomb & Bentler, 1988a). According to this theory, young adults who are heavily involved in the workforce, and therefore earning higher incomes, have perhaps prematurely acquired adult roles to the exclusion of further education. As a result, they tend to be more deviant and nontraditional, which is reflected in their higher rates of drug use. In addition, certain drugs such as cocaine are costly and are certainly more available to those with higher incomes.

Table 7.3   Factor Intercorrelations from the Final Confirmatory Factor Analysis Model

Factors	I	II	III	IV	V	VI	VII	VIII	IX	X	XI
I General Drug Use	1.00										
II Disruptive Drug Use	.66***	1.00									
III Job Instability	.20***	.17***	1.00								
IV Job Dissatisfaction	.08*	.09*	.22***	1.00							
V Work Involvement	.04	.06	.01	-.10*	1.00						
VI Earned Income	.06	.00	-.09*	-.07	.45***	1.00					
VII Public Assistance	.04	-.02	-.05	-.09*	-.20***	-.24***	1.00				
VIII Amount of Support for Work	-.12*	-.03	.01	-.05	.15**	.14**	-.12*	1.00			
IX Satisfaction with Support for Work	-.11*	-.07	.03	-.08*	-.04	.05	-.01	.55***	1.00		
X Vandalism at Work	.08*	.15**	.01	.15**	.05	-.04	-.01	-.02	-.14**	1.00	
XI Sought Advice about Work	.03	.08*	.07	.37***	-.03	.02	-.09*	.18**	.10*	.06	1.00

*p < .05; **p < .01; ***p < .001.

Table 7.4   Significant Correlations with Drug Use in the Final Second-order Factor Model

Drug-related Factor/Variable	Work-related Factor/Variable	Correlation
All Drug Use	Job Instability	.22***
All Drug Use	Job Dissatisfaction	.20***
All Drug Use	Earned Income	.12*
All Drug Use	Satisfaction with Support for Work	−.12**
All Drug Use	Vandalism at Work	.15**
All Drug Use	Sought Advice about Work	.11*
All Drug Use	amount of family support for work	−.13**
General Drug Use		
Drug Use	full-time job	.18**
Drug Use	income—October	.25***
Drug Use	satisfaction with organizational support for work	−.15**
alcohol frequency	amount worked	.12**
alcohol frequency	amount of friends' support for work	.08*
cannabis frequency	lost job past 6 months	.22***
cannabis frequency	unhappy with job	.07*
cannabis frequency	amount of friends' support for work	−.16**
cannabis frequency	satisfaction with friends' support for work	−.24***
cannabis frequency	Sought Advice about Work	−.09*
cocaine frequency	lost job past 6 months	.12**
cocaine frequency	collected food stamps past 4 years	−.14**
hard drug frequency	Vandalism at Work	.09*
hard drug frequency	Job Dissatisfaction	.09*
Disruptive Drug Use		
alcohol at work	lost job past 6 months	.08*
alcohol at work	amount of organizational support for work	−.14**
cannabis at work	lost job past 6 months	.18***
cannabis at work	Earned Income	−.13**
cocaine at work	Vandalism at Work	−.14**
hard drugs at work	satisfaction with organizational support for work	−.08*
hard drugs at work	Vandalism at Work	.13**
hard drugs at work	satisfaction with friends' support for work	−.07*

*$p < .05$; **$p < .01$; ***$p < .001$.

Indeed, disruptive cannabis use was significantly correlated with less Earned Income. This may indicate that among these young adult employees, those who are least successful, and therefore earning lower incomes, are more likely to use cannabis on the job. This lack of success may be related to their drug use, precocious development, or a personal disposition to deviance and nontraditionalism.

Although both general drug use and disruptive drug use were significantly correlated with Job Dissatisfaction when examined separately, it is the common portion of these types of drug use that appears to be actually related to Job Dissatisfaction. In other words, even though disruptive drug use was significantly related to Job Dissatisfaction, this association is based on a more general relationship between Job Dissatisfaction and All Drug Use. Thus, Job Dissatisfaction is related not solely to use of drugs on the job, but more broadly to drug use in all areas of life. This provides some support for the theories discussed earlier that relate work dissatisfaction and job stress with drug involvement, although the empirical tests of these theories were not able to separate disruptive from general drug use as in the present analyses.

Of course with cross-sectional data, it is impossible to determine whether drug use preceded job dissatisfaction and perhaps caused difficulties at work, or whether drug use occurred as a result of problems and dissatisfaction on the job. The theories discussed earlier hypothesize that drug use results from work difficulties. By contrast, the literature on alcohol and drug abuse by type of occupation noted that drug use patterns preceded job entry and probably job selection (e.g., Plant, 1978, 1979), suggesting that the drug use may lead to the job dissatisfaction. In previous analyses of the present data, we found that high school drug use predicted increased job instability among the subjects as young adults, but did not directly influence job dissatisfaction (Newcomb & Bentler, 1988a). The true relationship may be different for different people. Some people may be drawn to a job or have trouble with it as a result of drug use, whereas others may increase their drug involvement to handle problems and dissatisfaction at work. The present data do not include sufficient detail to determine what factors might generate these particular patterns. Still, we must conclude that the relationship between job satisfaction and any type of drug use is not a strong association, and we must consider other factors in order to understand more completely the patterns of disruptive drug use.

Job Instability, Vandalism at Work, and lack of organizational support for work problems were related to types of disruptive drug use. All types of drug use including specific aspects of disruptive drug use (particularly cannabis use at work) were associated with short-term and long-term losses of jobs. Although it is possible that the distress related to frequent job loss could generate drug use in all contexts of life, it seems more likely that a lifestyle of drug involvement, including drug use on the job, may severely restrict employment longevity. In simple terms, coming to work loaded or getting high on the job may lead to getting fired. This can be seen in the significant correlation between the specific use of cannabis at work during the past six months and loss of job during the past six months. Cannabis and cocaine use away from work during the past six months were also related to job loss during the past six months. Thus, it is clear that drug use on the job, as well as away from work, is associated with frequent loss of jobs.

Kandel (1980) has observed that those who are unemployed have substantially higher rates of general drug use than employed people. This conclusion is largely based on cross-sectional studies of adults, and somewhat different patterns are found among adolescent and young adult samples when longitudinal data are consulted. For instance, we found that high school drug use predicted greater workforce involvement and reduced college involvement (e.g., Newcomb & Bentler, 1985, 1986c). High school drug users are not interested in an academic lifestyle and may be eager to acquire adult roles of work and family involvement, perhaps prematurely, and may follow a pattern of precocious development (Newcomb, 1987; Newcomb & Bentler, 1988a). As a result, early workforce involvement may also be related to high levels of general drug use, as well as drug use on the job. This was evident in chapter 3, where it was shown that full-time employees had some of the highest rates of disruptive drug use.

Vandalism at Work was related to All Drug Use and to hard drug use aspects of General Drug Use and Disruptive Drug Use. Vandalism at Work was not specifically related to drug use on the job. Thus, disruptive hard drug use may share some motivation with destruction of an employer's property and may represent hostility to job or employer. On the other hand, since Vandalism at Work is correlated with All Drug Use, both may be indicators of a general tendency toward deviance or problem behaviors (e.g., Donovan & Jessor, 1985). This is supported by the specific correlations with hard drug use (both general and disruptive), which indicates an advanced degree of drug involvement. It is also interesting that cocaine use at work was negatively associated with Vandalism at Work, which disagrees with the general interpretation offered above, and may be related to the distinctive features of cocaine (i.e., it is a costly euphoriant).

Adequate amounts of and satisfaction with support regarding work problems were associated with lower drug use of all types. In particular, satisfaction with and amount of organizational support was related to specific aspects of not using alcohol and hard drugs on the job. When community or organizational support was available to address work-related difficulties, there was less use of drugs on the job. Thus, a work environment that is conducive to helping an employee handle job-related stress and problems may reduce the likelihood of disruptive drug use. Similar correlations were noted for All Drug Use and types of General Drug Use. This conforms to the hypothesis that a responsive social support network helps reduce the need for drug use in all contexts, and most likely the problems resulting from such use (e.g., Newcomb & Bentler, 1988b).

In conclusion, it appears that some work-related variables, in particular job instability, job dissatisfaction, lack of organizational support, and vandalism at work, are mildly related to disruptive substance use. But even significant associations tend to be small, and, therefore, these factors certainly cannot be considered the most important ones in understanding disruptive substance use. Thus, if disruptive substance use is not largely a function of the work environment, it must be related to other external influences, such as family problems, or to personal traits or predispositions. These areas are examined more closely in the next chapter.

Chapter 8

PSYCHOSOCIAL CORRELATES
OF DISRUPTIVE SUBSTANCE USE

One of the most well-researched topics in the area of drug use is the factors that generate various types of drug use behaviors in teenagers and young adults (see reviews by Chassin, 1984; Kandel, 1980; Long & Scherl, 1984). A wide range of antecedents or etiological factors have been proposed and investigated. Nevertheless, of the many theories proposed to help explain teenage drug use, most have been narrowly defined and focused on many separate and specific processes (see reviews in Lettieri, 1985; Lettieri, Sayers, & Pearson, 1980). Several broad distinctions have been drawn to help conceptualize these influences. For instance, Jessor and Jessor (1977, 1978) have proposed that both proximal influences (those close to or related to the person) and distal factors (social and cultural forces) have an impact on initiation into and maintenance of drug use behaviors. In a similar vein, Huba and Bentler (1982) delineate a variety of factors that fall into four general categories: biological (i.e., genetic), intrapersonal (e.g., personality, attitudes), interpersonal (peers, family), and sociocultural. Zucker and Gomberg (1986) have proposed a biopsychosocial model to explain drug use. These theories are broad, interactional in nature, and conceive of drug use as a multiply determined behavior that is not generated by a single cause or influence (see Sadava, 1987).

The number of diverse influences has prompted some researchers to consider a multicausal risk factor notion to explain teenage drug use (e.g., Bry, 1983; Bry, McKeon, & Pandina, 1982). From this perspective, no one factor is considered all important in generating drug use. Rather, it is the exposure to many different factors, each conducive to drug use, that increases the likelihood of drug involvement. This model has been tested empirically in several samples and found to be quite useful in explaining a large amount of variance in drug use behaviors (Bry, McKeon, & Pandina, 1982; Newcomb, Maddahian, & Bentler, 1986; Newcomb, Maddahian, Skager, & Bentler, 1987). This approach is used in chapter 13 of this book, in order to bring together the best risk factors for understanding disruptive drug use.

In this chapter, a number of measures that assess intrapersonal factors as well as interpersonal characteristics are used to understand disruptive drug use. The analyses are based on cross-sectional data, and, therefore, we cannot truly test for causal effects, but rather must examine how these factors are correlated or associated with disruptive substance use. The variables fall into four general areas of personal and interpersonal functioning: personality, personal distress, interpersonal relationships, and perceived competency.

As is the case with most research cited in this book, previous studies have not attempted to predict or understand drug use in the workplace, but rather have focused on drug use in general. Hence, there is a misleading assumption, and therefore false expectation, when using these more general studies to understand disruptive drug use. Although by definition, both types of use involve drugs, the contexts of use are different, and as a result may have different correlates and associations. Nevertheless, the data in those studies provide the best available background against which to explore the correlates of disruptive drug use. In addition, most of this research has been conducted on teenagers and young adults, since this is the period in life when drug-taking behaviors begin (e.g., Kandel & Logan, 1984).

A number of personality factors have been proposed and tested to help explain drug use among teenagers. Some of the more consistent personality traits related to drug use include independence and autonomy (e.g., Jessor & Jessor, 1977), rebelliousness (e.g., Smith & Fogg, 1978), low achievement motivation (e.g., Jessor & Jessor, 1977), sensation-seeking tendencies (Huba, Newcomb, & Bentler, 1981), lack of social conformity (Stein, Newcomb, & Bentler, 1987b), low religiosity (e.g., Tennant, Detels, & Clark, 1975), deviance and unconventionality (e.g., Donovan & Jessor, 1985), exhibition, impulsiveness, play (Labouvie & McGee, 1986), aggression, low responsibility (Brook, Whiteman, Gordon, & Cohen, 1986), extroversion, and liberalism (Wingard, Huba, & Bentler, 1979). Other personality traits have been examined in relation to drug use, but those listed above have demonstrated the most consistent and replicable associations.

Various types of personal or emotional distress have been found to be associated with and predictive of drug use. For instance, Kaplan (1985, 1986) suggests that drug use is a response to a negative self-image, expressing in particular self-derogation. In his studies, high self-derogation (and rejection by peers) increases drug use (and involvement with a deviant, drug-using subculture), which in turn has been associated with reduced self-derogation. Psychological distress has been examined in a variety of forms, although most variations tap a general factor of personal distress (e.g., Tanaka & Huba, 1984). These specific types of distress have included alienation, apathy, pessimism, low self-esteem, depression, low self-acceptance, anomie, anxiety, psychosis, neurosis, unhappiness, and low purpose in life (e.g., Aneshensel & Huba, 1984; Harlow, Newcomb, & Bentler, 1986; Huba, Newcomb, & Bentler, 1986; Newcomb & Harlow, 1986; Paton, Kessler, & Kandel, 1977; Smith & Fogg, 1978). The theoretical backing for these associations lies in a self-medicative model for drug use. If someone is feeling distressed and unhappy, he or she may choose to use drugs to ameliorate these negative or uncomfortable feelings. It appears that this process occurs over a relatively short period of time (i.e., several months or up to one year), and does not remain a significant predictive influence over several years (e.g., Newcomb & Bentler, in press b). In addition, it appears that for younger adolescents, using drugs as a coping mechanism or for the effects of drug use (e.g., Carman, 1979) is not fully established; using drugs as a coping style only develops during adolescence and young adulthood (e.g., Newcomb, Chou, Bentler, & Huba, in press; Newcomb & Harlow, 1986).

Drug users and abusers tend to have more negative and less satisfying relationships with other people than those who do not use drugs. One exception to this has been the finding that specific use of alcohol may facilitate or enhance social interactions and thus increase social support and reduce loneliness (e.g., Newcomb & Bentler, 1988a; Sadava & Thompson, in press). In general, however, those having greater involvement with drugs also have poorer relationships with family, friends, and romantic attachments. In fact, having a good social support network reduces problems in many areas of life, including trouble with drugs (Newcomb & Bentler, 1988b). It is not always clear, however, whether the drug use is engaged in to reduce the discomfort of social alienation or if drug use caused these problems in social or interpersonal relationships. It is possible that a third, unknown factor generates both poor social interactions and the tendency for drug use. Nevertheless, consistent associations have been noted between greater involvement with drugs and poorer relationships in all facets of one's social environment.

Finally, other research has indicated that personal competency, efficacy, and control are related to reduced involvement with drugs. For instance, Pentz (1985) found that increased personal efficacy and social skills reduced alcohol and cigarette use over a six-month period. Conversely, alcohol and cigarette use decreased personal efficacy and social skills over the same period of time. Powerlessness or a perceived lack of control has been found to be related to drug use both in general (e.g., Newcomb & Harlow, 1986) and within an organizational structure (e.g., Markowitz, 1984). Thus, it could be expected that those who do not feel in control, who have low personal efficacy, and who are not assertive may resort to disruptive drug use.

In this chapter, analyses are presented for three sets of variables that reflect the four areas reviewed above: personality, personal distress, interpersonal relationships, and competency. The first set of analyses examines fifteen personality traits, eight psychological functioning scales (assessing types of personal distress), and four measures of interpersonal relationships, and how these are related to disruptive drug use. The second set of analyses explores seven areas of life and their relationship to both disruptive drug use and general drug use. The seven areas include drug problems, psychosomatic complaints, relationship problems, emotional distress, health problems, family problems, and loneliness. The third set of analyses examines four personal competency factors and their relationship to disruptive and general drug use. These factors include leadership style, assertiveness, sense of control, and personal efficacy.

Measures

The composite disruptive substance use measures used in the previous chapters are used here as well. These include disruptive alcohol use, cannabis use, cocaine use, and hard drug use. For some analyses, a total score combining all four measures is used to reflect all disruptive drug use. In the latent-variable analyses, four frequency-of-use measures are used to reflect general drug use: frequency of alcohol use, cannabis use, cocaine use, and hard drug use.

Personality Traits.   Fifteen personality traits are included in the first set of analyses. These are from the Bentler Personality Inventory (BPI: Bentler & Newcomb, 1978; Stein, Newcomb, & Bentler, 1986b) and include (with period-free reliabilities in parentheses): ambition (.72), attractiveness (.67), congeniality (.48), deliberateness (.54), diligence (.53), extroversion (.66), generosity (.64), invulnerability (.68), law abidance (.83), leadership (.71), objectivity (.66), orderliness (.58), religious commitment (.77), and self-acceptance (.43). Each trait consists of four items, each rated on a five-point bipolar scale.

Psychological Functioning. Eight measures reflect various types of emotional distress, psychosomatic symptoms, and trust in the medical profession. These are from the Bentler Medical-Psychological Inventory (BMPI: Newcomb, Huba, & Bentler, 1981, 1986) and include (with alpha internal consistency measure of reliability in parentheses): headache prone (.87), insomnia (.74), injury hysteria (.79), depression (.74), trust physicians (.65), trust medicine (.78), illness sensitive (.79), and thought disorganization (.60). These were measured in the same manner as the BPI.

Social Support. Four scales assess the degree of good relationships (with reliability estimates in parentheses) with: parents (.82), family (.84), adults (.54), and peers (.74). These reflect a latent factor of Social Support and generally assess the extent of integration into a social network (Newcomb & Bentler, 1986e). These were measured in the same manner as the BPI and BMPI.

Problems in Life. The second set of analyses explores the relationships between disruptive drug use and seven areas of life. Each of these areas of life is represented by a latent factor and three indicators. Details regarding how each measure was assessed have been published elsewhere (e.g., Newcomb, in press; Newcomb & Bentler, 1988a; Newcomb & Bentler, 1986e; Stein, Newcomb, & Bentler, 1987a). The first area, Drug Problems, was assessed with three indicators: problems with drugs or alcohol, trouble with alcohol for the past four years, and trouble with drugs for the past four years (Stein, Newcomb, & Bentler, in press). A latent factor of Psychosomatic Complaints was reflected in scales for three indicators: headache prone (BMPI), insomnia (BMPI), and psychosomatic symptoms (Newcomb & Bentler, 1987c). Relationship Problems is a latent construct reflected in measures of trouble in relationship, unhappy in relationship, and lonely in relationship (Schmidt & Sermat, 1983). A latent construct of Emotional Distress was reflected in trouble handling feelings, unhappy handling feelings, and self-derogation (Kaplan, 1975). Health Problems is a latent factor reflected in trouble with health, unhappy with health, and health problems past four years. A latent factor of Family Problems was represented by unhappy with family, poor relationship with family past four years, and good relationship with family (the social support scale described above). Finally, a latent factor of Loneliness was created from the UCLA Loneliness Scale (Newcomb & Bentler, 1986e; Russell, Peplau, & Cutronia, 1980) by combining the items into three scales: lonely scale 1, 2, and 3.

Competency Measures. The third set of analyses examines the associations between four latent factors of competency and disruptive drug use. A latent construct of Leadership Style was reflected in three BPI traits: ambition, extroversion, and leadership. Assertiveness was a latent factor created from combining the nine items developed by Levenson and Gottman (1978) for measuring social competence into three scales (Newcomb, 1984): assertive 1, 2, and 3. A latent factor of Sense of Control is a reversed scored factor used by Newcomb & Harlow (1986) called Perceived Loss of Control or Powerlessness (Newcomb, 1986c). The three items used to identify this factor include: in control, feel powerful, and personal control. Finally, Personal Efficacy is a latent factor reflecting five items developed by Blatt, Quinlan, Chevron, McDonald, and Zuroff (1982) that were combined into three scales (McCarthy & Newcomb, 1987): inner resources, independence, and respect from others.

Results

As stated above, analyses for this chapter are presented in three sets. The first set examines the correlations and multiple regression associations between disruptive drug use and the personality, psychological functioning, and social support measures. Latent-variable models are not presented for this group of variables, since all do not reflect latent factors. Several of the variables that do represent latent constructs are included in the second and third sets of analyses. Thus, there is some overlap between the first set of analyses and the second and third sets of analyses. The second and third sets follow the pattern presented in the previous chapter. The second and third sets of analyses are kept separate for both conceptual reasons and also to limit the size of the models which become unmanageable if too large.

Personality, Psychosocial Functioning, and Social Support

Bivariate Correlations. Product-moment correlations were calculated between each disruptive drug use scale and the twenty-seven measures of personality, psychological functioning, and social support (see table 8.1).

Disruptive alcohol use was significantly correlated with only four of the twenty-seven variables. Disruptive alcohol use was significantly associated with more ambition, more extroversion, less law abidance, and less injury hysteria. Disruptive cannabis use was significantly correlated with less congeniality, less deliberateness, less law abidance, more liberalism, less self-acceptance, less injury hysteria, more depression, and poorer relationships with parents. Disruptive cocaine use was significantly related with less deliberateness, less law abidance, more liberalism, and less injury hysteria. Disruptive hard drug use was significantly correlated with less law abidance and more liberalism. Finally, disruptive use of all drugs was significantly correlated with more ambition, less congeniality, less deliberateness, more extroversion, less law abidance, more liberalism, less injury hysteria, and poorer relationships with parents.

Multiple Regression Analyses. Multiple regression analyses were used to predict each of the disruptive drug use scales simultaneously from the twenty-seven personality, psychological functioning, and social support variables (see table 8.1).

The equation for predicting disruptive alcohol use was significant, but accounted for only 6 percent of the variance. The only significant predictor of disruptive alcohol use was less law abidance. The equation to predict disruptive cannabis use was significant ($p < .01$) and accounted for 10 percent of the variance. Disruptive cannabis use was independently predicted from more invulnerability, less law abidance, more liberalism, and less injury hysteria. Disruptive cocaine use was reliably predicted from five variables, with 8 percent of the variance accounted for. Disruptive cocaine use was predicted from less deliberateness, less law abidance, more liberalism, less self-acceptance, and less injury hysteria. The equation for disruptive hard drug use was significant and accounted for 9 percent of the variance. Disruptive hard drug use was predicted from less law abidance, more liberalism, less self-acceptance, more headache proneness, less depression, and less illness sensitivity. Finally the equation for predicting disruptive drug use of all kinds was significant and accounted for 13

Table 8.1 Correlations and Multiple Regression Results of Disruptive Drug Use with Personality, Psychological Functioning, and Social Support Measures

Predictors	Alcohol		Cannabis		Cocaine		Hard Drugs		All Use	
	r	Beta	r	Beta	r	Beta	r	Beta	r	Beta
Personality										
Ambition	.08*	.03	.05	.00	.05	.00	.06	.01	.09*	.02
Attractiveness	.05	.02	.01	.01	.06	.04	.06	.02	.06	.03
Congeniality	−.07	−.02	−.09*	−.02	−.01	.05	−.04	.00	−.09*	−.01
Deliberateness	−.03	.03	−.09*	−.06	−.09*	−.08*	−.04	−.03	−.09*	−.05
Diligence	−.03	−.02	−.07	−.03	−.02	.02	−.03	−.02	−.06	−.02
Extroversion	.10**	.06	.01	−.02	.05	.02	.04	−.05	.08*	.01
Generosity	.02	.00	.00	.02	.06	.07	.06	.06	.04	.05
Invulnerability	.05	.04	.06	.10**	.01	.02	−.01	−.04	.06	.06
Law abidance	−.17***	−.13**	−.22***	−.16***	−.21***	−.18***	−.19***	−.15***	−.29***	−.22***
Leadership	.06	.00	.02	.02	.02	−.03	.07	.04	.07	.01
Liberalism	.07	.03	.19***	.16***	.13***	.08*	.14***	.11**	.19***	.15***
Objectivity	−.03	.01	−.04	.00	−.07	−.04	−.04	.00	−.06	−.01
Orderliness	−.04	−.02	−.01	.07	.02	.07	.01	.04	−.01	.06
Religiosity	−.06	.01	−.04	.06	−.04	.02	−.06	.00	−.07	.04
Self-acceptance	.03	.09	−.08*	−.06	−.05	−.13*	−.04	−.19**	−.05	−.07

Psychological Functioning							
Headache prone	-.02	-.07	-.01	.04	.10*	.01	.00
Insomnia	.06	.03	-.06	.01	-.01	.05	.02
Injury hysteria	-.10**	-.09**	-.08*	-.06	-.07	-.12**	-.11**
Depression	.08*	-.01	-.03	-.03	-.24***	.03	-.08
Trust physicians	-.02	.02	.01	-.05	-.03	-.03	.02
Trust medicine	.02	.01	.02	.00	.02	.00	.00
Illness sensitive	.02	.04	-.01	-.06	-.09*	-.01	-.02
Thought disorganization	.06	.05	-.01	-.01	-.01	.04	.05
Social Support							
Parents	-.08*	-.02	-.05	-.05	.00	-.09*	-.04
Family	-.05	.02	.05	-.07	-.07	-.07	-.01
Adults	-.06	-.01	-.03	-.02	-.01	-.07	-.03
Peers	-.05	-.03	-.02	.01	.02	-.03	-.02
Multiple Regression Summary							
R	.24	.32	.29		.30	.30	.36
R²	.06	.10	.08		.09	.09	.13
F(27,711)	1.55*	2.96***	2.38***		2.57***	2.57***	3.92***

*p < .05; **p < .01; ***p < .001.

percent of the variance. All disruptive use of substances was predicted from less law abidance, more liberalism, and less injury hysteria.

Problems in Life

Bivariate Correlations.   Product-moment correlations were calculated between each disruptive drug use scale and the twenty-one measures assessing problems in life (see table 8.2).

Disruptive alcohol use was significantly correlated with only four of these variables: more problems with drugs or alcohol, more psychosomatic symptoms, more trouble in relationships, and less unhappiness with health. Disruptive cannabis use was significantly correlated with more problems with all three of the Drug Problems variables (problems with drugs or alcohol, trouble with alcohol past four years, and trouble with drugs past four years), more self-derogation, poor relationship with family past four years, and more lonely scale 1. Disruptive cocaine use was significantly related with more of the three Drug Problems variables, more trouble in relationships, more trouble handling emotions, and more self-derogation. Disruptive hard drug use was significantly correlated with more of the three Drug Problems variables, more psychosomatic symptoms, more trouble in relationship, more trouble handling feelings, more trouble with health, reduced good relationship with family, and poorer relationship with family past four years. Finally, disruptive use of all drugs was significantly correlated with more of the the Drug Problems variables, more psychosomatic symptoms, more trouble in relationship, more trouble handling emotions, less good relationship with family, poorer relationship with family past four years, and more lonely scale 1.

Multiple Regression Analyses.   Multiple regression analyses were used to predict each of the disruptive drug use scales simultaneously from all twenty-one measures for problems in life (see table 8.2).

The equation for predicting disruptive alcohol use was significant, but accounted for only 5 percent of the variance. Disruptive alcohol use was predicted from more problems with drugs or alcohol, more psychosomatic complaints, more trouble in relationship, and less unhappiness with health. The equation to predict disruptive cannabis use was significant and accounted for 8 percent of the variance. Disruptive cannabis use was predicted from more of the three Drug Problems variables, poor relationship with family past four years, and more lonely scale 1. Disruptive cocaine use was reliably predicted from the variables, but with only 5 percent of the variance accounted for. Disruptive cocaine use was predicted from more problems with drugs or alcohol, more trouble with drugs past four years, more trouble handling emotions, and more self-derogation. The equation for disruptive hard drug use was significant and accounted for 8 percent of the variance. Disruptive hard drug use was predicted from only the three Drug Problems variables. Finally, the equation for predicting disruptive drug use of all kinds was significant and accounted for 9 percent of the variance. All use of disruptive substances was predicted from the three Drug Problems variables, more trouble in relationship, and more lonely scale 1.

Latent-variable Analyses. Two slightly different latent-variable models were developed for these data. Each model included a construct of General Drug Use that had indicators of alcohol frequency, cannabis frequency, cocaine frequency, and hard drug frequency, and a Disruptive Drug Use factor. All factors were identified as outlined above. The first model is a standard CFA model (see chapter 2). The other model uses a second-order factor to represent the two first-order drug use factors: General Drug Use and Disruptive Drug Use.

An initial CFA model that included nine latent factors was tested. These are General Drug Use, Disruptive Drug Use, Drug Problems, Psychosomatic Complaints, Relationship Problems, Emotional Distress, Health Problems, Family Problems, and Loneliness. This initial CFA model did not adequately reflect all of the data ($p < .001$), although the NFI revealed that many of the features of the model were accurate (.88). All hypothesized factor loadings were significant. Correlated errors were added to the model until an acceptable fit was achieved ($p = .20$, NFI = .96). All hypothesized factor loadings were significant and confirmed the proposed factor structure (see table 8.3; latent factors are identified by the measured variables).

Among factor intercorrelations, General Drug Use was significantly correlated with increased Disruptive Drug Use, increased Drug Problems, more Psychosomatic Complaints, more Emotional Distress, and more Health Problems (see table 8.4). Disruptive Drug Use was significantly correlated only with increased Drug Problems and was not significantly correlated with any of the other latent factors. (See table 8.4 for other factor intercorrelations.)

The final model for the life problem variables incorporated a second-order factor to represent the high association between General Drug Use and Disruptive Drug Use. In this way, life problem correlates can be examined for All Drug Use (the second-order factor) and then for the residuals of General Drug Use (drug

Table 8.2 Correlations and Multiple Regression Results of Disruptive Drug Use with Life Problem Variables

Predictors	Alcohol		Cannabis		Cocaine		Hard Drugs		All Use	
	r	Beta	r	Beta	r	Beta	r	Beta	r	Beta
Problems with drugs or alcohol	.07*	.07*	.16***	.09**	.14***	.09*	.19***	.13***	.20***	.13***
Trouble with alcohol past 4 years	.02	.00	.19***	.14***	.09*	.05	.15***	.09**	.17***	.11**
Trouble with drugs past 4 years	.01	−.03	.14***	.08*	.11**	.07*	.13***	.06*	.14***	.06*
Headache prone	.02	.00	−.02	−.03	−.02	.00	.04	.04	.01	−.01
Insomnia	.06	.05	.06	.04	−.02	−.04	.01	−.05	.05	.02
Psychosomatic symptoms	.07*	.10*	.03	−.04	.01	−.01	.09*	.06	.08*	.04
Trouble in relationship	.12**	.15***	.05	.03	.07*	.03	.10*	.06	.13**	.11**
Unhappy in relationship	.01	.05	.04	.01	.02	.02	.03	.04	.04	−.02
Lonely in relationship	.03	.05	.02	.01	.00	.03	.06	.08	.04	.04
Trouble handling emotions	.03	.06	.04	.02	.09*	.07*	.11**	.03	.09*	−.01
Unhappy handling feelings	−.01	.03	.06	.03	.01	.04	.06	.05	.04	.00

Self-derogation	.00	.05	-.05	.03	.10*	.07*	.03	.07*	-.05	-.02
Trouble with health	.00	.05	.03	.09*	.01	.01	.02	.02	.01	.02
Unhappy with health	-.02	-.01	.01	.04	.02	.03	.06	.03	-.11**	-.07*
Health problems past 4 years	-.03	.02	-.03	.01	-.03	-.03	.06	-.04	.03	.01
Unhappy with family	.06	.03	.03	.05	-.04	.00	.05	.00	.02	.04
Good relationship with family	-.06	-.07*	-.06	-.07*	-.02	-.01	-.06	-.05	-.02	-.05
Poor relationship with family past 4 years	.06	.09*	.04	.08*	.01	.03	.12**	.07*	.04	.04
Lonely scale 1	.11*	.07*	.02	.01	.04	.01	.12**	.09*	.08	.06
Lonely scale 2	-.04	-.02	-.01	-.02	-.07	-.02	.04	.03	-.06	-.01
Lonely scale 3	-.04	-.03	-.04	-.03	-.05	-.03	.02	.04	-.05	-.04
Multiple Regression Summary										
R	.30		.28		.21		.28		.22	
R^2	.09		.08		.05		.08		.05	
F-ratio	3.26		2.86		1.63		2.93		1.76	
p-value	<.001		<.001		.04		<.001		.02	

*p < .05; **p < .01; ***p < .001.

Table 8.3   Factor Loadings from the Final Confirmatory Factor Analysis Model for Problems in Life

Factor/Variable	Loading	Factor/Variable	Loading
General Drug Use		*Emotional Distress*	
alcohol frequency	.52	trouble handling emotions	.51
cannabis frequency	.68	unhappy handling feelings	.61
cocaine frequency	.85	self-derogation	.70
hard drug frequency	.56	*Health Problems*	
Disruptive Drug Use		trouble with health	.62
alcohol at work	.38	unhappy with health	.83
cannabis at work	.60	health problems past 4 years	.37
cocaine at work	.66	*Family Problems*	
hard drugs at work	.34	unhappy with family	.81
Drug Problems		good relationship with family	−.88
problems with drugs or alcohol	.68	poor relationship with family past 4 years	.57
trouble with alcohol past 4 years	.45	*Loneliness*	
trouble with drugs past 4 years	.61	lonely scale 1	.83
Psychosomatic Complaints		lonely scale 2	.95
headache prone	.48	lonely scale 3	.83
insomnia	.69		
psychosomatic symptoms	.84		
Relationship Problems			
trouble in relationship	.52		
unhappy in relationship	.80		
lonely in relationship	.73		

All factor loadings are significant ($p < .001$).

use that does not occur at work or school) and the residuals of Disruptive Drug Use (drug use that specifically occurs at work or school). Nonstandard correlations were added to capture the full associations between various types of drug use and the life problem variables and factors.

The final second-order factor model fit the data quite well ($p = .97$, NFI $= .97$) (see table 8.5; latent factors are capitalized and measured variables are in lower case). The second-order factor of All Drug Use was significantly correlated with increased Drug Problems, more Psychosomatic Complaints, more Emotional Distress, more Health Problems, more trouble in relationship, poorer relationship with family past four years, and lonely scale 1.

The residual of General Drug Use was significantly correlated with being less lonely in relationship. General alcohol frequency (while controlling for All Drug Use and General Drug Use) was significantly correlated with less Loneliness, less lonely scale 1, less headache prone, less unhappy handling feelings, and less self-derogation. General cannabis frequency (while controlling for the general factors) was significantly correlated with more problems with drugs or alcohol. General cocaine frequency was associated with less headache proneness. General hard drug frequency was correlated with more trouble in relationship, more trouble handling emotions, and more unhappy with family.

Finally, there were no significant correlations with the residual of the Disruptive Drug Use factor, although there were several significant correlations with specific types of disruptive substance use (after controlling for All Drug Use and Disruptive Drug Use). Alcohol at work (or disruptive alcohol use) was significantly correlated with more Psychosomatic Complaints, more Family Problems, more trouble in relationship, and more unhappy with health. The specific effect of cannabis use at work was uniquely correlated with more problems with alcohol past four years, more insomnia, and more unhappiness with family. Cocaine use at work was specifically related to more trouble handling emotions and more self-derogation. Hard drug use at work was uniquely correlated with more problems with alcohol past four years and more psychosomatic symptoms.

Competency and Control

Bivariate Correlations. Product-moment correlations were calculated between each disruptive drug use scale and the twelve measures of competency and control (see table 8.6).

Disruptive alcohol use was significantly correlated with four of

Table 8.4 Factor Intercorrelations from the Final Confirmatory Factor Analysis Model for Problems in Life

Factors	I	II	III	IV	V	VI	VII	VIII	IX
I General Drug Use	1.00								
II Disruptive Drug Use	.65***	1.00							
III Drug Problems	.48***	.34***	1.00						
IV Psychomatic Complaints	.10*	.03	.25***	1.00					
V Relationship Problems	.06	.08	.15**	.20***	1.00				
VI Emotional Distress	.10*	.06	.32***	.60***	.71***	1.00			
VII Health Problems	.14**	.01	.09*	.50***	.17***	.51***	1.00		
VIII Family Problems	.05	.03	.23***	.31***	.27***	.50***	.31***	1.00	
IX Loneliness	.01	.00	.24***	.49***	.47***	.71***	.27***	.44***	1.00

$*p < .05; **p < .01; ***p < .001.$

Table 8.5   Significant Correlations with Drug Use in the Final Second-Order Factor Model for Problems in Life

Drug-related Factor/Variable	Problems in Life Factor/Variable	Correlation
All Drug Use	Drug Problems	.52***
All Drug Use	Psychosomatic Complaints	.10**
All Drug Use	Emotional Distress	.11**
All Drug Use	Health Problems	.15***
All Drug Use	trouble in relationship	.12**
All Drug Use	poor relationship with family past 4 years	.08*
All Drug Use	lonely scale 1	.12*
General Drug Use		
Drug Use	lonely in relationship	−.40***
alcohol frequency	Loneliness	−.12***
alcohol frequency	lonely scale 1	−.09*
alcohol frequency	headache prone	−.10**
alcohol frequency	unhappy handling feelings	−.12**
alcohol frequency	self-derogation	−.16***
cannabis frequency	problems with drugs or alcohol	.10**
cocaine frequency	headache prone	−.13**
hard drug frequency	trouble in relationship	.08*
hard drug frequency	trouble handling emotions	.06*
hard drug frequency	unhappy with family	.07*
Disruptive Drug Use		
alcohol at work	Psychosomatic Complaints	.09**
alcohol at work	Family Problems	.06*
alcohol at work	trouble in relationship	.09**
alcohol at work	unhappy with health	.14**
cannabis at work	trouble with alcohol past 4 years	.13***
cannabis at work	insomnia	.09*
cannabis at work	unhappy with family	.08*
cocaine at work	trouble handling emotions	.07*
cocaine at work	self-derogation	.10**
hard drugs at work	trouble with alcohol past 4 years	.07*
hard drugs at work	psychosomatic symptoms	.11**

*$p < .05$; **$p < .01$; ***$p < .001$.

these variables: more ambition, more extroversion, more assertive 3, and less feeling of power. Disruptive cannabis use was significantly correlated only with less feeling of power. Disruptive cocaine use was not significantly correlated with any of the twelve control or competency variables. Disruptive hard drug use was significantly correlated only with more leadership. Finally, disruptive use of all drugs was significantly correlated with more ambition, more extroversion, more leadership, and less feeling of power.

Multiple Regression Analyses.   Multiple regression analyses were used to predict each of the disruptive drug use scales

Table 8.6 Correlations and Multiple Regression Results of Disruptive Drug Use with Competency and Control Variables

Variable	Alcohol		Cannabis		Cocaine		Hard Drugs		All Use	
	r	Beta	r	Beta	r	Beta	r	Beta	r	Beta
ambition	.08*	.07	.05	.06	.05	.05	.06	.03	.09*	.08*
extroversion	.10**	.08*	.01	.00	.05	.05	.04	.01	.08*	.05
leadership	.06	-.01	.02	.01	.02	-.02	.07*	.05	.07*	.01
assertive 1	.06	.02	.01	.00	.02	.01	.06	.04	.05	.02
assertive 2	.04	-.01	.02	.00	.02	.02	.04	-.01	.04	.00
assertive 3	.07*	.04	.02	.02	.03	.01	.03	-.01	.06	.03
in control	.04	.06	-.05	.05	.00	.03	-.01	-.04	-.01	.00
feel powerful	-.07*	-.08*	-.08*	-.08*	-.03	-.02	.01	.01	-.07*	-.08*
personal control	-.03	-.05	-.02	.03	-.05	-.07	-.01	-.03	-.04	-.04
inner resources	.02	.01	.02	.05	.00	.00	.05	.05	.03	.05
independent	.02	-.02	-.01	-.02	.00	-.01	.06	.05	.02	-.01
respect from others	.03	.01	-.02	-.04	.00	-.01	-.03	-.09*	-.01	-.05
Multiple Regression Summary										
R	.16		.12		.10		.13		.16	
R^2	.03		.01		.01		.02		.02	
F-ratio	1.64		.89		.57		1.02		1.49	
p-value	.08		>.50		>.50		.43		.12	

*$p < .05$; **$p < .01$.

simultaneously from all twelve control and competency measures (see table 8.6).

All equations for predicting types of disruptive drug use were nonsignificant and accounted for between 1 percent and 3 percent of the variance. Disruptive alcohol use was marginally nonsignificant (p = .08), and accounted for 3 percent of the variance. Disruptive alcohol use was predicted from more extroversion and less feeling of power. Disruptive cannabis use was predicted only from less feeling of power. Disruptive cocaine use was not predictable from any of these variables. Disruptive hard drug use was predicted only from receiving less respect from others. All use of disruptive substances was predicted from more ambition and less feeling of power.

Latent-variable Analyses. Two latent-variable models were developed; each model includes General Drug Use and Disruptive Drug Use factors. All factors were identified as outlined above.

An initial CFA model that included six latent factors was tested. These included General Drug Use, Disruptive Drug Use, Leadership Style, Assertiveness, Sense of Control, and Personal Efficacy. The initial CFA model did not adequately reflect all of the data (p < .001), although the NFI revealed that many of the features of the model were accurate (.91). All hypothesized factor loadings were significant. Correlated errors were added to the model until an acceptable fit was achieved (p = .25, NFI = .97). All hypothesized factor loadings were significant and confirmed the proposed factor structure (see table 8.7; latent factors are identified by the measured variables).

Among latent factor intercorrelations, General Drug Use was significantly correlated with increased Disruptive Drug Use and higher Leadership Style (see table 8.8). Disruptive Drug Use was significantly correlated only with increased Leadership Style. (See table 8.8 for other factor intercorrelations).

The final model for the competency and control variables incorporated a second-order factor to represent the high association between General Drug Use and Disruptive Drug Use. In this way, competency and control correlates can be examined for All Drug Use (the second-order factor) and then for the residuals of General Drug Use (drug use that does not occur at work or school) and the residuals of Disruptive Drug Use (drug use that specifically occurs at work or school). Nonstandard correlations were added to capture the full associations between various types of drug use and the life problem variables and factors.

The final second-order factor model fit the data quite well (p = .99, NFI = .98) (see table 8.9; latent factors are capitalized and

Table 8.7   **Factor Loadings from the Final Confirmatory Factor Analysis Model for Competency and Control**

Factor/Variable	Factor Loading	Factor/Variable	Factor Loading
General Drug Use		*Assertiveness*	
alcohol frequency	.50	assertive 1	.85
cannabis frequency	.67	assertive 2	.85
cocaine frequency	.86	assertive 3	.86
hard drug frequency	.58		
Disruptive Drug Use		*Sense of Control*	
alcohol at work	.35	in control	.63
cannabis at work	.60	feel powerful	.47
cocaine at work	.60	personal control	.78
hard drugs at work	.38		
Leadership Style		*Personal Efficacy*	
ambition	.40	inner resources	.67
extroversion	.49	independence	.70
leadership	.85	respect from others	.49

All factor loadings are significant ($p < .001$).

Table 8.8   **Factor Intercorrelations from the Final Confirmatory Factor Analysis Model for Competency and Control**

	Factors	I	II	III	IV	V	VI
I	General Drug Use	1.00					
II	Disruptive Drug Use	.73***	1.00				
III	Leadership Style	.12**	.11*	1.00			
IV	Assertiveness	.06	.07	.71***	1.00		
V	Sense of Control	−.06	−.06	.35***	.37***	1.00	
VI	Personal Efficacy	−.06	−.01	.61***	.52***	.50***	1.00

$*p < .05; **p < .01; ***p < .001$.

measured variables are in lower case). The second-order factor of All Drug Use was significantly correlated with increased Leadership Style and more Assertiveness.

There were no significant correlations with the residual of General Drug Use. General alcohol frequency (while controlling for All Drug Use and General Drug Use) was significantly correlated with more Assertiveness, more ambition, feeling more in control, and having many inner resources. General cocaine frequency was associated with more assertive 1.

Finally, there were no significant correlations with the residual of the Disruptive Drug Use factor, although there were significant correlations with specific types of disruptive substance use (after controlling for All Drug Use and Disruptive Drug Use). Alcohol at

Table 8.9   Significant Correlations with Drug Use Variables in the Final
Second-order Factor Model for Competency and Control

Drug-related Factor/Variable	Competency and Control Factor/Variable	Correlation
All Drug Use	Leadership Style	.33***
All Drug Use	Assertiveness	.09*
General Drug Use		
alcohol frequency	Assertiveness	.05*
alcohol frequency	ambition	.06*
alcohol frequency	in control	.17***
alcohol frequency	inner resources	.13**
cocaine frequency	assertive 1	.17**
Disruptive Drug Use		
alcohol at work	in control	.07*
alcohol at work	feel powerful	− .07*
cannabis at work	feel powerful	− .08*
hard drugs at work	inner resources	.11**

*p < .05; **p < .01; ***p < .001.

work was significantly correlated with feeling more in control and less feeling of power. Cannabis use at work was correlated with less feeling of power. Finally, using hard drugs at work was correlated with more inner resources.

Interpretation

The main conclusion from these analyses is that disruptive drug use is moderately related to a few psychosocial functioning measures, modestly related to a few more, and generally unrelated to most of them. The best multiple regression equation could account for no more than 13 percent of the variance in all disruptive use of substances. In the equation for the personality, psychological functioning, and social support measures, only three of the twenty-seven variables contributed independently. The life problem variables could predict no more than 9 percent of the variance in disruptive drug use, and the control and competency measures could not as a group predict disruptive substance use reliably. From these findings, we can conclude that disruptive drug use is most highly associated with personal factors, less related to various problems in life, and least related to competency and control.

Of the personality, psychological functioning, and social support variables, disruptive drug use was most closely related to a lack of law abidance, more liberalism, and a lack of injury history . Law abidance and a lack of liberalism are two components of a latent factor called Social Conformity, which is discussed in the next chapter. The present results confirm that disruptive drug use, like regular drug use, is highly associated with deviance, rebelliousness, and lack of traditionalism. This is one of the most consistent findings in the general drug use literature and appears to characterize disruptive drug use as well. The finding for injury history, on the other hand, needs to be interpreted somewhat differently. This finding suggests that those who are not fearful and guarded about physical danger, and thus may be more likely to take risks, are more likely to engage in disruptive drug use. This extends previous research, which has found positive association between high sensation seeking (thrills and adventure), low harm avoidance, and drug use (e.g., Huba, Newcomb, & Bentler, 1981; Labouvie & McGee, 1986), as well as extending the negative relationship of cocaine use and panic-phobia symptoms (e.g., Newcomb, Bentler, & Fahy, 1987) to injury hysteria and disruptive drug use.

Some of the smaller effects noted in this group of variables are related to a lack of deliberateness, low self-acceptance, and poor relationship with parents being associated with disruptive drug use. A lack of deliberateness involves being spontaneous, making few plans, and a lack of forethought. Low self-acceptance clearly relates to low self-esteem and few positive personal feelings. Poor relationship with parents is characterized by alienation, lack of communication, and low mutual respect. Although these associations with disruptive drug use were small, they add a little more substance to understanding the kind of person who engages in such behavior.

Clear patterns also emerged from the results based on the life problems analyses. First, various types of disruptive drug use were best predicted from all three measures of Drug Problems, psychosomatic symptoms, trouble in relationship, family problems, and some loneliness. Second, it seems that most of these associations are attributable to All Drug Use and not specifically to Disruptive Drug Use. In fact, the associations between General Drug Use and the life problem factors are generally large, and thus more systematic than such associations with disruptive drug use. Third, some of the positive effects of specific alcohol use (while controlling for general drug use) confirm some of the research cited above; this was only apparent for residuals of the general drug use frequency measures, however, and not for the residuals of the disruptive substance use variables. If there are indeed some positive aspects to alcohol use (when such use is not related to polydrug use), this does not hold true for alcohol use at work. In fact, disruptive alcohol use was correlated with more Psychosomatic Complaints, more Family Problems, more trouble in relationships, and more unhappiness with health. Hence, disruptive alcohol use is quite different from general alcohol use, at least in regard to the correlates noted here. Similarly, other types of drug use occurring specifically at work were related to several other problems such as insomnia, self-derogation, psychosomatic symptoms, and experiencing problems with alcohol during the past four years. Interestingly, the specific use of cocaine away from work was significantly correlated with a lack of headache proneness. In other analyses, headache proneness in high school predicted decreased cocaine use four years later (Newcomb & Bentler, 1986b). It is possible that a predisposition to headaches may prevent cocaine use, perhaps as a result of the psychoactive properties of the drug or the "cut" often put in cocaine (e.g., Washton & Gold, 1984).

It is interesting that the latent factor of Drug Problems was more highly correlated with General Drug Use than with Disruptive Drug Use. Although the strongest correlate of Drug Problems was the second-order factor of All Drug Use, it may be that those who use drugs in inappropriate settings such as work or school are less likely to perceive this as a problem than heavy drug users in general contexts. If this is true, and it is only speculation, then those who engage in disruptive substance use may not appreciate the problems associated with such use. Thus, if they do not perceive their drug use at work as a problem, they may be less likely to seek help or less amenable to prevention efforts. Clearly, as part of a prevention strategy, the employee must first recognize the problems of such use.

Among the control and competency correlates, we found that very few of these variables were significantly related to disruptive drug use (or general drug use for that matter). As a group, these variables could not significantly predict any of the disruptive drug use scales in the multiple regression analyses. Small associations were noted with ambition, extroversion, leadership, and not feeling powerful, although none of these accounted for more than 1 percent of the variance. Among the latent factors, both General Drug Use and Disruptive Drug Use were significantly correlated positively with Leadership Style, but not with any other constructs. These associations were the result of All Drug Use, since no residual effects were left with Leadership Style when this second-order factor was introduced. A few small effects were found for the residuals of the disruptive drug use scales. Alcohol at work was uniquely associated with feeling in control and not feeling powerful. Cannabis use at work was associated with a lack of feeling powerful. Hard drug use at work was associated with the feeling of having many inner resources.

Overall, these associations appear to be stronger than the work-related ones identified in chapter 7, but they still tend to be quite modest, and certainly do not capture an appreciable amount of variance in disruptive drug use. The two exceptions are law abidance and liberalism. These variables are explored further in the next chapter.

Chapter 9

DISRUPTIVE DRUG USE AND OTHER DEVIANT ATTITUDES AND BEHAVIORS

In this chapter, I explore the association between disruptive drug use and other types of deviant behavior. Other deviant behavior includes high levels of sexual involvement, selling illegal drugs, polydrug use, and various types of criminal behavior. Deviant attitudes include a lack of social conformity or conventionalism. These analyses can help determine whether disruptive drug use occurs as a relatively independent form of disruptive behavior, or whether it is linked to a general lifestyle of problematic attitudes and irresponsible behavior. This has important implications for treating disruptive drug use at work or school. If disruptive drug use is strongly associated with other types of deviant behavior, simply reducing the inappropriate drug use may not correct a general problem of deviance. Other types of deviance, such as selling drugs, theft, and property damage, may cause disruption and special problems in the workplace.

The problem behavior theory was developed by the Jessors (Jessor & Jessor, 1977, 1978) and provides one of the best conceptualizations of the idea that teenage drug use is one aspect of a deviance-prone lifestyle. Adolescent substance use is considered to be only one facet of a constellation of attitudes and behavior that may be considered problematic, unconventional, or nontraditional. This "behavior that is socially defined as a problem, a source of concern, or as undesirable by the norms of conventional society . . . and its occurrence usually elicits some kind of social control response" (Jessor & Jessor, 1977, p. 33). Behaviors are considered

121

inappropriate according to age-determined norms. For adolescents, these deviant behaviors can include heavy alcohol abuse, illicit drug use, precocious sexual activity, frequency of various sexual activities, and general delinquent behavior. More recently the Jessors' theory has been tested in a series of confirmatory factor analysis models (Donovan & Jessor, 1985), which have attempted to identify a syndrome of problem behaviors among adolescents and young adults. They found that one common latent factor accounted for the correlations among several indicators of problem behavior including frequency of drunkenness, frequency of marijuana use, extent of sexual experience, general deviant behaviors (i.e., shoplifting, vandalism, lying, and fighting), lack of church attendance, and poor school performance. Similarly, high associations have been found in other studies between drug use and various types of deviant attitudes. In our study (Newcomb & Bentler, 1988a), we found that teenage drug use was correlated quite highly with low social conformity ($r = -.69$), criminal activities ($r = .42$), deviant friendship network ($r = .46$), early sexual involvement ($r = .52$), and low academic potential ($r = -.34$).

Unfortunately, most of these studies have focused on teenagers, in whom many of these behaviors are considered offenses; they would not be considered problematic at an older age. Some research has indicated that this cluster of problem behaviors may lose its coherence and unidimensionality later in life (e.g., Osgood, 1985). Rather than retaining a general deviant lifestyle, young adults may retain only certain unconventional behaviors as a result of the pressures to conform to adult roles. For instance, even though drug use may continue as a lifestyle into young adulthood and later life (e.g., Newcomb & Bentler, 1987a), other aspects of general deviance may be abandoned or may now conform to age-related norms and lose their systematic associations with drug use. Further, these studies have focused solely on general drug use and have never examined use of drugs at school or in the workplace. Although it seems reasonable to assume that similar associations would be found for disruptive drug use, this speculation has not been tested. It is possible that disruptive drug use and general drug use are related differently to other forms of deviant behavior.

An alternate theory is that other deviant behaviors replace those of adolescence as the person grows into adulthood. For instance, teenage delinquency may turn into adult criminality. Age-status offenses may only precede truly illegal behavior. In addition, criminal behaviors that are only feasible for an adult may emerge and coalesce into a lifestyle of adult problem behaviors.

In the analyses for this chapter, both disruptive drug use and general drug use are examined in relation to latent constructs of Social Conformity (with indicators of law abidance, liberalism, and religious commitment), Dealing Drugs (cannabis, cocaine, and hard drugs), Criminal Behaviors (with indicators of confrontational acts, thefts, and property damage), and Sexual Involvement (with indicators for the number of steady and sexual partners, and age at first intercourse). I follow the established series of analyses, with one exception: I have added an additional latent-variable model that tests the hypothesis that all six factors are generated by a higher-order factor of General Deviance. This is a second-order factor model (e.g., Bentler & Newcomb, 1986), analogous to the analyses presented by Donovan & Jessor (1985), but at a higher level of abstraction. They examined whether a first-order latent factor could account for variation among several measured variable indicators of deviance, whereas the present analyses attempt to identify several different types of deviance as first-order factors (with multiple indicators for each specific type), and then use a second-order factor to account for the association among the first-order factors.

Measures

The same four composite disruptive substance use measures and four combined general drug use measures used in the previous chapters are used here. These include disruptive alcohol use, cannabis use, cocaine use, and hard drug use. For some analyses, a total score combining all four of these measures is used to reflect all disruptive drug use. In the latent-variable analyses, the four frequency of general drug use measures are used to reflect General Drug Use: frequency of alcohol use, cannabis use, cocaine use, and hard drug use.

Three measures that assess attitudes or personality characteristics of conventionality or deviance are included from the Bentler Personality Inventory (see the previous chapter) and are used to reflect a latent factor of Social Conformity: law abidance, liberalism, and religious commitment. The personal development of the values behind this construct has been traced through adolescence (Huba & Bentler, 1983a) and reflects adherence to traditional values and conformity to societal norms. It does not indicate conformity to one's particular friendship network or peer culture. It represents a continuous latent tendency, which at the low end reflects a rejection of traditional values or societal norms, and acceptance or tolerance of deviance, radical social change, and rejection of social control (e.g., laws and the legal system). At the high end, it reflects an adoption of and belief in traditional values and social norms, a disinclination toward deviance, and a conventinal or traditional view of life.

Three variables were used to reflect a latent factor of Criminal Behavior: confrontational acts, thefts, and property damage. The young adults indicated how often during the past six months they had engaged in sixteen different criminal acts, ranging from minor thefts and fights to major acts of violence and property damage. Items relating to automobile theft were eliminated because of little variance. The remaining items were grouped into the three scales based on factor analyses (Huba & Bentler, 1984).

Three variables were used to represent a latent factor of Sexual Involvement: number of steady partners, number of sexual partners, and age at first intercourse. The two variables on number of partners were based on lifetime occurrence, and the age variable was based on the age reported (if they had not yet engaged in sexual intercourse, their present age was used as datum).

Three variables were used to reflect a latent construct of Dealing Drugs: amount of cannabis sold, amount of cocaine sold, and amount of hard drugs sold. The respondents were asked to indicate the value of six different types of drugs they had sold or dealt for the past six months. Responses were given on seven-point scales that ranged from none to more than $250. Marijuana and hashish were combined for the cannabis variable. Uppers, downers, and heroin were combined for the hard drug variables. Selling cocaine was kept as a single item.

Results

Bivariate Correlations

Product-moment correlations were calculated between each disruptive drug use scale and the twelve deviance-related variables (see table 9.1).

Disruptive alcohol use was significantly correlated with all of the deviance-related variables except four. Disruptive alcohol use was significantly associated with less law abidance, more liberalism, more confrontational acts, more thefts, more property damage, more sexual partners, and more dealing of cannabis and hard drugs. Disruptive cannabis use was significantly correlated with all variables except two; disruptive cannabis use was not significantly correlated with religious commitment or property damage. All significant correlations were in the expected directions. Disruptive cocaine use was significantly correlated with eight of the twelve variables: less law abidance, more liberalism, more thefts, more sexual partners, a young age at first sexual intercourse, and selling all three types of drugs. Disruptive hard drug use was significantly correlated with all variables except religious commitment. All correlations were in hypothesized directions. Finally, disruptive use of all drugs was significantly correlated with all twelve deviance-related variables in the expected directions.

Multiple Regression Analyses

Multiple regression analyses were used to predict each of the disruptive drug use scales simultaneously from all twelve deviance-related variables (see table 9.1).

The equation for predicting disruptive alcohol use was significant, but accounted for only 6 percent of the variance. The predictors of disruptive alcohol use were low law abidance, more confrontational acts, and more selling of cannabis. The equation to predict disruptive cannabis use was highly significant ($p < .001$) and accounted for 32 percent of the variance. Disruptive cannabis use was predicted from low law abidance, more liberalism, more confrontational acts, many steady partners, and selling cannabis. Disruptive cocaine use was significantly associated with four variables and accounted for 20 percent of the variance. Disruptive cocaine use was predicted from low law abidance, more thefts, and more selling of cocaine and hard drugs. There were five significant predictors of disruptive hard drug use, which accounted for 36 percent of the variance. Disruptive hard drug use was predicted from less law abidance, more liberalism, more steady partners, and more selling of cannabis and hard drugs. Finally, the equation for predicting disruptive drug use of all kinds was significant and accounted for 32 percent of the variance. All use of disruptive substances was predicted from less law abidance, more liberalism, more confrontational acts, and more selling of cannabis and hard drugs.

Latent-variable Analyses

Three latent-variable models were developed; each included a construct of General Drug Use. All factors were identified as outlined above. The first model is a standard confirmatory factor analysis model (see chapter 2). The second model uses a second-

Table 9.1 Correlations and Multiple Regression Results of Disruptive Drug Use with Other Deviant Behaviors

Variables	Alcohol		Cannabis		Cocaine		Hard Drugs		All Use	
	r	Beta	r	Beta	r	Beta	r	Beta	r	Beta
law abidance	-.17***	-.14***	-.22***	-.06*	-.21***	-.08*	-.19***	-.07*	-.29***	-.13***
liberalism	.07*	.02	.19***	.10**	.12**	.04	.14***	.05*	.19***	.08**
religious commitment	-.06	.00	-.04	.03	-.04	.01	-.06	-.01	-.07*	.01
confrontational acts	.17***	.17***	.12**	.09**	.05	.04	.08*	.04	.17***	.09*
thefts	.07*	.04	.17***	.05	.15***	.07*	.10*	.00	.18***	.02
property damage	.08*	.04	.04	.00	.00	.05	.07*	.04	.08*	.04
number of steady partners	.03	.01	.11**	.07*	.05	.05	.10*	.05*	.11**	.04
number of sexual partners	.08*	.02	.13**	.03	.14***	.04	.11**	.01	.16***	.00

age at first sexual intercourse	−.02	.02	−.14***	−.05	−.11**	−.03	−.10*	−.04	−.14***	−.03
amount of cannabis sold	.10*	.08*	.53***	.46***	.26***	.01	.27***	.08*	.45***	.29***
amount of cocaine sold	.06	.07	.35***	.03	.39***	.29***	.27***	.03	.37***	.04
amount of hard drugs sold	.12**	.06	.24***	.04	.28***	.16***	.56***	.57***	.40***	.25***
Multiple Regression Summary										
R	.25		.57		.45		.56***	.60	.57	.25***
R²	.06		.32		.20			.36	.32	
F-ratio	3.89		28.73		15.10		34.47	28.60		
p-value	<.001		<.001		<.001		<.001	<.001		

*p < .05; **p < .01; ***p < .001.

order factor to account for the associations among the first-order factors. The third model uses a second-order factor to represent the two first-order drug use factors: General Drug Use and Disruptive Drug Use.

Confirmatory Factor Analysis Model. An initial CFA model that included six latent factors was tested. These included General Drug Use, Disruptive Drug Use, Social Conformity, Criminal Behavior, Sexual Involvement, and Dealing Drugs. This initial CFA model did not adequately reflect all of the data ($p < .001$), although the NFI revealed that many of the features of the model were accurate (.81). All hypothesized factor loadings were significant. Correlated errors were added to the model until an acceptable fit was achieved ($p = .59$, NFI $= .98$). Many of the largest correlations between residual or unique terms added to the model were between variables related to similar substances, such as between cannabis frequency and amount of cannabis sold. These were not unexpected and reflect small method factors related to specific substances. All hypothesized factor loadings were significant and confirmed the proposed factor structure (see table 9.2; latent factors are identified by measured variables).

Among latent factor intercorrelations, all six factors were significantly correlated with each other, with many pairs of factors quite highly correlated (see table 9.3). Both General Drug Use and Disruptive Drug Use were significantly correlated with less Social

Table 9.2   Factor Loadings from the Final Confirmatory Factor Analysis Model of Deviance Measure

Factor/Variable	Loading	Factor/Variable	Loading
General Drug Use		*Sexual Involvement*	
alcohol frequency	.45	number of steady partners	.35
cannabis frequency	.71	number of sexual partners	.80
cocaine frequency	.81	age at first sexual intercourse	− .37
hard drug frequency	.68		
Disruptive Drug Use		*Dealing Drugs*	
alcohol at work	.33	amount of cannabis sold	.67
cannabis at work	.53	amount of cocaine sold	.83
cocaine at work	.55	amount of hard drugs sold	.46
hard drugs at work	.45		
Social Conformity		*Criminal Behavior*	
law abidance	− .77	confrontational acts	.40
liberalism	.35	thefts	.86
religious commitment	.33	property damage	.37

All factor loadings are significant ($p < .001$).

Conformity, more Criminal Behaviors, more Sexual Involvement, and more Dealing Drugs. It is interesting that General Drug Use was more highly correlated with Sexual Involvement than was Disruptive Drug Use, whereas the reverse effect was evident for Dealing Drugs: Disruptive Drug Use was more substantially correlated with Dealing Drugs than was General Drug Use. Other factor intercorrelations among the deviance-related constructs support the expectation that these forms of deviance would be significantly correlated (see table 9.3).

General Deviance Model. The general deviance model is built upon the final CFA model. Rather than allowing the six factors to correlate, however, each was predicted from a single second-order factor. This tests the notion that the associations among the six first-order factors, which were quite high, can be accounted for by a higher-order latent construct. In other words, this tests whether a higher-order factor of General Deviance, reflecting a syndrome of problem behavior, can explain the relationships among the six first-order factors of specific deviance. The initial model tested did not accurately reflect the data ($p < .001$, NFI $= .96$) and was a significantly poorer fit than the final CFA model (difference chi-square $p < .001$). The Lagrangian multiplier test was used to select three pairs of first-order disturbance variables to correlate (Bentler & Chou, 1986). With the inclusion of these correlations, this model fit the data ($p = .41$, NFI $= .97$) and did not have a significantly worse fit than the final CFA model ($p > .05$) (see figure 9.1).

For the sake of clarity, I have depicted only the first-order and second-order factors in the final model of General Deviance; the measured variable factor structure was the same as in the final CFA model. The strongest indicators of General Deviance (as gauged by the magnitude of the standardized factor loadings) were General Drug Use, Disruptive Drug Use, lack of Social Conformity, and Dealing Drugs. Sexual Involvement and Criminal Behavior were moderately good indicators of the General Deviance second-order factor. The small circles with numbers are the residual variances of each first-order factor remaining after prediction from the General Deviance construct. The three additional correlations represent significant associations that were not captured in the general factor. Sexual Involvement had additional associations with General Drug Use and low Social Conformity, whereas Disruptive Drug Use was uniquely correlated with Dealing Drugs.

Second-order Factor Model. The final model incorporated a second-order factor to represent the high association between General Drug Use and Disruptive Drug Use. By doing so, the deviance-related correlates can be examined for All Drug Use (the

Table 9.3   Factor Intercorrelations from the Final Confirmatory Factor Analysis Model for Deviance Measures

Factors	I	II	III	IV	V	VI
I General Drug Use	1.00					
II Disruptive Drug Use	.78***	1.00				
III Social Conformity	−.63**	−.53***	1.00			
IV Criminal Behaviors	.32***	.37***	−.37***	1.00		
V Sexual Involvement	.64***	.39***	−.49***	.19***	1.00	
VI Dealing Drugs	.64***	.84***	−.41***	.31***	.29***	1.00

**p < .01; ***p < .001.

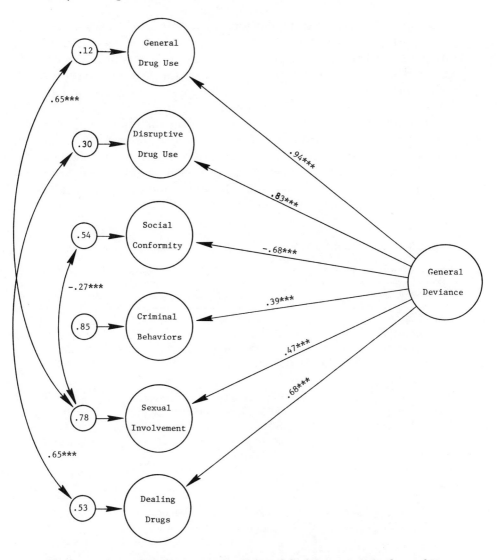

Figure 9.1   Second-Order Latent Factor Model of Deviant Attitudes and Behaviors.   The measurement portion of the model is not depicted for simplicity. The large circles are latent factors and the small circles are disturbance or factor residual terms. Parameter estimates are standardized, residual variables are variances, and significance levels were determined by critical ratios (*** *p* < .001).

second-order factor) and then for the residuals of General Drug Use (drug use that does not occur at work or school) and the residuals of Disruptive Drug Use (drug use that specifically occurs at work or school). Nonstandard correlations were added to capture the full associations between various types of drug use and the deviance-related variables and factors.

The final second-order factor model fit the data quite well (p = .99, NFI = .98) (see table 9.4; latent factors are capitalized and measured variables are in lower case). The second-order factor of All Drug Use was significantly correlated with decreased Social Conformity, increased Criminal Behavior, increased Sexual Involvement, and increased Dealing Drugs.

Table 9.4 Significant Correlations with Drug Use in the Final Second-order Factor Model for Deviance

Drug-related Factor/Variable	Deviance Factor/Variable	Correlation
All Drug Use	Social Conformity	−.68***
All Drug Use	Criminal Behavior	.37***
All Drug Use	Sexual Involvement	.54***
All Drug Use	Dealing Drugs	.67***
General Drug Use		
Drug Use	number of steady partners	.20***
alcohol frequency	Social Conformity	−.90***
alcohol frequency	religious commitment	−.12**
alcohol frequency	number of sexual partners	.16***
cannabis frequency	liberalism	.08*
cannabis frequency	amount of cannabis sold	.44***
hard drug frequency	confrontational acts	.14**
hard drug frequency	number of steady partners	.12**
hard drug frequency	number of sexual partners	.14***
hard drug frequency	amount of hard drugs sold	.37***
Disruptive Drug Use		
Drug Use	amount of hard drugs sold	.23***
alcohol at work	law abidance	−.08*
alcohol at work	confrontational acts	.12**
cannabis at work	amount of cannabis sold	.54***
cocaine at work	thefts	.12**
cocaine at work	Dealing Drugs	.25***
cocaine at work	amount of cannabis sold	.25***
cocaine at work	amount of hard drugs sold	.16***
hard drugs at work	amount of cannabis sold	.09*
hard drugs at work	amount of hard drugs sold	.49***

*p < .05; **p < .01; ***p < .001.

The residual of General Drug Use was significantly correlated with more steady partners. General alcohol frequency was significantly correlated with less Social Conformity, less religious commitment, and more sexual partners. Cannabis frequency was significantly associated with more liberalism and more selling of cannabis. Hard drug frequency was correlated with more confrontational acts, more steady partners, more sexual partners, and more selling of hard drugs.

The residual of the Disruptive Drug Use factor was associated only with more selling of hard drugs. Alcohol at work (or disruptive alcohol use) was correlated with less law abidance and more confrontational acts. Cannabis use at work was associated with more selling of cannabis. Cocaine use at work was correlated with more thefts, more Dealing Drugs, and more selling of cannabis and hard drugs. Finally, hard drug use at work was related to more selling of cannabis and hard drugs.

Interpretation

Of all the variables thus far examined as correlates of disruptive drug use, the deviance measures appear to be the strongest. One obvious conclusion from the analyses is that disruptive drug use is indeed one aspect of general deviance. Using drugs at work or school was highly associated with a lack of Social Conformity (and in particular with low law abidance) and Dealing Drugs, and moderately related to Sexual Involvement and Criminal Behaviors. Thus, although there may be a variety of psychogenic theories to explain disruptive drug use as a response to stress, family problems, or emotional distress of various sorts, one clear and incontrovertible pattern is that disruptive drug use is engaged in by those who practice other deviant behaviors and hold nontraditional values.

In terms of magnitude of associations, various types of disruptive substance use were most highly correlated with low law abidance and selling drugs, followed by thefts and confrontational acts, and then the sexual involvement variables. Disruptive alcohol use was less tightly bound to other types of deviance, compared to disruptive use of other drugs. This can be seen in the amount of variance accounted for in the multiple regression analyses by the deviance variables for each type of disruptive substance use. Although significant, these variables accounted for only 6 percent of the variance of disruptive alcohol use, whereas these variables accounted for approximately 20 percent of the variance of disruptive cocaine use and 36 percent of the variance in disruptive hard drug use.

It again appears that disruptive alcohol use may be somehow different from inappropriate use of the other three categories of drugs. This finding certainly may be related to the legal nature of alcohol, since to obtain any of the other drugs the young adult must make connections with dealers and the illicit drug trade. Thus, those who are willing to risk procuring illicit substances may be different from those who are not willing to deal with the drug underworld and prefer to obtain their drugs at the liquor store. Therefore, even though they may be practicing similar behavior (i.e., getting high at work or school), the type of person may differ with the type of drug. Those who use cannabis, cocaine, and hard drugs at work may be more likely to engage in other illegal behaviors than those who get high on alcohol at work. This does not mean that one type of drug is any more or less problematic when used in an inappropriate situation, only that the type of person who uses illicit drugs on the job may be more likely to engage in other illegal activities.

If we look at the correlates of specific types of disruptive drug use while controlling for All Drug Use, we find that the only correlates of alcohol at work were increased confrontational acts (i.e., arguments and aggression) and a slight association with less law abidance, an attitude rather than a behavior variable. By contrast, all the correlates of cannabis, cocaine, and hard drug use at work were illegal behaviors. These included theft and selling all types of illegal drugs.

This leads to another critical finding. Although General Drug Use and Disruptive Drug Use had associations roughly equivalent in magnitude with Social Conformity and Criminal Behavior, quite different associations were found for Sexual Involvement and Dealing Drugs. With only a very few exceptions, Disruptive Drug Use was associated with Dealing Drugs (and the specific indicators of this factor), whereas General Drug Use was associated with increased Sexual Involvement. This indicates that General Drug Use is more strongly related to noncriminal deviance (i.e., heightened sexual involvement) than is Disruptive Drug Use, which was more strongly related to Dealing Drugs, a decidedly illegal activity. From this perspective, it appears that disruptive drug use may be more deviant in the legal sense than is general drug use, which may be more deviant in a social sense.

Although these differential effects are intriguing and shed important light on the nature of disruptive drug use, a more general conclusion is that disruptive drug use is, in fact, an indicator of

General Deviance. Using drugs at work must be considered a sign of a general lifestyle of deviance and illegal behavior. This pattern may not be as pronounced for alcohol at work as it is for illicit drug use at work. Nevertheless, it is clear that only treating the problem of using drugs at work ignores the larger syndrome of deviance-prone behavior. It will be necessary to address the general lifestyle of deviant and illegal behavior and attitudes of the drug user at work, in order to create a lasting and complete rehabilitation.

Chapter 10

STABILITY AND CHANGE OF DISRUPTIVE DRUG USE

In this chapter, longitudinal data are used to examine the associations between the disruptive drug use of adolescents and the disruptive drug use of young adults. Four years separate these two assessments, leaving time for the young adults to grow and mature (e.g., Havighurst, 1952, 1972). It is possible that disruptive drug use as a teenager (and primarily at school) may reflect a phase or stage of rebellion and acting-out behavior that could diminish or disappear with the maturity and responsibility of young adulthood. This would indicate that those who engage in disruptive drug use as a teenager may not be the same people who engage in such behavior as a young adult. On the other hand, if there is a great deal of consistency between those who use drugs at work or school as a teenager and those who do so as a young adult, such behavior may reflect a stable disposition of the person and not simply a response to environmental pressures or stress.

It is also possible that a lifestyle of drug use may remain stable from adolescence to young adulthood, even if a consistent pattern of disruptive drug use is not evident. General drug use as a teenager may be the best predictor of later disruptive drug use despite a lower consistency of disruptive drug use. This would indicate that high general drug involvement at a younger age may precede and perhaps help generate disruptive drug use later in life. This would reflect a stability in a lifestyle characterized by the use of drugs.

To date, there are no data on the long-term consistency of disruptive drug use. The sources most relevant are on recidivism rates of workers caught using drugs on the job and longitudinal

136

studies of general drug use over time. The data on recidivism rates are disparate, since the rates vary greatly based upon the employer's response to the drug use, available treatment, and type of follow-up and monitoring (e.g., Backer, 1987). These data are not directly relevant to the present analyses, because they represent effects of intervention rather than natural patterns of usage.

There has been considerable research on the stability and change in general drug use over varying lengths of time. One of the most consistent findings is that early drug use predicts later drug use (e.g., Chassin, 1984; Kandel, 1980; Long & Scherl, 1984). This has been found over short and long periods of time.

Two differential relationships have been observed in regard to the stability of drug use. First, the greater the length of time between assessments, the lower will be the consistency or stability in drug use. This is a common-sense conclusion regarding the inverse relationship between stability and time. In general, for example, there is a higher correlation between drug use assessments that are measured one month apart than between those measured one year apart. Second, stability increases with age. In our study, we found that stability effects for latent constructs of alcohol, cannabis, and hard drugs were substantially smaller between early and late adolescence than between late adolescence and young adulthood (Newcomb & Bentler, 1986d). This was also apparent for measured variables of cigarette and nonprescription drugs. Further, a latent factor of General Drug Use was found to be twice as stable in the later compared to the earlier time period (Stein, Newcomb, & Bentler, 1987a). In fact, a factor of general drug use in high school accounted for 60 percent of the variance in young adult drug use measured four years later (Newcomb & Bentler, 1987a). Looking at specific substances, we find that males showed greater stability than the females over this period in their use of cannabis. No other sex differences on stability were evident. In a sample of adults, Aneshensel and Huba (1983) found a very high level of stability for alcohol use (as a latent factor) over a one-year period. Thus, in regard to general drug use, there evolves a lifestyle that becomes more established with age.

Slightly more relevant to the present work is a study by Donovan, Jessor, and Jessor (1983) which examined stability and change in problem drinking from adolescence to young adulthood. Problem drinking in the subjects was defined as producing "negative consequences due to their drinking at two or more times during the past year in each of three or more out of six different life-areas: trouble with teachers, difficulties with friends, trouble with parents, criticism from dates, trouble with the police, and driving

while under the influence of alcohol" (p. 113). Prevalence rates for
problem drinking were similar for the adolescent and young adult:
about 30 percent for the men and half that for the women.
Interestingly, however, less than half of the teenage problem
drinkers remained problem drinkers as young adults. The conti-
nuity of problem drinking was greater for the men than it was for
the women.

In another study, adult regular marijuana users were surveyed
twice over six years (Halikas, Weller, Morse, & Hoffman, 1984). At
the initial interview, 12 percent reported almost daily use of
marijuana and 50 percent of this group maintained this pattern at
the follow-up, whereas 23 percent of the sample were almost daily
users at the second testing. Those initially classified as moderate
users (one to four times per week) were the least stable over time:
23 percent of this group escalated their usage to almost daily use,
and 43 percent reduced their level of use. Vicary and Lerner (1983)
followed a group of subjects from childhood to adulthood and found
that severe use of alcohol and marijuana increased during middle
adolescence and then decreased in young adulthood, with prevalence rates of 1 percent for alcohol and 4 percent for marijuana at
that time. These rates seem surprisingly small and may reflect the
nature of the sample (from New York and predominantly Jewish)
and historical effects (subjects were originally assessed in 1956).

Bachman, O'Malley, and Johnston (1984) examined the stability
of general drug use in a group of teenagers; they were assessed
when they were seniors and again at one, two, and three years
after high school. As expected, the stabilities decreased with time.
At the three-year follow-ups, the correlations between high school
and later alcohol and marijuana use were the largest (.58 and .59),
whereas the correlations for heavy drinking and other illicit drug
use were smaller (both .42). Kandel, Davies, Karus, and Yamaguchi (1986) presented correlations over a longer period of time,
between ever using a drug by age fifteen or sixteen and frequency
of use at age twenty-five. The correlation for cigarettes was .32,
.18 for alcohol, .29 for marijuana, and .23 for other illicit drugs.
Unfortunately, these data are distorted because of the use and
nonuse measures from adolescence, for which no degree or extent
of involvement can be determined.

Overall, it seems that general drug use is fairly stable over time,
particularly at older ages. Severe or problematic drug use, however, perhaps more akin to disruptive drug use, tends to be more
volatile and less stable over time. The present analyses examine
the prevalence of disruptive drug use during late adolescence and
compare this to young adult estimates. Next, multivariate analyses

are used to explore how the degree of involvement in disruptive substance use during adolescence generates disruptive substance use in young adults. Finally, measures of general drug use during late adolescence are introduced as predictors of young adult disruptive substance use.

Measures

The measures of disruptive drug use in young adulthood incorporated in previous chapters are used in these analyses. These include prevalence and frequency of use for the eight separate drugs, the four composite scales, and the total scores. During late adolescence, the subjects indicated their frequency of being high, drunk, or stoned on beer, wine, liquor, cannabis, and other illicit (hard) drugs at work or school on a seven-point scale that ranged from none (1) to more than forty times (7). The responses were based on the past six-month period (as were the young adult assessments). For some analyses the three alcohol items are combined into a composite scale of disruptive alcohol use, and all measures are combined into a scale of disruptive use of all drugs. Both frequency and prevalence (use and nonuse) scorings of these items and scales are used. Finally, in late adolescence, subjects indicated their frequency of general use during the past six months for twenty-one different substances. Responses were indicated on rating scales that ranged from never (1) to more than once per day (7). These items were combined into four scales: alcohol frequency (beer, wine, and liquor), cannabis frequency (marijuana and hashish), cocaine frequency (a single item), and hard drug frequency (fourteen different drugs including stimulants, hypnotics, psychedelics, inhalants, narcotics, and PCP). Both prevalence and frequency scorings of these scales are used.

Results

Since all of the analyses in this chapter (and the two following chapters) utilize information from the late adolescent assessment in the longitudinal study, fewer subjects are used. In these analyses, a total of 654 cases are included; 192 are men and 462 are women.

Prevalence Rates of Disruptive Drug Use

Rates for the prevalence of different types of disruptive substance use during late adolescence and young adulthood are given for the total sample and separately for men and women (see table 10.1). Chi-square differences in proportion tests are used to compare rates between assessment periods and between sexes. In order to make the young adult scales comparable to the late adolescent scales, disruptive cocaine and hard drug use were combined in the young adult measures for this analysis only.

For the total sample, prevalence rates of disruptive alcohol use and any disruptive drug use did not change from adolescence to young adulthood. The prevalence rate of disruptive cannabis use decreased into young adulthood, whereas the prevalence rate of disruptive hard drugs increased over the same period. For the males, prevalence rates at both times were not different except for disruptive hard drug use, which increased into young adulthood. For the women, prevalence rates were equivalent at the two times, except for a decrease of disruptive cannabis use into young adulthood. Men reported greater prevalence of disruptive alcohol and any use during adolescence. These differences were continued in young adulthood, but a significant difference emerged on disruptive cannabis use. Even though both men and women decreased

Table 10.1   Prevalence of Disruptive Substance Use among Late Adolescents and Young Adults

	Alcohol	Cannabis	Hard Drugs	Any Use
Total Sample (N = 654)				
Late Adolescence	21.1	22.2	7.3	31.3
Young Adulthood	18.3	16.2	11.8	30.1
χ^2 =	1.56	7.50**	7.44**	.23
Males Only (N = 192)				
Late Adolescence	28.1	25.5	6.8	37.0
Young Adulthood	28.6	21.4	13.0	37.5
χ^2 =	.01	.93	4.21*	.01
Females Only (N = 462)				
Late Adolescence	18.2	20.8	7.6	29.0
Young Adulthood	14.1	14.1	11.3	27.1
χ^2 =	2.89	7.23**	3.67	.44
Sex Differences				
Late Adolescence χ^2 =	8.06**	1.77	.13	4.01*
Young Adulthood χ^2 =	19.24***	5.30*	.41	7.03**

$*p < .05; **p < .01; ***p < .001.$

their disruptive cannabis use into young adulthood, the reduction for the women was much greater than that for the men.

Conditional Prevalence of Disruptive Drug Use over Time

Of those who used beer at work or school during adolescence, 52 percent used some drug in these contexts in young adulthood (see table 10.2). The strongest predictor for using any disruptive drug in young adulthood was disruptive hard drug use as a teenager; 62 percent of those who used a hard drug at work or school during adolescence also used a drug at work or school as a young adult. The strongest predictor of disruptive beer use as a young adult was disruptive beer use as an adolescent. Similar specific effects were apparent for wine and liquor. The best predictor of use of marijuana, stimulants, and cocaine at work or school by young adults was disruptive hard drug use by the teenager.

Table 10.2 Conditional Prevalence of Disruptive Substance Use during Late Adolescence and Young Adulthood

Young Adult Use	Adolescent Use[a]					
	Any Use	Beer	Wine	Liquor	Cannabis	Hard Drugs
Any Use	52.2	52.1	49.1	54.1	56.8	62.5
	(16.4)	(7.5)	(4.1)	(7.0)	(12.5)	(4.6)
Beer	22.9	29.8	20.0	25.9	22.8	20.8
	(7.2)	(4.3)	(1.7)	(3.4)	(5.0)	(1.5)
Wine	9.8	10.6	14.5	9.4	6.9	8.3
	(3.1)	(1.5)	(1.2)	(1.2)	(1.5)	(0.6)
Liquor	13.7	13.6	16.4	16.5	11.0	8.3
	(4.3)	(2.0)	(1.4)	(2.1)	(2.4)	(0.6)
Marijuana	30.2	29.8	23.6	31.8	38.6	39.6
	(9.5)	(4.3)	(2.0)	(4.1)	(8.6)	(2.9)
Hashish	3.4	5.3	7.3	5.9	4.8	0.0
	(1.1)	(0.8)	(0.6)	(0.8)	(1.1)	(0.0)
Stimulants	13.7	13.8	7.3	15.3	17.2	27.1
	(4.3)	(2.0)	(0.6)	(2.0)	(3.8)	(2.0)
Hypnotics	1.5	1.1	1.8	2.4	2.1	2.1
	(0.5)	(0.2)	(0.2)	(0.3)	(0.5)	(0.2)
Cocaine	22.0	22.3	20.0	25.9	24.1	27.1
	(6.9)	(3.2)	(1.7)	(3.4)	(5.4)	(2.0)

[a]The first number indicates the percentage of subjects who used a specific drug as a young adult if they had used a specific drug as a late adolescent. The number in parentheses indicates the percentage of the sample that used the one substance during young adulthood and the other during late adolescence.

The rates for total use are comparable: 16.4 percent of the sample used at least one drug at work or school as an adolescent and also as a young adult. Aside from the any/all disruptive substance use scales, disruptive beer and cannabis use in late adolescence were associated with the highest prevalences of disruptive drug use in young adulthood.

Across-Time Correlations of Disruptive Drug Use

With one exception, all three teenage disruptive drug use scales were significantly correlated with the five young adult disruptive drug use scales (see table 10.3). (Disruptive cocaine use as a young adult was not significantly correlated with hard drug use at work as a teenager.) Although significant, these correlations ranged in magnitude from small to moderate. The largest correlation was between disruptive cannabis use at both times ($r = .40$).

Separate correlations were generated for men and women and most corresponding correlations were not significantly different when statistically compared (using the Fisher r to z conversion). The primary exception was on disruptive cannabis use at the two times; this correlation was significantly larger for the men than the women. No difference was found on the any/all use scales.

In the multiple regression analyses, young adult disruptive alcohol use was the most difficult to predict, with only alcohol at work as a teenager being a predictor and the entire equation accounting for only one percent of the variance (although significant). The other four young adult disruptive drug use scales were predicted more strongly from the teenage disruptive drug use scales, ranging in magnitude from 7 percent of disruptive cocaine use to 16 percent of disruptive cannabis use (see table 10.3). Disruptive cannabis use (in young adulthood) was predicted from cannabis at work (as a teenager), disruptive hard drugs was predicted from cannabis and hard drugs at work, and, finally, disruptive use of all substances was predicted from cannabis at work.

Test of Stage Theory of Disruptive Drug Use

In chapter 3 I presented cross-sectional data as a test of the application of the stage theory of drug use to disruptive drug use. We found that disruptive alcohol use leads to disruptive cannabis use, which then leads to disruptive hard drugs. Since those data were cross-sectional, however, they cannot provide a definitive test of the theory. With the longitudinal data available in the present analyses, a much stronger test can be made.

A latent-variable model was tested that included a latent factor of Alcohol at Work (with indicators of beer, wine, and liquor at work), and measured variables of cannabis and hard drugs at work (both treated as factors, although they are single indicators) from late adolescence. From young adulthood three latent factors were included: Alcohol at Work (with indicators of beer, wine, and liquor at work), Cannabis at Work (with indicators of marijuana and hashish at work), and Hard Drugs at Work (with indicators of stimulants, hypnotics, and cocaine at work). All factors in adolescence were allowed to correlate, as were all factor residuals in young adulthood. All young adult constructs were predicted initially from all teenage constructs. This initial model was modified by adding necessary paths and deleting nonsignificant ones. The final model fit the data quite well ($p = .23$, NFI = .99) (see figure 10.1).

There is no stability effect for the Alcohol at Work construct, whereas moderate stabilities were evident for Cannabis at Work and Hard Drugs at Work. There were small stability effects for the specific alcohol substance of beer at work and wine at work. Two cross-substance effects were found over time. Early use of hard drugs at work predicted later Alcohol at Work, and teenage cannabis at work increased later cocaine at work. Except for this last effect, no other support for the stage theory of disruptive drug use was found.

General Drug Use during Late Adolescence

Teenage general drug use is now contrasted with later disruptive drug use. The drug use prevalence rates during late adolescence (during the past six months) are: 82 percent had used alcohol, 49 percent had used cannabis, 18 percent had used cocaine, and 25 percent had used some type of hard or illicit drug (see table 10.4). Alcohol use during adolescence only slightly increased the prevalence of any type of disruptive drug use as a young adult. In contrast, using cannabis as a teenager increased the likelihood of using a drug disruptively as a young adult by about 50 percent; use of hard drugs, and in particular cocaine, increased the likelihood even more substantially. For instance, a teenager who has used cocaine at least once during a six-month period is over three times more likely to use cocaine or hard drugs at work or school as a young adult.

In terms of the most prevalent pairing of teenage general drug use and young adult disruptive drug use, general alcohol use and disruptive use of any substance captured 29 percent of the sample.

Table 10.3   Correlations and Multiple Regression Results of Young Adult Disruptive Drug Use with Late Adolescent General and Disruptive Drug Use

	Young Adult Disruptive Drug Use									
	Alcohol		Cannabis		Cocaine		Hard Drugs		All Use	
Late Adolescent Predictors	*r*	*Beta*	*r*	*Beta*	*r*	*Beta*	*r*	*Beta*	*r*	*Beta*
Disruptive Drug Use										
alcohol at work	.11**	.09*	.21***	.00	.16***	.04	.05	−.01	.21***	.02
cannabis at work	.08*	.01	.40***	.43***	.25***	.26***	.22***	.17***	.35***	.32***
hard drugs at work	.07*	.04	.09*	−.02	.04	−.02	.31***	.27***	.18***	.04
Multiple Regression Summary										
R		.12		.41		.26		.34		.35
R²		.01		.16		.07		.11		.12
F-ratio		3.02		42.65		16.02		28.09		30.87
p-value		.03		<.001		<.001		<.001		<.001
General Drug Use										
alcohol frequency	.18***	.15***	.20***	−.01	.19***	.02	.15***	−.01	.27***	.03
cannabis frequency	.13**	−.02	.43***	.48***	.29***	.22***	.24***	.07	.40***	.27***
cocaine frequency	.18***	.14***	.30***	.08*	.27***	.19***	.25***	.07	.36***	.17***
hard drug frequency	.11**	.00	.19***	−.05	.12***	−.01	.32***	.25***	.27***	.02
Multiple Regression Summary										
R		.21		.45		.32		.34		.43
R²		.05		.20		.10		.11		.18
F-ratio		7.77		40.19		18.76		20.71		35.96
p-value		<.001		<.001		<.001		<.001		<.001

*p < .05; **p < .01; *** p <.001.

In regard to specific substances, the highest proportion of the sample used alcohol in general as a teenager and alcohol at work as a young adult (17 percent).

General Drug Use Predictors of Later Disruptive Drug Use

General use scales of alcohol, cannabis, cocaine, and hard drugs as a teenager were correlated with and used as multiple predictors of the five disruptive substance use scales in young adulthood (see table 10.3).

All four of the adolescent general drug use scales were correlated significantly with each of the five young adult disruptive substance use scales. These ranged from a low of .11 between teenage hard drug frequency and young adult disruptive alcohol use, to a high of .43 between teenage cannabis frequency and young adult disruptive cannabis use.

In the multiple regression analyses, the four teenage drug use scales were able to account for 5 percent of the variance in young adult disruptive alcohol use, with predictors of alcohol and cocaine frequency. Twenty percent of the variance of disruptive cannabis use was accounted for by the four drug scales, with cannabis and cocaine being predictors. Disruptive cocaine use and all use were predicted from cannabis and cocaine frequency. Finally, only hard drug frequency was a predictor of disruptive hard drug use.

Total Model of General and Disruptive Drug Use

Finally, a latent model was developed to examine simultaneously General Drug Use and Drug Use at Work during adolescence as predictors of young adult Drug Use at Work. The latent factor of late adolescent General Drug Use had indicators of alcohol, cannabis, cocaine, and hard drug frequencies. The adolescent factor of Drug Use at Work had indicators of alcohol, cannabis, and hard drugs at work. The young adult latent factor of Drug Use at Work had indicators of alcohol, cannabis, cocaine, and hard drugs at work. Initially, both teenage constructs were allowed to correlate freely and to predict young adult Drug Use at Work. Nonsignificant paths were deleted and other necessary paths were added. The final model fit the data well ($p = .95$, NFI $= .99$) (see figure 10.2).

Young adult Drug Use at Work was directly predicted from teenage General Drug Use, cocaine frequency, and cannabis at work, but *not* from teenage Drug Use at Work. There was an

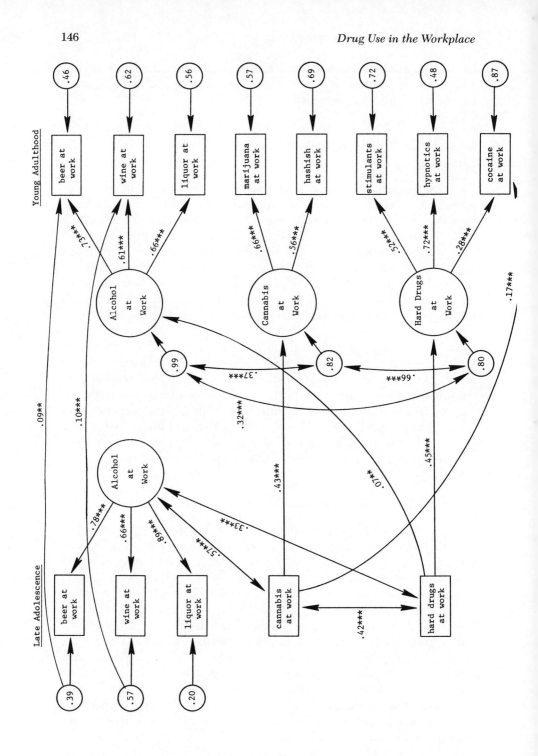

Table 10.4 Conditional Prevalences of General Drug Use during Late Adolescence and Disruptive Drug Use during Young Adulthood

Young Adult Disruptive Drug Use	Prevalence	Late Adolescent General Drug Use			
		Alcohol	Cannabis	Cocaine	Hard Drugs
Prevalence		81.8	48.6	18.2	25.5
Alcohol	18.3	21.3	24.8	32.8	25.7
		(17.4)	(12.1)	(6.0)	(6.6)
Cannabis	16.2	18.9	27.7	36.1	31.1
		(15.4)	(13.5)	(6.6)	(8.0)
Cocaine	9.0	11.0	15.7	28.6	21.6
		(9.0)	(7.6)	(5.2)	(5.5)
Hard Drugs	5.7	6.7	10.7	18.5	18.6
		(5.5)	(5.2)	(3.4)	(4.7)
Any Use	30.1	35.3	44.7	60.5	54.5
		(28.9)	(21.7)	(11.0)	(13.9)

indirect effect of this factor on later Drug Use at Work, given the high correlation with General Drug Use ($r = .84$). In regard to specific substances, alcohol at work (as a young adult) was directly predicted from alcohol and cocaine frequencies (as a late adolescent), and cannabis at work was directly predicted from teenage cannabis at work and cannabis frequency. Finally, hard drugs at work was predicted from teenage hard drugs at work and hard drug frequency.

Interpretation

These analyses provide some interesting insights into how disruptive drug use changes or remains stable over time. Of course, the time period reflected in these data is a special one, which may influence the applicability of the results to other periods in life. For instance, disruptive drug use may be more stable at an older age, by which time it could be a firmly established behavioral style (barring, of course, detection and intervention). Most types of drug use behavior are established during the period from adolescence

Figure 10.1 Longitudinal Latent-Variable Model of Disruptive Drug Use over Time. The large circles are latent factors, the rectangles are measured variables, and the small circles are residuals or factor disturbance terms. Parameter estimates are standardized, residual variables are variances, and significance levels were determined by critical ratios (** $p < .01$; *** $p < .001$).

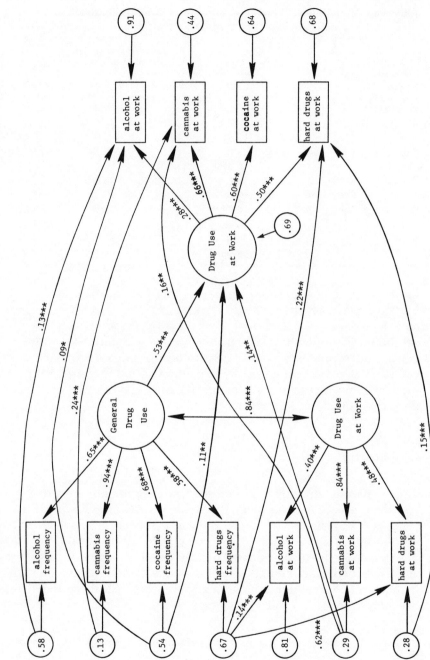

to young adulthood, and it does not seem unreasonable to assume disruptive drug use behavior may become established at this time as well. Certainly disruptive drug use is engaged in at both of these age periods: nearly 30 percent of the sample reported at least one instance of being high or stoned while at work or school during a six-month period in adolescence and young adulthood. It is interesting that this 30 percent prevalence figure is close to that reported for problem drinking by Donovan, Jessor, and Jessor (1983). It appears that for people in the age group from late adolescence to young adulthood, almost one-third of them have some trouble with drugs, including use at work or school.

Disruptive drug use tends to be modestly to moderately stable over time, but not as stable as general drug use. Disruptive drug use resembles severe or problematic drug use: it is more volatile over time when compared to a general tendency to use drugs (perhaps nonproblem use). This suggests that it is a drug-using lifestyle that is developed and is most stable over time, one component of which may be disruptive drug use. In fact, general drug use, and cocaine frequency in particular, were both direct predictors of later disruptive drug use (the Drug Use at Work latent factor). These were stronger factors than earlier disruptive drug use (or drug use at work, with the exception of a moderate direct effect of teenage cannabis use at work). This suggests that general drug use as a teenager may be a better predictor of later disruptive drug use than knowing whether that person used drugs at work or school as a teenager. According to our evidence, the propensity to use drugs is more stable than is the tendency to use drugs in inappropriate environments.

It is somewhat curious that disruptive alcohol use was the least successfully predicted type of disruptive drug use as a young adult. There was no direct stability effect from earlier Alcohol at Work to later Alcohol at Work when these were assessed as latent factors. There were small specific tendencies to use particular types of alcohol in these contexts (e.g., beer and wine), but not to use alcohol. A consideration here is that alcohol became legal for these subjects over the four-year period between adolescence and young adulthood, and different styles of disruptive drug use may be

Figure 10.2 Longitudinal Latent Variable Model of General and Disruptive Drug Use over Time. The large circles are latent factors, the rectangles are measured variables, and the small circles are residuals or factor disturbance terms. Parameter estimates are standardized, residual variables are variances, and significance levels were determined by critical ratios (* $p < .05$; ** $p < .01$; *** $p < .001$).

reflected in the legality of the substance (as noted in the previous chapter).

The longitudinal data did not support the application of the stage theory of drug involvement to disruptive substance use. The one exception here is the effect of earlier cannabis use at work to increase later cocaine use at work. This supports previous work on general drug use, which has consistently found that cannabis use leads to and increases cocaine use over time (e.g., Kandel, Murphy & Karus, 1985; Newcomb & Bentler, 1986a, in press a). With this exception, there was no support for a theory of sequential development of disruptive drug use. In fact, if anything, a reverse sequence seems to appear; teenage hard drugs at work increased later Alcohol at Work. This conforms with the earlier findings in chapter 6, where disruptive drug use was found to occur at a moderate to high level of general drug involvement. Thus, even though disruptive alcohol use involves using alcohol (typically considered an entry-level drug), it in fact represents a fairly high level of general drug involvement, well into the illicit substances. This can be seen in the effect of teenage cocaine frequency increasing or generating later Drug Use at Work. In general, however, disruptive drug use can be characterized by moderate stability for specific types of substances (and not general alcohol use) with little cross-germination over time.

It must be remembered that these effects were found over a fairly lengthy period, suggesting that more subtle influences may have gone undetected. In addition, types of disruptive drug use in both adolescence and young adulthood were quite highly intercorrelated; this and the stability effects just discussed make it more difficult to isolate direct cross-effects. Many of these may be indirect.

Although disruptive cannabis use decreased from late adolescence to young adulthood, particularly for women (as did the general use of cannabis [Newcomb & Bentler, 1987a]), cannabis remained the second most prevalent type of substance used disruptively. This may mean that early experimental or infrequent use of cannabis during the teenage years does not continue into young adulthood; either the drug is abandoned or use escalates (e.g., Halikas et al., 1984). Thus, while the proportion of cannabis users decreases, the involvement of the continuing users increases.

From these analyses we can conclude that general drug use is certainly a feature of one's personality; the same is true of disruptive drug use but to a lesser extent. Intrapersonal factors play an important role in disruptive drug use, since such behavior is moderately maintained over many years and presumably across

varied contexts. Other personal factors, as well as external influences, may contribute to increasing or decreasing disruptive drug
use, and in fact may have greater success in modification than
altering general tendencies to use drugs (which appear to be more
deeply ingrained).

Although disruptive substance use is moderately stable over
time, it is much less so than general drug use, which tends to be
highly consistent over time among adults (e.g., Aneshensel &
Huba, 1983). Thus, it is important to locate, if possible, the factors
that influence the stability in disruptive substance use over time.
Such information could be useful in developing interventions to
reduce disruptive drug use.

Chapter 11

ADOLESCENT PERSONALITY AND PSYCHOLOGICAL FUNCTIONING AS PREDICTORS OF LATER DISRUPTIVE DRUG USE

Using the longitudinal data from late adolescence, this chapter examines the influence of several psychological functioning variables on generating changes in disruptive drug use from adolescence to young adulthood. Several types of psychological functioning measures are included from the late adolescent assessment, including personality, life satisfaction, and emotional distress. Measures of both general drug use and disruptive drug use from adolescence are also included in these analyses. It is essential to incorporate these drug use measures so that when an effect is noted between an adolescent variable and later disruptive drug use, we can conclude that the effect generated a change in the level of disruptive drug use and was not simply a correlation over time. Several of the psychological measures included in the cross-sectional analyses of chapter 8 are included in the present analyses. Chapter 8 provided correlations between disruptive drug use and various types of psychological functioning, and no unidirectional effects could be tested. The present analyses can determine the impact of earlier psychological functioning on changes in disruptive drug use, and can establish directional relationships. Such information is vital when attempting to design effective programs to modify or reduce drug use at work or school.

According to previous research, drug use is not generated by a single factor, but rather results from a variety of different attitudinal, personality, family, social, and environmental forces. Unlike most previous etiological work on predicting drug involvement (e.g., Kandel, Kessler, & Margulies, 1978; Newcomb, Maddahian, & Bentler, 1986; Yamaguchi & Kandel, 1984), which has addressed initiation into and changes in general patterns of drug use, the present analyses focus on explaining changes in a specific type of drug abuse, which I have called disruptive drug use. Few studies have examined the etiological factors for abuse of drugs using panel data. None, to my knowledge, has examined the antecedents of disruptive drug use.

The precursors of general drug use and of drug abuse have similarities and differences. The literature in this area is certainly not definitive or conclusive (e.g., Long & Scherl, 1984), so my discussion provides generalities and tentative conclusions rather than definitive answers. It is apparent that most teenage drug use is initiated in peer settings (e.g., Kandel, 1980), but peer influences do not lead to abusing drugs. Many years ago, Freud made the somewhat circuitous statement that "only the addiction prone become addicted" (Freud, 1905). Nevertheless, there may be a great deal of truth to this self-evident statement, for of the many adolescents and adults who use drugs, only a small percentage develop severe problems with such use. Other factors than those related to initiation or use of drugs must come into play to generate or predispose someone to misuse or abuse drugs. For instance, in a cross-sectional study, Carman (1979) found that nonproblem use of drugs was associated with social facilitation factors, whereas abuse was related to personal effects motivation (i.e., to reduce negative feelings). In addition, some research has noted that those who initiate drug use earlier than their peers are more prone to abuse than those who begin using drugs later in their life (e.g., Robins & Przybeck, 1985). In this case, the factors involved in generating early drug use may be related to the eventual abuse of drugs. Such factors might include precocious development (Newcomb, 1987), genetic predispositions, or familial influences (e.g., Long & Scherl, 1984; Zucker & Gomberg, 1986). Early use of drugs may also preclude or prevent the acquisition of adaptive coping skills that are not based on drug use, placing the burden of later adjustment on the coping function (albeit inadequate) of drugs (e.g., Newcomb & Bentler, 1988a, in press a).

A few studies have used longitudinal data to separate the long-term precursors of general drug use from those of problem drug use. Donovan, Jessor, and Jessor (1983) compared a range of psychosocial variables over a seven-year period for a group of teenagers assessed when all subjects were nonproblem drinkers. They found that those who developed problem drinking patterns were more alienated, had greater tolerance of deviance, had more sex disjunction, engaged in more deviant behavior, had greater marijuana involvement, were more often engaged in solitary drinking, and attended church more infrequently as teenagers compared to those who did not become problem drinkers. Margulies, Kessler, and Kandel (1977) found that social influences were most salient in predicting onset of alcohol use, whereas personality tendencies were most important in determining those who became problem drinkers. Two studies from my data have also attempted to differentiate precursors of use and abuse of drugs. In one study, we found that general use of drugs was predicted by social learning variables such as prior use, peer models, and adult models, whereas problem use was generated by internal factors such as low social conformity and family disruption (Stein, Newcomb, & Bentler, 1987a). This confirms cross-sectional research that has found that general use is generated by external factors such as peer influences, whereas abuse or problem use is generated by internal factors such as personality tendencies or distress (e.g., Carman, 1979). In another study based on the same sample, we found that later problems with drugs were predicted from negative personal feelings, low social support, and low social conformity, as well as prior drug use (Newcomb & Bentler, in press c).

Several criteria have been established when attempting to draw causal inferences from statistical analyses (e.g., Clayton & Tuchfeld, 1982; Hirschi & Selvin, 1973): (1) a statistically reliable relationship must exist between the cause and the effect; (2) the cause must precede the effect in time; and (3) the association between cause and effect cannot be spurious (i.e., the result of a third variable that generates both cause and effect variables). A fourth criterion incorporated in my research is that the cause must generate a change in the effect variable (e.g., Newcomb, 1987; Newcomb & Bentler, 1988a). The fourth point requires that a prior measure of the effect variable must be included at the time the cause variable was assessed in order to control for the base line association between the cause and effect and to establish an estimate of the stability or state dependence of the effect (e.g., Gollob & Reichardt, 1987). Each of these criteria is applied in the present analyses so that we can draw causal inferences from the results. In particular, I want to determine which, if any, psychosocial factors in adolescence caused or contributed to disruptive drug use in young adulthood.

Analyses in this chapter include only the disruptive drug use variables from the young adult data; all other variables were assessed during late adolescence. From the late adolescent data, twenty-five variables were selected to represent eight constructs or latent factors. These are used to predict young adult disruptive substance use. The eight constructs are General Drug Use (with indicators of frequency of alcohol, cannabis, cocaine, and hard drug use), Disruptive Drug Use (with indicators of alcohol at work, cannabis at work, and hard drugs at work), Social Conformity (with indicators of law abidance, liberalism, and religious commitment), Perceived Opportunity (with indicators of happy with future, happy with schooling, and happy with chances to be what you want), Leadership Style (with indicators of deliberateness, diligence, and orderliness), Emotional Distress (with indicators of self-acceptance, depression, and self-derogation), Conscientiousness and Psychosomatic Complaints (with indicators of headache prone, insomnia, and illness sensitivity). I follow the sequence of analysis used in most of the preceding chapters. All analyses are based on 654 subjects.

Measures

Many of the variables used in this chapter have been described in earlier chapters, including the composite disruptive substance use measures from young adulthood (i.e., disruptive alcohol use, cannabis use, cocaine use, and hard drug use). As before, for some analyses, a total score combining all four measures is used to reflect all disruptive drug use. The three disruptive drug use measures and four general drug use measures assessed during late adolescence that were used in chapter 10 are included here. Social Conformity is reflected in the three personality scales described in chapter 9. The three scales used to represent the Leadership Style construct were described in chapter 8. The Psychosomatic Complaints construct and variables headache prone and insomnia were defined in chapter 8; the variable illness sensitivity (also from the BMPI) is used here instead of psychosomatic symptoms, which was not assessed during late adolescence. The Emotional Distress latent factor is reflected in three scales: self-derogation (also used in chapter 8), self-acceptance (from the BPI), and depression (from the BMPI). Conscientiousness is a latent construct represented by three traits from the BPI: deliberateness, diligence, and orderliness. Finally, Perceived Opoportunity is reflected in three single-item variables that were assessed on five-point scales (Newcomb,

Bentler, & Collins, 1986): happy with future, happy with schooling up to now, and happy with chances to be what you want.

Results

Bivariate Correlations

Product-moment correlations were calculated between each young adult disruptive drug use scale and the twenty-one variables assessed during late adolescence (the four general drug use scales from late adolescence were not included in these analyses because of their high correlations with the adolescent disruptive drug use scales).

Disruptive alcohol use was significantly correlated with all three disruptive drug use scales, low law abidance, low religiosity, low happiness with future, more ambition, more leadership, and less illness sensitivity (see table 11.1). Disruptive cannabis use was significantly correlated with all three disruptive drug use variables, in addition to less law abidance, more liberalism, less religious commitment, less happiness with future, less happiness with school, and more ambition. Disruptive cocaine use was significantly correlated with more alcohol at work, more cannabis at work, less law abidance, and more liberalism. Disruptive hard drug use was significantly correlated with more cannabis at work, more hard drugs at work, less law abidance, more liberalism, less religiosity, less happiness with school, and less orderliness. Finally, disruptive use of all drugs was significantly correlated with all three disruptive drug use scales, less law abidance, more liberalism, less religiosity, less happiness with future, less happiness with school, more ambition, more leadership, and less illness sensitivity.

Multiple Regression Analyses

Multiple regression analyses were used to predict each of the disruptive drug use scales simultaneously from the twenty-one variables of disruptive drug use and psychological functioning from late adolescence (see table 11.1).

The equation for predicting disruptive alcohol use was significant, but accounted for only 6 percent of the variance. The predictors of disruptive alcohol use were more alcohol at work (a stability effect), less happiness with future, more ambition, and less illness sensitivity. The equation to predict disruptive cannabis

Table 11.1 Correlations and Multiple Regression Results of Young Adult Disruptive Drug Use with Late Adolescent Disruptive Drug Use and Psychological Ranking Variables

Adolescent Predictors	Young Adult Outcomes									
	Alcohol		Cannabis		Cocaine		Hard Drugs		All Use	
	r	Beta	r	Beta	r	Beta	r	Beta	r	Beta
alcohol at work	.11**	.08*	.21***	–.01	.16***	.03	.05	–.03	.21***	.00
cannabis at work	.08*	.01	.40***	.40***	.25***	.21***	.22***	.13***	.35***	.27***
hard drugs at work	.07*	.06	.09*	–.04	.04	–.02	.31***	.27***	.18***	.05
law abidance	–.09*	–.04	–.20***	–.08*	–.19***	–.13**	–.18***	–.12**	–.24***	–.12**
liberalism	.06	.02	.19***	.07*	.13**	.06*	.10**	.01	.18***	.06*
religiosity	–.07*	–.04	–.07*	–.02	–.01	.04	–.11**	–.07*	–.10**	–.04
happy with future	–.07*	–.10*	–.07*	–.08*	–.02	–.05	–.05	–.07*	–.07*	–.11**
happy with school	–.06	–.03	–.09*	–.05	–.06	–.03	–.09*	–.02	–.11**	–.05
happy with chances	–.03	.01	.00	.03	.01	–.06	.01	.05	–.01	.05
ambition	–.11**	.09*	.07*	.01	.02	–.02	.06	.02	.11**	.05
extroversion	.01	–.05	–.03	–.08*	.01	–.03	.02	–.05	.00	–.08*
leadership	.08*	.05	.02	.00	.02	.02	.05	.04	.07*	.04
deliberateness	–.05	–.05	–.04	–.03	–.05	–.04	–.03	.01	–.06	–.04
diligence	–.02	–.06	–.01	.06	–.04	.02	–.06	.03	–.02	.01
orderliness	–.04	–.06	.00	.00	.00	.04	–.07*	–.07	–.04	–.04
self-acceptance	.00	–.03	.01	.05	–.04	–.07	–.05	–.06	–.02	–.03
depression	.00	–.05	.02	–.03	.03	–.06	.03	–.07	.02	–.06
self-derogation	.01	.03	.02	–.02	.05	.02	.03	–.01	.04	.01
headache-prone	–.02	.05	–.02	–.02	–.03	–.04	.00	.05	–.03	.02
insomnia	–.02	–.04	.04	.05	–.02	–.03	.02	–.01	.01	.00
illness sensitivity	–.09*	–.11**	–.05	–.04	–.01	.01	–.05	–.11**	–.09*	–.10**
Multiple Regression Summary										
R	.24		.44		.31		.39		.42	
R²	.06		.20		.09		.15		.18	
F-ratio	1.85		7.30		3.11		5.46		6.53	
p-value	.01		<.001		<.001		<.001		<.001	

*p < .05; **p < .01; ***p < .001.

use was quite significant ($p < .001$) and accounted for 20 percent of the variance (the best predicted of all disruptive drug use scales). Disruptive cannabis use was predicted from more cannabis at work (a stability effect), less law abidance, more liberalism, less happiness with future, and less extroversion. Disruptive cocaine use was significantly predicted from three of the late adolescent variables and accounted for 9 percent of the variance. Disruptive cocaine use was predicted from more cannabis at work, less law abidance, and more liberalism. There were six significant predictors of disruptive hard drug use, which accounted for 15 percent of the variance. Disruptive hard drug use was uniquely predicted from more cannabis at work, more hard drugs at work (a stability effect), less law abidance, less religiosity, less happiness with future, and less illness sensitivity. Finally, the equation for predicting disruptive drug use of all kinds had six significant predictors and accounted for 18 percent of the variance. All use of disruptive substances was predicted from more cannabis at work, less law abidance, more liberalism, less happiness with future, less extroversion, and less illness sensitivity.

Latent-variable Analyses

Two latent-variable models were developed for predicting young adult disruptive drug use from adolescent factors. The first is a standard confirmatory factor analysis model used to verify the factor structure, as well as to examine the correlations among the latent factors. The second is a structural or path model that includes a second-order factor of All Drug Use to reflect the two drug use constructs from adolescence. The three drug use constructs from the previous chapter are included in each of these models (General Drug Use and Disruptive Drug Use from adolescence and Disruptive Drug Use from young adulthood).

Confirmatory Factor Analysis Model. An initial CFA model that included nine latent factors was tested. The factors from late adolescence are General Drug Use, Disruptive Drug Use, Social Conformity, Perceived Opportunity, Leadership Style, Conscientiousness, Emotional Distress, and Psychosomatic Complaints; the factor from young adulthood is Disruptive Drug Use. This initial CFA model did not adequately reflect the data ($p < .001$), although the NFI revealed that many of the features of the model were accurate (.89). All hypothesized factor loadings were significant ($p < .001$). Correlated errors were added to the model until an acceptable fit was achieved ($p > .50$, NFI $= .96$). All hypothesized factor loadings were significant and confirmed the proposed factor structure (see table 11.2; latent factors are identified by measured variables).

Late adolescent General Drug Use was significantly correlated with Disruptive Drug Use at both times, as well as with less Social Conformity, less Perceived Opportunity, more Leadership Style, less Conscientiousness, more Emotional Distress, and more Psychosomatic Complaints (see table 11.3). A similar pattern of significant associations was apparent for late adolescent Disruptive Drug Use, although the correlations tended to be smaller in magnitude. Finally, Disruptive Drug Use as a young adult was significantly correlated with the two drug use constructs from adolescence, less Social Conformity, and no other constructs. Other factor intercorrelations among the psychological functioning constructs from late adolescence are given in the table, and are in expected directions. For instance, Perceived Opportunity was negatively correlated with Emotional Distress and positively correlated with Conscientiousness.

Structural Model. The structural model is built upon the final CFA model, but instead of allowing all nine factors simply to correlate, the adolescent factors were used to predict simultaneously the young adult factor of Disruptive Drug Use. In order to reduce colinearity problems and to capture the large association between General Drug Use and Disruptive Drug Use during adolescence, a second-order construct of All Drug Use was introduced to generate these two first-order drug use constructs. In the initial structural model, All Drug Use and the other six late adolescent constructs were allowed to correlate freely and each to predict young adult Disruptive Drug Use. Across-time correlations were deleted and modification indices (Bentler & Chou, 1986) were used to include these effects as direct predictors in the model. The model was overfit and then nonsignificant paths were deleted as recommended by MacCallum (1986). The final structural model fit the data quite well ($p > .50$, NFI $= .96$).

This final model is presented in two sections for clarity: correlations between latent factors only (see figure 11.1) and correlations that include at least one measured variable (see table 11.4). Correlations between the six psychological functioning constructs are not included; the final values were essentially identical to those reported above (table 11.3). Factor loadings on the measured variables are not included, but vary only slightly from those given above (table 11.2).

All Drug Use was a highly reliable second-order factor of the two adolescent drug use constructs. This factor was correlated with low Social Conformity, low Perceived Opportunity, low Conscien-

Table 11.2 Factor Structure and Loadings for the Final Confirmatory Factor Analysis Model

Factor/Variable	Standardized Loading	Factor/Variable	Standardized Loading
Late Adolescence			
General Drug Use		*Leadership Style*	
alcohol frequency	.66	ambition	.51
cannabis frequency	.91	extroversion	.38
cocaine frequency	.69	leadership	.74
hard drug frequency	.58	*Conscientiousness*	
Disruptive Drug Use		deliberateness	.10
alcohol at work	.40	diligence	1.00[a]
cannabis at work	.83	orderliness	.48
hard drugs at work	.48	*Emotional Distress*	
Social Conformity		self-acceptance	−.88
law abidance	.66	depression	.82
liberalism	−.45	self-derogation	.54
religious commitment	.30	*Psychosomatic Complaints*	
Perceived Opportunity		headache prone	.43
happy with future	.74	insomnia	.71
happy with schooling up to now	.57	illness sensitivity	.37
happy with chances to be what you want	.75		
Young Adulthood			
Disruptive Drug Use			
alcohol at work	.27		
cannabis at work	.65		
cocaine at work	.60		
hard drugs at work	.51		

All factor loadings are significant.

[a]The residual of this variable was constrained at zero to prevent it from being estimated as negative.

tiousness, high Emotional Distress, and high Psychosomatic Complaints. All Drug Use also significantly predicted Disruptive Drug Use in young adulthood. The only other adolescent construct to have a direct effect on young adult Disruptive Drug Use was adolescent Social Conformity. Less Social Conformity as a teenager increased Disruptive Drug Use as a young adult (see figure 11.1).

There are several direct effects on young adult Disruptive Drug Use and its four indicators (see table 11.4). Disruptive Drug Use as a young adult was increased by more cannabis at work, more cocaine frequency, and less law abidance as a teenager. Alcohol at work as a young adult was increased by more alcohol frequency and less illness sensitivity as an adolescent. Increased levels of cannabis at work were generated by earlier cannabis at work, cannabis frequency, less extroversion, and more insomnia. There were no predictors for changes in cocaine at work. Finally, use of hard drugs at work or school increased as a function of earlier use of hard drugs (both in general and at work), as well as having low levels of illness sensitivity.

The within-time correlations between the disruptive and general drug use scales and the psychological functioning variables during adolescence are strictly correlations and have no causal implications (see table 11.4). Alcohol frequency was significantly correlated with less law abidance, less religiosity, more ambition, less Conscientiousness, more insomnia, and less headache proneness. Cocaine frequency was significantly correlated with less ambition. Hard drug frequency was significantly correlated with less happiness with schooling and more extroversion. The residual of the Disruptive Drug Use construct was significantly correlated with less diligence and more self-derogation. Alcohol at work was associated with less law abidance, and hard drugs at work was related to less self-acceptance.

Interpretation

In general, the findings from these analyses are fairly clear. After controlling for the modest stability of disruptive drug use over time, the strongest predictor of increased use of drugs at work or school was a lack of Social Conformity, and in particular low law abidance, as a teenager. There were several other smaller effects worth noting, but the clearest conclusion is that teenagers with deviant and nonconforming attitudes are the most likely to initiate or increase their use of drugs at work or school.

In previous analyses of the data, several personal and social

Table 11.3 Factor Intercorrelations for the Final Confirmatory Factor Analyses of Personality, Life Satisfaction, Emotional Distress, and Drug Use

Factor	I	II	III	IV	V	VI	VII	VIII	IX
Late Adolescence									
I General Drug Use	1.00								
II Disruptive Drug Use	.84***	1.00							
III Social Conformity	-.79***	-.62***	1.00						
IV Perceived Opportunity	-.17***	-.09*	.27***	1.00					
V Leadership Style	.08*	.10*	-.14**	.24***	1.00				
VI Conscientiousness	-.17***	-.17***	.41***	.43***	.32***	1.00			
VII Emotional Distress	.21***	.16**	-.31***	-.69***	-.47***	-.44***	1.00		
VIII Psychosomatic Complaints	.09*	.07	-.18**	-.38***	-.23***	-.26***	.59***	1.00	
Young Adulthood									
IX Disruptive Drug Use	.54***	.46***	-.51***	-.08	.09	-.07	.05	-.05	1.00

*p < .05; **p < .01; ***p < .001.

Table 11.4 Significant Across-Time Effects and Within-Time Correlations Not Depicted in Figure 11.1 Related to Late Adolescent Psychosocial Factors and Young Adult Disruptive Drug Use

Adolescent Psychosocial Factor/Variable	Drug-related Factor/Variable	Regression Path or Correlation[a]
Across-Time Effects[b]		
cannabis at work	Disruptive Drug Use	.34***
cocaine frequency	Disruptive Drug Use	.15**
law abidance	Disruptive Drug Use	− .12**
alcohol frequency	alcohol at work	.12**
illness sensitivity	alcohol at work	− .09*
cannabis at work	cannabis at work	.19***
cannabis frequency	cannabis at work	.29***
extroversion	cannabis at work	− .06*
insomnia	cannabis at work	.08*
hard drugs at work	hard drugs at work	.18***
hard drug frequency	hard drugs at work	.20***
illness sensitivity	hard drugs at work	− .09**
Within-Time Correlations[c]		
All Drug Use (see figure 11.1)		
	General Drug Use	
law abidance	alcohol frequency	− .34***
religiosity	alcohol frequency	− .15***
ambition	alcohol frequency	.12**
Conscientiousness	alcohol frequency	− .15***
insomnia	alcohol frequency	.10*
headache prone	alcohol frequency	− .08*
ambition	cocaine frequency	− .09*
happy with schooling	hard drug frequency	− .08*
extroversion	hard drug frequency	.11**
	Disruptive Drug Use	
diligence	Disruptive Drug Use	− .18**
self-derogation	Disruptive Drug Use	.13*
law abidance	alcohol at work	− .11**
self-acceptance	hard drugs at work	− .13**

*p < .05; **p < .01; ***p < .001.

[a] The regression effects are in standardized form.

[b] Drugs are from young adulthood.

[c] Drugs are from late adolescence.

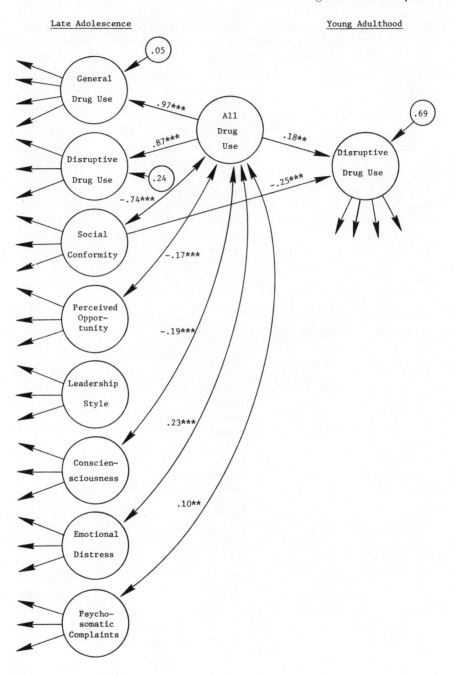

constructs from adolescence were used to predict drug use, problems with drugs, and disruptive drug use as young adults (Stein, Newcomb, & Bentler, 1987a). Although peer and adult models of drug use played a prominent role in generating changes in general drug use, these influences had little direct impact on later disruptive drug use. Prior drug use predicted later disruptive drug use, but not as strongly as it predicted later general drug use. In other words, disruptive drug use appears to behave like a type of problem drug use and is not strongly influenced directly by social or environmental factors (such as peer drug use). Disruptive drug use appears to be a function of personal traits and tendencies, which may have their roots in disturbed functioning of the family of origin. Specifically, we have shown that teenagers from a divorced or disrupted family tend to develop more deviant and rebellious attitudes than their peers from intact families. This lack of traditionalism or social conformity then propels the youngster toward various types of problem behavior, including drug use (e.g., Newcomb & Bentler, in press a; Stein, Newcomb, & Bentler, 1987a).

Several other smaller effects for predicting changes in disruptive drug use were found. These were apparent in the multiple regression and latent-variable analyses. Disruptive drug use, the general factor and specific types, increased with little happiness about the future, low extroversion, high insomnia, and low illness sensitivity. Thus, those who are unhappy about their future prospects, who tend toward introversion, who show difficulties in sleeping, and who do not feel vulnerable to diseases increased or initiated disruptive drug use from adolescence to young adulthood. Although the Emotional Distress factor and its indicators had no direct impact on changes in disruptive drug use, it appears that a particular type of distress related to introversion and dissatisfaction with future plans, and perhaps reflected in insomnia, can increase disruptive drug use. The effect of illness sensitivity on reducing disruptive drug use has been noted in other research on general patterns of drug use. My interpretation of this small but consistent

Figure 11.1 Longitudinal Latent Variable Model of Adolescent Psychosocial Factors Predicting Changes in Disruptive Drugs Use over Time. Measured variables and correlations among psychosocial constructs are not included for clarity (see Tables 11.2 and 11.3). Nonstandard effects and correlated residuals are given in Table 11.4. The large circles are latent factors and the small circles are factor disturbance terms. All Drug Use is a second-order factor. Parameter estimates are standardized, disturbance terms are variances, and significance levels were determined by critical ratios (** $p < .01$; *** $p < .001$).

finding is that those who feel sensitive to illnesses and other external invasions are vulnerable to environmental impositions on their life. This supports the small effect of invulnerability on higher disruptive cannabis use noted in chapter 8. In other words, those who are fearful and concerned about external controls and sanctions, and thus value a high degree of internal control, are not willing to engage in behavior when this control is threatened, such as drug use in general, and at work in particular (Newcomb, Bentler, & Fahy, 1987). Conversely, those who have little fear of external dangers (whether real or imagined) will take more risks, such as using drugs. This supports the findings of previous research, which have found an association between drug use and sensation seeking (e.g., Huba, Newcomb, & Bentler, 1981), if we assume that low illness sensitivity reflects high sensation seeking.

The few significant cross-sectional correlations also support the general points above. Low diligence, high self-derogation, low law abidance, and low self-acceptance were associated with various types of disruptive substance use as a teenager (see table 11.4). These verify the conclusion that disruptive drug use is associated with and predicted by internal factors related to deviance and negative personal feelings. This supports the thesis that is emerging from these analyses: that disruptive drug use differs from general drug use; the former represents more problem use or abuse (even at relatively low levels) and is generated by internal rather than external factors. These internal factors include deviance, dissatisfaction with the future, invulnerability, introversion, and distress. It must be emphasized, however, that these effects, although significant, tend to be small in magnitude and do not account for a large proportion of disruptive drug use. For instance, in the final structural model developed in this chapter, only 31 percent of the variance in young adult disruptive drug use was accounted for by knowing a wide range of theoretically important and meaningful aspects of the teenager's behavior, emotional responses, and attitudes.

A four-year span is a fairly lengthy period of time, particularly when it encompasses such a critical developmental stage as that from adolescence to young adulthood. Even though personality and behavior are substantially more established during this period than in early adolescence (e.g., Stein, Newcomb, & Bentler, 1986b, 1987a), it is quite likely that personal behavior and tendencies become even more firmly established with age. Indeed, it is quite possible that disruptive drug use may be more systematic and predictable at an older age than among this group of relatively young people. Despite this increasing stability in development, it is crucial to identify and study those factors that are associated with and help generate behavior and attitudes that characterize the remainder of one's life. Many young adults are in the workforce and are using drugs on the job. Detailed information about this process can help prevent this behavior from becoming more firmly established as the person matures. Thus, although the present data and analyses cannot enlighten us about disruptive drug use among older people, it can help us understand such behavior at its inception.

The present analyses, when combined with previous work in this area, stress the importance of internal and personal factors (in contrast to social and environmental influences) on generating disruptive drug use. Some of these factors relate to negative feelings and internal distress. These can represent specific motivations that may differentiate general from disruptive drug use. Knowing the reasons for using drugs may allow us to better predict different types of drug use, such as at work or school. This is the focus of the next chapter, which uses adolescent data on motivations for drug use to predict general and disruptive drug use over time.

Chapter 12

ADOLESCENT REASONS FOR DRUG USE AS PREDICTORS OF LATER DISRUPTIVE DRUG USE

In this chapter, reasons for using alcohol and cannabis reported in year four of the study are used to predict general drug use in year five and disruptive drug use in years five and nine. When attempting to understand various types of purposeful and directed behavior, such as drug use, we must consider the self-acknowledged reasons for engaging in such behavior. Although these motivations are certainly influenced by such factors as cognitive consistency (a desire to have thoughts match behavior), stereotypes, social desirability, and other biases, and do not capture unconscious and psychodynamic reasons for engaging in a particular behavior, they can still be useful in understanding a portion of the behavior. In particular, drug abuse prevention and intervention programs often have a cognitive focus, and the success of the program depends in part on knowing what motivations generate drug use and abuse.

Although a number of influences related to and predictive of drug use have been identified and can be conceptualized as risk factors (e.g., Newcomb, Maddahian, & Bentler, 1986), many of these influences are mediated by cognitive or motivational processes (e.g., Newcomb, Huba, & Bentler, 1983). For instance, drug use has been related to negative life events (e.g., divorce, job loss, or death of a family member) in both teenagers (Newcomb, Huba, & Bentler, 1986) and adults (Newcomb & Harlow, 1986). One possible reason for this association that makes intuitive sense is that drug use in this instance might reduce the discomfort and unhappiness associated with the changes. Drug use in these cases may be motivated by a need to reduce emotional distress. Drug use in other cases may relate to peer pressure. If a teenager has many friends who are using drugs and feels left out by not joining them with their use, this adolescent might use drugs to satisfy peers or simply to fit in. In more general terms, the teenager may use drugs among peers in order to increase social cohesion. Both motivations to use drugs—to reduce negative feelings and to increase social cohesion—can be known and articulated by the teenager. Therefore, they may be important cognitive factors in generating drug use and abuse that may also be amenable to modification in prevention or intervention efforts. Nevertheless, it is essential to determine first whether certain motivations are related to and predictive of drug use.

Research in this area has been focused on three perspectives. These include understanding the reasons for using particular drugs, reasons to avoid drug use, and expectations regarding the use of particular substances.

The literature on the last topic has focused largely on alcohol and has identified expectations such as enhanced experience, increased social pleasure, enhanced sexual functioning, augmented power and assertiveness, and reduced tension (e.g., Brown, Goldman, Inn, & Anderson, 1980; Christiansen, Goldman, & Inn, 1982; Smith, 1980). These expectations are moderately correlated and reflect a general factor of alcohol expectancy (e.g., Brown et al., 1980). This research has demonstrated that anticipation of alcohol effects contributes to alcohol use, and this occurs over and above the pharmacologic effects of alcohol (Christiansen, Goldman, & Inn, 1982; see review by Marlatt & Rohsenow, 1980) and demographic and background factors (Christiansen & Goldman, 1983).

The reasons for drug use are slightly different. Although the distinction between reasons for drug use and expectancies is not perfectly clear, since they both represent motivations, the research on reasons takes a broader perspective on why drugs are used and has considered reasons for using drugs other than alcohol. The broader perspective is reflected in the types of motivations entertained to account for drug use. For example, Murry and Perry (1984) identified evidencing adulthood as one motive for adolescent drug use; Thorne and DeBlassie (1985) cited acting-out, status, and identity; and Johnston and O'Malley (1986) list such motives as defying parents, defying society, and being self-destructive. Nevertheless, the bulk of the research on reasons for drug use focuses on "immediate affective states and consequences" of drug use (Johnston & O'Malley, 1986, p. 32), which appear quite similar to expectancies.

Researchers have identified a wide range of motivations for drug use: to have a good time with friends, experiment, feel good, get high (Johnston & O'Malley, 1986), insight seeking, therapeutic needs, sentience, pleasure (Butler, Gunderson, & Bruni, 1981), to relieve boredom, to have fun, make friends, personal energy, reduce stress (Murry & Perry, 1984), peer pressure, creativity (Kamali & Steer, 1976), enhance feelings and creativity, reduce negative feelings, addiction, and social cohesion (Newcomb, Chou, Bentler, & Huba, 1987). Many of these specific motivations are highly correlated and reflect one or more general factors. For instance, Butler, Gunderson, and Bruni (1981) located one general factor underlying their four dimensions and termed it General Sensation Seeking. Similarly, we found a general factor underlying alcohol motivations, and another reflecting marijuana motivations (although even these two were highly correlated). Similarly, Segal, Huba, and Singer (1980) located two general factors related to increasing positive feeling and reducing negative feeling.

A less researched area is the reasons to avoid, limit, or abstain from drug use. Reeves and Draper (1984) identified three reasons to reduce alcohol use: to safeguard health, not to disappoint parents, and to increase self-esteem. Traub (1983) studied a group of college women, who reported that important reasons to discontinue marijuana use were problems associated with jobs, friends, and parents. Newcomb, Fahy, and Skager (in press) studied several reasons to avoid drug use among teenagers. These reasons included addiction, punishment, disappoint self, disappoint parents, lose friends, and harmfulness of the drugs. Newcomb, Fahy, and Skager (in press) found that only perceived harmfulness was substantially related to lower levels of drug use; the other reasons were only slightly related to drug use levels.

Although most of these studies have examined motivations for drug use in relation to general alcohol or drug use, several have made a distinction between general use and abuse or heavy use of drugs, which is relevant to our focus on disruptive drug use. Carman (1979; Schilling & Carman, 1978) has noted that beliefs in external (versus internal) control were associated with problem-oriented motivations for drug use and social complications of drug use. Problem-oriented motivations were, in turn, associated with problematic drug use (defined as troubles with friends, family, or authorities, accidents, injuries, and property damage related to using drugs). Problem-oriented motivations were those associated with personal effects factors such as coping with stress and altering self-perceptions. Interestingly, social effects motivations—those related to enhancing social interactions and having a good time with friends—were associated with using drugs, but were not significantly related to problem drug use (negative consequences and frequent intoxications). Similar findings have been reported by Levy and Rasher (1981). They found that social reasons for drug use were associated with the lowest frequency and intensity levels of alcohol and marijuana, although different patterns emerged for the other illicit drugs. Brown (1985) found several similarities and differences in expectancies for alcohol use among three types of drinkers: context-determined drinkers, heavy drinkers, and problem drinkers. Those in all three groups had high levels of social assertion and social-physical pleasure expectations of their drinking. Only the heavy and problem drinkers indicated high expectations for tension reduction, sexual enhancement, and arousal aggression. Finally, Donovan and Marlatt (1982) found three reasons were frequently reported by those who had been arrested for drinking while intoxicated: reducing external tension (interpersonal problems), reducing internal tension (negative feelings), and to be social and convivial.

According to this research, different motivations may generate general drug use in contrast to problem drug use. The following analyses attempt to determine whether motivations for alcohol and marijuana (each a latent factor reflected in four scales) relate differently to general drug use and disruptive drug use over time. Controls for social conformity are included. Some research suggests that drug use motivations become established during adolescence (e.g., Cutter & Fisher, 1980; Newcomb & Harlow, 1986) and may govern or dictate patterns of drug involvement later in life.

Measures

Most of the variables used in this chapter have been described earlier. The four composite disruptive substance use measures (and total score for all use) from young adulthood, the three disruptive drug use measures, and four general drug use measures assessed during late adolescence (year five of the study) used in chapters 10 and 11 are included here. Data from one year earlier in the study (year four) are also included, since this was the only occasion when drug use motivations were assessed. Measures taken from year four are the three personality traits that reflect

Social Conformity (law abidance, liberalism, and religious commitment as defined in chapter 9), four general drug use measures
assessed in an identical fashion to those in year five (alcohol,
cannabis, cocaine, and hard drug frequencies, as described in
chapter 10), and eight measures of alcohol and cannabis motivations. Fifteen reasons for using drugs were assessed separately for
alcohol and marijuana, resulting in thirty items. Exploratory and
confirmatory factor analyses of these items resulted in four identical scales for each substance that were reliable for boys and girls
(Newcomb, Chou, Bentler, & Huba, in press). These four scales
included social cohesion (four items, such as to feel good around
people), addiction (three items, such as to help me get through
the day), reduce negative feeling (three items, such as to get rid of
anxiety or tension), and enhancement/creativity (five items, such
as to enjoy what I am doing more). The four scales for alcohol and
the four scales for marijuana were correlated sufficiently high to
reflect latent factors of Alcohol Motivations and Marijuana Motivations, respectively.

Results

Bivariate Correlations

Product-moment correlations were calculated between each young
adult disruptive drug use scale and the fifteen scales assessed in
year four and the seven variables measured in year five. All
analyses in this chapter are based on 621 subjects, who provided
complete data at year four, year five, and year nine (young adulthood) (see table 12.1).

   Disruptive alcohol use was significantly correlated with eleven
of the adolescent measures: reduce negative affect (for both alcohol
and marijuana), alcohol and cannabis frequencies (at years four and
five), low law abidance, high liberalism, cocaine frequency at year
five, and alcohol and cannabis at work. Disruptive cannabis use
was significantly correlated with all year five scales in expected
directions, and all year four scales with the exception of social
cohesion, addiction motivations for alcohol, cocaine frequency,
and religious commitment. Disruptive cocaine use was significantly correlated with all year five scales except hard drugs at
work, and ten of the fifteen year-four variables. Disruptive hard
drug use was significantly correlated with all year four variables
except cocaine frequency and liberalism and all of the year five
scales except alcohol at work. Finally, disruptive use of all drugs

was significantly correlated with all of the year five variables, and all of the year four scales with two exceptions: addiction motivation for alcohol and cocaine frequency.

Multiple Regression Analyses

Multiple regression analyses were used to predict each of the disruptive drug use scales in young adulthood simultaneously from all twenty-two scales from years four and five, when the subjects were middle adolescents (see table 12.1).

The equation for predicting disruptive alcohol use was significant ($p < .01$), but accounted for only 6 percent of the variance. The predictors of disruptive alcohol use were more alcohol at work (a stability effect) and more alcohol and cocaine frequencies at year five. The equation to predict disruptive cannabis use was highly significant ($p < .001$) and accounted for 27 percent of the variance. This was the best predicted of all disruptive drug use scales, as mentioned in previous chapters. Disruptive cannabis use was predicted from more liberalism, more cannabis at work (a stability effect), and more cannabis and cocaine frequencies in year five. Disruptive cocaine use was significantly predicted from cannabis and cocaine frequencies at both years four and five, and accounted for 15 percent of the variance. There were five significant predictors of disruptive hard drug use, which accounted for 14 percent of the variance. Disruptive hard drug use was predicted from less law abidance, more cannabis at work, more hard drugs at work (a stability effect), and more cocaine and hard drug frequencies in year five. Finally, the equation for predicting disruptive drug use of all kinds had four significant predictors and accounted for 22 percent of the variance. All use of disruptive substances was predicted from less law abidance in year four, more cannabis at work, and more cannabis and cocaine frequencies in year five. In none of these multiple regression analyses were the motivation scales from year four predictors of young adult disruptive drug use. This occurred largely because the year five drug use measures were also included in the analyses. In other words, the year five drug use measures were better predictors of young adult disruptive drug use than the year four motivations. As a result, the significant correlations between some of the motivation scales and young adult disruptive drug use variables were captured and mediated by the year five drug use measures. Thus, we would expect that the year four variables would predict the year five variables, which in turn would influence the young adult measures. This sequence can be seen better in the latent-variable models developed next.

Table 12.1   Correlations and Multiple Regression Analyses between Young Adult Disruptive Drug Use and Adolescent Drug Use Motivations, Social Conformity, and Drug Use

Adolescent Variables	Alcohol		Cannabis		Cocaine		Hard Drugs		Any Use	
	r	Beta	r	Beta	r	Beta	r	Beta	r	Beta
Year 4 Variables										
Alcohol Motivations										
social cohesion	.04	.05	.05	.04	.07*	.07	.08*	.05	.08*	.03
addiction	.03	−.01	.04	.03	.03	.03	.07*	.06	.06	.01
reduce negative affect	.07*	.01	.10*	.05	.03	.01	.08*	.04	.12**	.04
enhancement/creativity	.05	.02	.12**	.04	.09*	.06	.10*	.05	.13**	.04
Marijuana Motivations										
social cohesion	.03	.00	.15***	.08	.09*	.08	.10*	.07	.14**	.08
addiction	.00	.03	.15***	.01	.07	.04	.08*	.10	.12**	.03
reduce negative affect	.07*	.03	.22***	.04	.12**	.09	.18***	.05	.22***	.01
enhancement/creativity	.05	.02	.22***	.00	.11**	.08	.16***	.06	.21***	.08
General Drug Use										
alcohol frequency	.13**	.06	.12**	.06	.16***	.05	.13**	.00	.20***	.02
cannabis frequency	.07*	.05	.29***	.01	.26***	.14**	.20***	.08	.30***	.03
cocaine frequency	.01	.03	.04	.04	.45***	.22***	.05	.01	.05	.00
hard drug frequency	.01	.01	.13**	.02	.10*	.00	.14**	.02	.13**	.01

Social Conformity										
law abidance	-.07*	-.21***	-.08*	-.15***	-.04	-.15***	-.05	-.18***	-.02	-.09*
liberalism	.05	.14**	.02	.06	.01	.05	.08*	.15***	.05	.08*
religious commitment	.01	-.07*	-.05	-.09*	-.04	.00	.00	-.06	-.03	-.03
Year 5 Variables										
General Drug Use										
alcohol frequency	.02	.27***	.05	.14**	.01	.19***	.06	.20***	.14**	.17***
cannabis frequency	.17**	.40***	.07	.21***	.11*	.28***	.34***	.44***	.01	.10**
cocaine frequency	.22***	.34***	.09*	.21***	.22***	.26***	.12**	.30***	.16**	.13**
hard drug frequency	.01	.19***	.12*	.24***	.07	.10*	.01	.19***	.07	.01
Young Adult Outcomes										
Disruptive Drug Use										
alcohol at work	.03	.22***	.06	.04	.06	.17***	.06	.23***	.08*	.11**
cannabis at work	.19***	.37***	.21***	.24***	.07	.26***	.20***	.41***	.01	.08*
hard drugs at work	.08	.10*	.13**	.23***	.03	.02	.03	.08*	.06	.02
Multiple Regression Summary										
R	.47		.37		.39		.52		.25	
R²	.22		.14		.15		.27		.06	
F-ratio	8.63		4.84		5.30		10.84		1.93	
p-value	<.001		<.001		<.001		<.001		<.01	

*$p < .05$; **$p < .01$; ***$p < .001$.

Latent-variable Analyses

Two latent-variable models were developed. The first is a standard confirmatory factor analysis model used to verify the factor structure, as well as to provide an opportunity to examine the correlations among the latent factors. The second is a structural or path model that spans data obtained from the three years. A second-order factor, however, was not included in the structural model, since the year five data were mediational. The three drug use constructs from previous chapters were included in each of these models (General Drug Use and Disruptive Drug Use from year five and Disruptive Drug Use from young adulthood). From year four, four constructs were included: Social Conformity (with three indicators), General Drug Use (with four indicators), Alcohol Motivations, and Marijuana Motivations (each reflected in four scales).

Confirmatory Factor Analysis Model. An initial CFA model that included seven latent factors was tested. Two complex factor loadings in year four were included on an a priori basis: alcohol frequency was allowed to load on Alcohol Motivations and cannabis frequency was allowed to load on Marijuana Motivations, in addition to both loading on General Drug Use. Several correlated residuals were also included on an a priori basis: between similar substances over time and between pairs of similar motivation scales (i.e., between addiction motivation for alcohol and for marijuana). This initial CFA model did not adequately reflect the data ($p <$ .001), although the NFI revealed that the important features of the model (i.e., factor loadings) were accurate as hypothesized (.87). Correlated residuals were added to the model until an acceptable fit was achieved ($p >$ .50, NFI = .97). All hypothesized factor loadings were significant and confirmed the proposed factor structure (see table 12.2; latent factors are identified by measured variables).

All correlations were highly significant ($p <$ .001) and in expected directions (see table 12.3). For instance, Disruptive Drug Use as a young adult was significantly correlated with more Alcohol and Marijuana Motivations, more General Drug Use at years four and five, less Social Conformity, and more Disruptive Drug Use in year five. As expected, the largest correlations were with the year five constructs, and the smallest correlations were with the year four factors. The two motivation factors were more highly correlated with General Drug Use than with Disruptive Drug Use.

Structural Model. The structural model was built upon the final CFA model. Rather than allowing all nine factors simply to correlate, the year four factors were allowed to predict simultane-

Table 12.2   Factor Loadings in the Final Confirmatory Factor Analysis Model of Drug Use Motivations and Disruptive Drug Use

Factor/Variable	Standardized Loading	Factor/Variable	Standardized Loading
Year 4		Year 5	
Alcohol Motivations		*General Drug Use*	
social cohesion	.61	alcohol frequency	.64
addiction	.61	cannabis frequency	.89
reduce negative affect	.78	cocaine frequency	.73
enhancement/creativity	.80	hard drug frequency	.64
Marijuana Motivations		*Disruptive Drug Use*	
social cohesion	.71	alcohol at work	.56
addiction	.63	cannabis at work	.89
reduce negative affect	.84	hard drugs at work	.52
enhancement/creativity	.84		
General Drug Use		Year 9	
alcohol frequency[a]	.46		
cannabis frequency[b]	.63	*Disruptive Drug Use*	
cocaine frequency	.62	alcohol at work	.28
hard drug frequency	.67	cannabis at work	.75
Social Conformity		cocaine at work	.53
law abidance	.71	hard drugs at work	.43
liberalism	−.47		
religious commitment	.32		

All factor loadings are significant ($p < .001$).
[a]Also loads on Alcohol Motivations (.40).
[b]Also loads on Marijuana Motivations (.37).

Table 12.3   Factor Correlations in the Final Confirmatory Factor Analyses Model of Drug Use Motivations and Disruptive Drug Use

Factor	I	II	III	IV	V	VI	VII
Year 4							
I Alcohol Motivations	1.00						
II Marijuana Motivations	.70	1.00					
III General Drug Use	.38	.57	1.00				
IV Social Conformity	−.63	−.71	−.70	1.00			
Year 5							
V General Drug Use	.47	.70	.78	−.66	1.00		
VI Disruptive Drug Use	.29	.52	.64	.47	.83	1.00	
Year 9							
VII Disruptive Drug Use	.20	.34	.36	−.37	.59	.48	1.00

All correlations are significant ($p < .001$).

ously the year five constructs, which in turn were allowed to predict young adult Disruptive Drug Use. In the initial structural model, the year four constructs were allowed to correlate freely, as were the residuals of the two year-five constructs. Residuals correlated over time that were not hypothesized and included a priori were deleted, and modification indices (Bentler & Chou, 1986) were used to include these effects as direct predictors in the model. The model was overfit and then nonsignificant paths were deleted as recommended by MacCallum (1986). The final structural model fit the data quite well ($p > .50$, NFI $= .98$).

The final model is presented in two sections for clarity: correlations that are strictly between latent factors (see figure 12.1) and correlations that include at least one measured variable (nonstandard effects) (see table 12.4).

Among the correlations between latent factors, both Marijuana Motivations and General Drug Use from year four significantly predicted year five General Drug Use and Disruptive Drug Use. Because of the many correlations among the year four constructs, indirect effects of Alcohol Motivations and Social Conformity on the two year-five constructs were also evident. Finally, only year

Table 12.4 Direct Across-Time Effects Not Depicted in Figure 12.1

Year 4 Predictors	Year 5 Predictors/Consequences	Year 9 Consequences	Standardized Path Estimate
Alcohol Motivation	alcohol frequency		.18***
Social Conformity	alcohol frequency		.24***
reduce negative affect-alc	alcohol frequency		.10**
social cohesion-alc	alcohol frequency		.14***
Marijuana Motivations	cannabis frequency		.13**
cocaine frequency	cocaine frequency		.41***
law abidance	cocaine frequency		− .08*
cocaine frequency	hard drug frequency		.24***
Alcohol Motivations	alcohol at work		.08*
addiction-mj	cannabis at work		.13***
cannabis frequency	cannabis at work		.15***
reduce negative affect-mj	hard drugs at work		.09**
cocaine frequency	hard drugs at work		.10**
hard drug frequency	hard drugs at work		.24***
	cocaine frequency	Disruptive Drug Use	.23***
	alcohol frequency	alcohol at work	.13***
liberalism		cannabis at work	.06*
	cannabis at work	cannabis at work	.68***
	hard drug frequency	hard drugs at work	.10**
	cannabis at work	hard drugs at work	.14***
	hard drugs at work	hard drugs at work	.14***

*$p < .05$; **$p < .01$; ***$p < .001$.

Latent constructs are capitalized and measured variables are in lower case.

five General Drug Use directly increased young adult Disruptive Drug Use. The influence of year five Disruptive Drug Use and the year four constructs on young adult Disruptive Drug Use were mediated through General Drug Use in year five (see figure 12.1).

Several other direct effects are apparent among correlations that include both latent constructs and variables. Again we find that year four variables influenced year five variables, which then influenced young adult disruptive substance use assessments. Only one variable had a direct effect from year four to young adulthood: Liberalism increased the frequency of cannabis use at work in young adulthood. This effect occurred because we did not include the Social Conformity construct in year five; if we had, the effect would probably have been from the year five liberalism scale. As in previous analyses, cocaine frequency in year five directly increased Disruptive Drug Use as a young adult. Year five alcohol frequency was predicted from year four Alcohol Motivations, low Social Conformity, and specific alcohol motivations to reduce negative affect and for social cohesion. Year five cannabis frequency was directly increased by earlier Marijuana Motivations. Year five cocaine frequency was significantly predicted by earlier cocaine use and lack of law abidance. Year five hard drug frequency was influenced by year four cocaine use. Alcohol at work in year five was predicted from earlier Alcohol Motivations. Year five cannabis at work was directly influenced by earlier cannabis frequency and addiction motivation for marijuana. Year five hard drugs at work was predicted from earlier cocaine and hard drug frequencies, as well as the motivation to reduce negative feelings with marijuana. The separate measures of disruptive substance use as a young adult were only predicted from the year five scales (except for liberalism, discussed above) (see table 12.4).

Interpretation

The findings from these analyses were not as definitive as would be expected from suggestions in the literature. With a few exceptions, motivations for drug use were related to both general drug use and disruptive drug use. Only a few differential effects suggested that disruptive drug use is more likely to be generated by problem-oriented or personal effects motivations than is general drug use, which is more likely to be influenced by social facilitation motives. This is reinforced by the finding that alcohol frequency was predicted by the effect of social cohesion, whereas cannabis at work was predicted by addiction for cannabis. These two effects

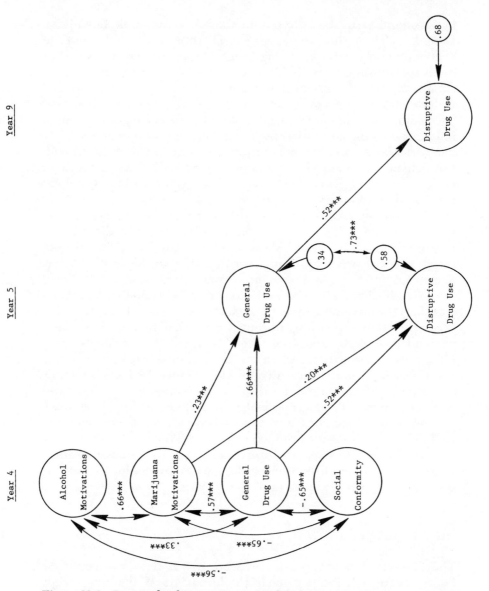

Figure 12.1 Longitudinal Latent Factor Model of Drug Use Motivations, Social Conformity, General Drug Use, and Disruptive Drug Use.   Measured variables are not included for clarity and nonstandard effects are given in Table 12.4. The large circles are latent factors and the small circles are factor disturbance terms. Parameter estimates are standardized, residual terms are variances, and significance levels were determined by critical ratios (*** $p < .001$).

certainly support the hypothesis, but few other effects result in such clear differentiation. For instance, the specific motivation to reduce negative feelings was associated with both alcohol frequency (with the alcohol motivation variant) and hard drugs at work (with the marijuana motivation variant).

One reason for the apparent difficulty in confirming the hypothesis is the general drug use factor. This factor does not simply measure beginning drug use (nonproblematic use), but also reflects possible abuse and misuse of drugs at the high end of the scale. For instance, the high end of the General Drug Use latent construct indicates frequent use of alcohol, cannabis, cocaine, and hard drugs. This would certainly indicate a lifestyle of heavy drug involvement and someone who is having problems with drugs. A better way to operationalize the hypothesis of differential effects of varying motivations would have been to include assessments of nonproblem use, which unfortunately was not done. Thus, high levels of General Drug Use must also be considered to be broadly indicative of drug problems, and disruptive drug use to be indicative of a specific drug problem.

When considered from this perspective, we can see that drug use motivations, and in particular motivations for marijuana use, predict increased general drug use to perhaps problematic levels, as well as disruptive drug use. It is interesting that elements of Marijuana Motivations were able to predict both General and Disruptive Drug Use, particularly in light of the high correlation between these two constructs ($r = .83$). This suggests that there may be cognitive motivations that are only associated with disruptive drug use. Unfortunately, the present measures do not provide sufficient detail to tease these out further. The strongest correlate between the eight drug use motivation scales and the scale of any use of disruptive substances as a young adult was the motivation for marijuana to reduce negative feelings. This may indicate which type of motivation leads to the problem of using drugs at work or school. This conjecture along with the effect of addiction motivations for marijuana on predicting cannabis at work suggests that personal effects motivations may have a specific influence on generating disruptive drug use. Those who need to use drugs to get through the day, who feel bad without them, and who use them to alleviate their feelings of emotional distress are more likely to use drugs in inappropriate settings such as work or school. It may be, therefore, that some people use drugs at work because they have not learned alternative ways to handle stress.

This view agrees nicely with the meta-analysis of drug prevention programs reported by Tobler (1986). She examined the effect-

iveness of 147 drug prevention programs for teenagers and con-
cluded that the best approach for those students at high risk for
abuse and negative drug consequences was one that taught the
students alternatives to their daily activities. This approach may
have indirectly increased the coping skills of the vulnerable youth,
so that when faced with stressful situations, they had other options
than using drugs (e.g., Labouvie, 1986).

If this theory is accurate, it has important implications for
identifying and ameliorating drug use on the job. If the employer
is aware that at least one reason for drug use on the job is a lack of
viable options in the employee's life, teaching the employee about
options would reduce disruptive drug use. Additional coping models can be provided and skills taught, so that drug use is not the
only option for an employee when confronted with internal distress. The employer might consider standard employee assistance
programs (EAPs), granting greater power to employees, and life
enrichment programs.

The motivations discussed in this chapter are only some of the
multiple predictors of disruptive substance use. Attitudinal deviance or lack of social conformity was quite important in previous
chapters. In the current analyses, however, when prior levels of
drug use were controlled, the Social Conformity construct and
variables were less important than drug use motivations. Thus,
aside from the problem-oriented motivations, there remains the
critical factor of nonconformity. Apparently, high levels of drug
use motivations go hand in hand with a lack of socially conforming
attitudes.

No single factor can explain disruptive drug use. It appears to be
a function of a variety of influences, some of which have been
identified in the present and earlier analyses. Like general drug
use, disruptive drug use requires a multicausal perspective, just as
successful prevention and intervention efforts require multifaceted
approaches (e.g., Segal, 1986).

In the next chapter, I investigate the multicausal notion of
disruptive drug use. This will help summarize the analyses and
findings from previous chapters, and provide the foundation for
future research. In addition, the next chapter examines the extent
to which disruptive drug use overlaps with other types of drug
problems.

Chapter 13

OTHER DRUG PROBLEMS AND THE DEVELOPMENT OF RISK FACTOR INDICES: Relations with Disruptive Drug Use

Two tasks are addressed in this chapter. First, I examine how disruptive drug use is related to other drug problems experienced by this sample of young adults. Second, I develop a risk factor index that can optimally predict the prevalence of disruptive drug use.

In line with the emerging perspective that disruptive drug use is a form of drug abuse, it is likely that disruptive drug use may be associated with a variety of other problems related to drug use. In other words, disruptive drug use may be only one symptom of a general pattern of having problems with drugs.

Certain drug-related problems have been identified in the work environment. For instance, Lodge (1983) has noted that the employed drug user is "late three times more often, requests time off 2.2 times more often, has 2.5 times as many absences of eight days or more, uses three times the normal level of sick benefits, is five times more likely to file a workmen's compensation claim, and is involved in accidents 3.6 times more often than other employees" (p. 57). Gardner (1982) cites other employment problems from drug use such as lunch-time lateness, many short-term absences, especially on Mondays and Fridays, and injuries, particularly on the afternoon shift. I suspect that there are other problems more directly associated with using drugs at work or school.

In this chapter, I examine the association between disruptive drug use and eight other drug-related occurrences: subjective reports of having had trouble with alcohol, trouble with drugs, a drug-related car accident, arrest or conviction for driving while intoxicated, arrest or conviction for selling or possessing illegal drugs, attendance at an alcohol treatment program, sale of illegal drugs, and a negative reaction to using marijuana.

The second focus of this chapter is on the development of a risk factor index to predict involvement with disruptive drug use. Based on the findings in the preceding chapters, I develop two risk factor indices that are maximally related to disruptive drug use. Although the risk factor theory has been used often by epidemiologists to study the spread of infectious and other types of disease (e.g., Jenkins, 1976a, 1976b; Kraus, Borhani, & Franti, 1980; Stern, Haskell, Wood, Osann, King, & Farqubar, 1975), it has only lately been used by drug researchers. This application to drug use has been formulated by Bry (1983) and initially operationalized by Bry, McKeon, and Pandina (1982).

According to this theory, there are many diverse factors related to drug use and these can help explain this behavior, but none of these is sufficient alone to fully explain the phenomenon. In other words, there is not one common pathway to drug use, but rather multiple pathways, each providing an increment in risk for getting involved with drugs. A risk factor is any measurable quality that can distinguish one who uses drugs from one who does not. In my analysis, each factor is scored dichotomously: zero (0) if the risk is not present and one (1) if the risk is present. These individual risk factors are then combined into a single index, with low values reflecting little chance of drug involvement and high values indicating great chance of drug involvement.

The few previous studies that have used this approach have focused on general drug use among adolescents. For instance, Bry et al. (1982) identified six risk factors: low grade-point average, lack of religiosity, early alcohol use, low self-esteem, psychopathology, and poor relationship with parents. Newcomb, Maddahian, and Bentler (1986) expanded these to ten by adding high levels of peer drug use, adult drug use, deviance, and sensation seeking. The pool of risk factors was further expanded by Newcomb et al. (1987) by adding unhappiness in life and few educational plans.

Unfortunately, these risk factors may not be as useful for understanding disruptive drug use for two reasons. First, some of these factors, such as grade-point average, may not be relevant for an older group. Second, and perhaps more important, many of these risk factors were not found to be strongly related to disruptive drug use in the analyses already presented in this book. Therefore, a new index based on the present findings must be created.

For this index, I selected variables related to disruptive drug use (focusing most strongly on the any use scale) from each of the preceding empirical chapters (3 to 12). To make the index practical to an employer or corporation, I had to consider certain restrictions. For instance, it is unlikely that an employer would have access to detailed information about an employee's adolescence. Thus, no variables from the longitudinal analyses were included. Second, it is also not likely that an employee will be perfectly honest about illegal behavior, such as using or selling illegal drugs or committing vandalism at work (e.g., Gardner, 1982). As a result, no extremely illegal behavior was included. Finally, since it is possible that some information on drug use (from drug testing, collateral contacts, previous work records) could be obtained, prevalence of cannabis and cocaine use is included in one risk factor index. A second index that did not include any use of illegal substances was created.

The variables were used as predictors in multiple regression analyses with the any disruptive drug use scale as the dependent variable. Only those variables that contributed significantly to the equation were retained as risk factors. These variables were dichotomized by one of two criteria. If there was a natural break in the responses (e.g., male versus female, use versus nonuse), risk was assigned accordingly. In the other instances (i.e., multi-item scales), the quartile at risk was chosen as the cut point (e.g., Newcomb, Maddahian, & Bentler, 1986; Newcomb et al., 1987). Eleven risk factors were chosen in this manner. Two of these were any use of cocaine and any use of cannabis during the past six months (not the disruptive drug use scales). Results are presented for two risk factor indices: one without and one with these drug variables.

When the individual risk factors were combined into the two indices, there were very few people at the high end of the scale, which would make it unstable and distort results. Therefore anyone receiving more than seven risk factors in the nondrug risk scale was categorized as having seven or more; in the risk index that included the two drug items, those scoring higher than nine risk factors were categorized as having nine or more. These modifications yielded much more uniform descending functions of risk factors as predicted by the theory (e.g., Newcomb, Maddahian, & Bentler, 1986).

Analyses are first presented for the associations between disruptive drug use and other drug problems. Following this, the description and analyses of the risk factor indices are given.

Other Drug Problems

Measures

Eight variables or scales were used to assess having problems with drug use other than using drugs at work or school. Trouble with drugs past four years and trouble with alcohol past four years were based on a series of questions that asked the respondents to indicate whether they felt that they had had a drug problem or alcohol problem in each of the four years preceding the young adult assessment. Subjects were coded as having a problem if in any of those four years they indicated they had had a problem with alcohol (for the alcohol item) or with drugs (for the drug item). Six items were used to create a drug-involved accident item. This item was coded affirmative if the young adults indicated that they had had an accident during the past six months after drinking alcohol, smoking marijuana, or getting high on another drug, or if an accident occurred because of using any of these three substances. Driving while intoxicated past four years was coded affirmative if the young adults indicated they had been arrested or convicted of this offense in any of the past four years. Similarly, drug law violation past four years was coded affirmative if the subjects indicated they had been arrested or convicted of selling or possessing illegal drugs in any of the four previous years. Attended alcohol treatment past four years was scored affirmative if the young adults indicated they had participated in an alcohol treatment program in any of the four years preceding the young adult assessment. Sold illegal drugs was coded affirmative if the subjects indicated that during the past six months they had sold any marijuana, hashish, uppers, downers, cocaine, or heroin. Finally, negative reaction to marijuana was coded affirmative if the young adults indicated they had had at least one of eight possible uncomfortable experiences with marijuana during the past six months. The negative experiences included such feelings as persecution, panic about time distortions, fear of losing control, and paranoia.

Results

I have calculated the prevalence of eight other drug problems on the basis of the prevalence of disruptive drug use (the total ever use scale) (see table 13.1). I have also given the chi-squared value for each two-by-two analysis between prevalence of disruptive drug use and prevalence of another drug problem (table 13.1, column 6). Five of the contrasts were significant at the $p < .05$ level, two were marginally nonsignificant ($p < .10$), and one was decidedly nonsignificant (on attended alcohol treatment). The lack of significant association between disruptive drug use and attending alcohol treatment was largely the result of the infrequent occurrence of obtaining treatment for an alcohol problem: only 0.5 percent of the sample had attended an alcohol treatment program during the past four years (no one in the sample had ever attended a drug treatment program).

The most prevalent problem was a negative reaction to marijuana, reported by 23.7 percent of the sample. This was followed in magnitude by sold drugs (12.6 percent), had trouble with drugs (6.6 percent), had trouble with alcohol (6.4 percent), driving while intoxicated (2.7 percent), drug law violation (2.0 percent), had a drug-involved accident (1.8 percent), and attended alcohol treatment (0.5 percent). The prevalence of disruptive drug use is based on whether or not the subject had experienced one of the other drug problems. For instance, 57.4 percent of those who had sold illegal drugs during the past six months had also used drugs at work or school. I have also given the ratio between the prevalences of disruptive drug use with and without having another problem with drugs. For example, if someone was arrested or convicted of driving while intoxicated, the person was 1.7 times more likely to have used drugs on the job than if he or she had not been arrested or convicted. Similarly, if someone has had a negative reaction to marijuana (possibly reflecting greater involvement or heavier use of cannabis), the person was 3.0 times more likely to have used drugs on the job than if he or she had not experienced a bad reaction to marijuana.

I have also given the prevalence of having a problem in the eight areas depending on whether the subjects have or have not used drugs at work or school. For example, one percent of the young adults who have not used drugs at work or school have been arrested or convicted for selling or possessing drugs (drug law violation). For those who have engaged in disruptive drug use, this percentage increased to 4.4 percent. The ratio between these two prevalence rates is also given. In this instance, those who used drugs at work were 4.4 times more likely to have been caught committing a drug law violation compared to those who had not participated in disruptive drug use. The highest ratio is on sold illegal drugs: those who have used drugs at work were 12.8 times

Table 13.1 Prevalence of Other Drug Problems by Prevalence of Disruptive Drug Use

Other Drug Problems	Sample Prevalence %	Prevalence of Disruptive Drug Use %	Ratio	Prevalence of Other Drug Problems			
				Disruptive Drug Use		Ratio	$\chi^2(1)$
				No %	Yes %		
Trouble with alcohol past 4 years							
No	93.6	29.0		3.9			
Yes	6.4	57.4	2.0		11.8	3.1	16.64***
Trouble with drugs past 4 years							
No	93.4	28.6		3.5			
Yes	6.6	63.3	2.2		13.6	3.9	25.84***
Drug-involved accident							
No	98.2	30.4		1.2			
Yes	1.8	53.8	1.8		3.1	2.6	3.28+
Driving while intoxicated past 4 years							
No	97.3	30.3		2.0			
Yes	2.7	50.0	1.7		4.4	2.2	3.53+
Drug law violation past 4 years							
No	98.0	30.1		1.0			
Yes	2.0	66.7	2.2		4.4	4.4	9.21*
Attended alcohol treatment past 4 years							
No	99.5	30.7		0.4			
Yes	0.5	50.0	1.6		0.9	2.3	.69ns
Sold illegal drugs							
No	87.4	23.1		2.7			
Yes	12.6	57.4	3.7		34.6	12.8	145.92***
Negative reaction to marijuana							
No	76.3	20.9		12.7			
Yes	23.7	62.9	3.0		48.2	3.8	110.07***

+$p < .10$; * $p < .05$; *** $p < .001$.

more likely to have sold illegal drugs than if they had not used drugs at work. The smallest ratio was for driving while intoxicated, which was 2.2 times more prevalent for those who have engaged in disruptive drug use.

Risk Factors

Measures

Eleven risk factors were selected: sex of the respondent, marital status, educational plans, cohabitation history, being fired from a job in the past four years, having trouble in an intimate relationship (past three months), law abidance, liberalism, any cigarette use (past six months), any cannabis use (past six months), and any cocaine use (past six months). (See table 13.2 for the definition of each risk factor, the cut point, and percentage of the sample at risk based on each factor.) A person was considered at risk for disruptive drug use if male, not married or not living with spouse, had no educational interest beyond high school, had cohabited, had been fired, had at least some difficulty with an intimate relationship, reported low law abidance, high liberalism, smoked cigarettes, used cannabis, and used cocaine (each at least once during the past six months).

Results

Distribution of Risk Factors. In the index without drugs, the number of risk factors ranged from zero to seven or more with a mode of 3 and an average of 2.98 (table 13.3). In the risk factor index with drugs, the number of risk factors ranged from zero to nine or more with a mode of 2 and an average of 3.74. The distribution for both indices appears appropriately even and smooth.

Prevalence of Disruptive Drug Use by Number of Risk Factors. For each risk factor index, the prevalence of disruptive drug use was contrasted with the number of risk factors (see table 13.4 and table 13.5). Disruptive drug use was broken down into alcohol, cannabis, cocaine, hard drugs, and a total score of any or all use. I have also given point-biserial and rank-order correlations between the use and nonuse of each category of drug use and number of risk factors.

The number of risk factors excluding drug use was significantly related to the prevalence of using drugs at work or school (see

Table 13.2 Items, Scales, Cut Points, and Percents for Eleven Risk Factors

Risk Factor	Items	Cut Point	Percent at Risk
Sex	Sex of subject: male or female?	Male	30
Marital Status	Current living arrangement?	Not married or living with spouse	82
Educational Plans	Long-range educational plans?	No interest beyond high school	19
Cohabitation History	Ever lived with a lover at least five nights per week without being married?	Yes	34
Fired Past 4 Years	Ever been fired from a job during the past 4 years?	Yes	16
Trouble in Intimate Relationship	Extent of difficulty in a relationship with a lover or spouse or date in the past three months: great, much, some, little, or no difficulty?	Great, much or some difficulty	34
Low Law Abidance	Which describes you most of the time? 5 4 3 2 1 willing to keep extra change / return incorrect change 1 2 3 4 5 afraid of getting caught / might use a false ID 1 2 3 4 5 wouldn't know how or want to / might shoplift 5 4 3 2 1 not quite so honest / goodie-goodie honest type	≤ 11	24
High Liberalism	Which describes you most of the time? 5 4 3 2 1 don't feel women need or want it / support women's liberation 1 2 3 4 5 see cops as pigs / see cops as law enforcers 1 2 3 4 5 think cops shouldn't carry guns / think police should carry guns 5 4 3 2 1 approve of few protests / approve of many protests	≥ 12	20
Cigarette Smoker	Ever smoked a cigarette during the past six months?	Yes	38
Marijuana User	Ever used marijuana or hashish during the past six months?	Yes	43
Cocaine User	Ever used cocaine during the past six months?	Yes	34

Table 13.3   Number of Risk Factors for Each Index

Number of Risk Factors	Prevalence			
	Index without Drugs		Index with Drugs	
	N	%	N	%
0	20	2.7	16	2.2
1	125	16.9	108	14.6
2	163	22.1	124	16.8
3	168	22.7	119	16.1
4	134	18.1	110	14.9
5	81	11.0	89	12.0
6	31	4.2	82	11.1
7[a]	17	2.3	61	8.3
8			20	2.7
9[b]			10	1.4
Average Number	2.98		3.74	

[a]7 or more without drugs.
[b]9 or more with drugs.

Table 13.4   Prevalence of Disruptive Drug Use by Number of Risk Factors without Drug Use

Number of Risk Factors	Prevalence of Disruptive Drug Use				
	Alcohol	Cannabis	Cocaine	Hard Drugs	All Use
All Subjects	18.3	16.6	9.3	5.5	30.9
0	0.0	5.0	0.0	0.0	5.0
1	8.0	1.6	1.6	0.0	10.4
2	11.7	6.1	3.7	1.8	18.4
3	20.2	16.1	7.1	5.4	31.0
4	23.9	22.4	9.0	5.2	40.3
5	28.4	40.7	23.5	13.6	54.3
6	25.8	35.5	35.5	16.1	67.7
7 or more	52.9	52.9	41.2	35.3	76.5
$\chi^2(6) =$	47.77***	96.52***	82.51***	58.13***	105.49***
Correlations					
Point-biserial	.23***	.35***	.30***	.25***	.38***
Rank order	.22***	.34***	.28***	.22***	.37***

***$p < .001$.

table 13.4). This risk factor index was most highly related to the any use category and least related to the prevalence of disruptive alcohol use. The magnitude of the correlations ranged from modest to moderate. Having two or fewer risk factors was associated with low prevalence of disruptive drug use, whereas having five or more was associated with high prevalence rates. For instance, over three-quarters of those who had seven or more risk factors had used drugs at work or school during the past six months.

The risk factor index with drugs (cannabis use and cocaine use as risk factors) achieved better predictions. It is worth remembering that the improvement in predictability is based on knowing whether the person had used illegal drugs during the past six months, which may be difficult to ascertain under typical conditions.

The risk factor index with drug use was most strongly related to the prevalence of any disruptive drug use and disruptive cannabis use (see table 13.5). It was least related to the prevalence of disruptive alcohol use. Those with three or fewer risk factors had the lowest prevalence of disruptive drug use; those with five or more had rather high rates. Fully 90 percent of those with nine or more risk factors had used drugs at work or school during the past six months. In fact, those with nine or more risk factors were from

Table 13.5 Prevalence of Disruptive Drug Use by Number of Risk Factors with Drug Use

Number of Risk Factors	Prevalence of Disruptive Drug Use				
	Alcohol	Cannabis	Cocaine	Hard Drugs	All Use
All Subjects	18.3	16.6	9.3	5.5	30.9
0	0.0	0.0	0.0	0.0	0.0
1	7.4	0.9	0.0	0.0	8.3
2	8.9	0.0	0.0	0.0	8.9
3	15.1	5.9	3.4	2.5	21.8
4	20.0	12.7	6.4	2.7	30.0
5	23.6	30.3	11.2	9.0	46.1
6	29.3	30.5	17.1	6.1	51.2
7	31.1	50.8	27.9	21.3	65.6
8	25.0	55.0	55.0	30.0	85.0
9 or more	70.0	70.0	60.0	30.0	90.0
$\chi^2(8) =$	54.10***	174.77***	142.22***	83.53***	169.41***
Correlations					
Point-biserial	.25***	.46***	.39***	.29***	.47***
Rank order	.24***	.45***	.36***	.27***	.46***

***$p < .001$.

three to six times more likely to use drugs at work or school than the sample taken as a whole.

Frequency of Disruptive Drug Use by Number of Risk Factors. The frequency of disruptive drug use, rather than the prevalence, was contrasted with the number of risk factors. Thus, analyses of variance and product-moment correlations were used (see table 13.6).

All correlations and *F*-ratios were significant, with those associated with the risk factor index with drugs being higher than the index without drugs, as expected. The correlations were somewhat smaller than those obtained with the prevalence variables, and indicate that the risk factors may better predict prevalence than extent of involvement with disruptive drug use. As before, the associations between risk factors and disruptive drug use were strongest for the any use category and weakest for disruptive alcohol use.

The associations between risk factors and the frequency of all disruptive drug use are dramatic and indicate an increasing, almost exponential, relationship between risk factors and frequency of all disruptive drug use (see figures 13.1 and 13.2). Frequency of disruptive drug use was strongly related to the number of risk factors.

Heavy Disruptive Drug Use by Number of Risk Factors. A prevalence index of heavy disruptive drug use was generated by categorizing all subjects who indicated that they had been drunk or stoned on any of the eight substances eleven or more times at work or school during the past six months. In the total sample, 8.1 percent had used drugs at work or school this frequently (see table 13.7).

The chi-squares and correlations indicate that heavy disruptive drug use was moderately associated with both risk factor indices,

Table 13.6   Frequency of Disruptive Drug Use by Number of Risk Factors

	Disruptive Drug Use				
	Alcohol	*Cannabis*	*Cocaine*	*Hard Drugs*	*All Use*
Risk Factor Index without Drugs					
Correlation	.19	.32	.22	.19	.35
F-ratio (7, 731)	4.65	15.65	8.48	5.67	17.28
Risk Factor Index with Drugs					
Correlation	.20	.40	.30	.23	.43
F-ratio (9, 729)	4.92	22.26	13.23	7.32	23.98

All correlations and *F*-ratios are significant ($p < .001$).

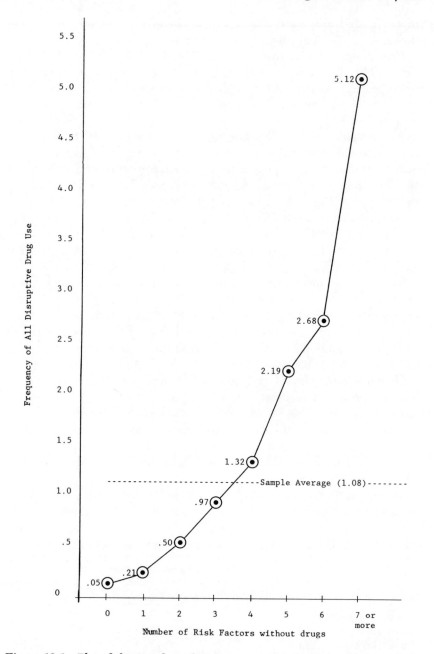

Figure 13.1   Plot of the Number of Risk Factors That Exclude Drug Use with the Frequency of All Disruptive Drug Use.   The dotted line indicates the total sample average.

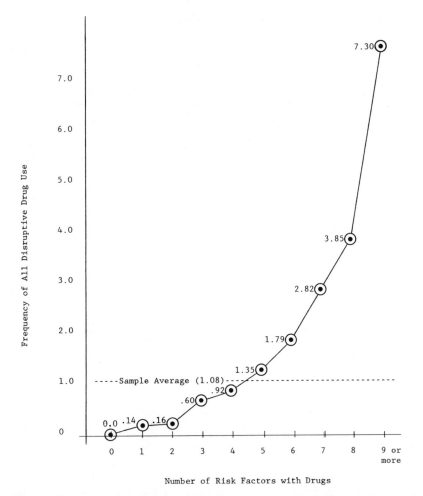

Figure 13.2   **Plot of the Number of Risk Factors That Include Drug Use with the Frequency of All Disruptive Drug Use.**   The dotted line indicates the total sample average.

and somewhat higher, as expected, with the index with drugs. Those receiving zero or one risk factor were extremely unlikely to be using drugs heavily at work. Those receiving six or more risk factors were from 2.8 to 8.6 times more likely to be using drugs heavily at work than the sample as a whole.

Finally, the hazard rates of using drugs heavily were calculated for each risk factor and plotted against the risk factor index without drugs (see figure 13.3) and the index with drugs (see figure 13.4). The hazard rate was calculated by dividing the prevalence rate for heavy disruptive drug use for a certain number of risk factors by

Table 13.7   Prevalence of Heavy Disruptive Drug Use by Number of Risk Factors

	Prevalence Rates	
Number of Risk Factors	Without Drugs	With Drugs
All Subjects	8.1	8.1
0	0.0	0.0
1	0.8	0.0
2	3.1	0.8
3	6.5	2.5
4	10.4	5.5
5	17.3	11.2
6	22.6	13.4
7[a]	47.1	26.2
8		30.0
9[b]		70.0
	$\chi^2(7) = 70.22$***	$\chi^2(9) = 121.12$***
Correlations		
Point-biserial	.28***	.35***
Rank order	.26***	.32***

***$p < .001$.

[a]7 or more without drugs.

[b]9 or more with drugs.

the sample base rate for heavy use (8.1) and multiplying by 100. Thus, a hazard rate of 100 would indicate no more or no less likelihood than the sample taken as a whole (e.g., Newcomb, Maddahian, & Bentler, 1986). Hazard rates under 100 indicate less likelihood of heavy disruptive drug use, and hazard rates over 100 signify greater risk for heavy disruptive drug use. The data reveal a dramatic association between number of risk factors and the hazard rate of using drugs heavily at work.

Interpretation

Disruptive drug use can be considered one aspect of a lifestyle characterized by heavy and problematic use of drugs, based on both subjective perceptions of the person and objective events (Stein, Newcomb, & Bentler, in press). The extent of the association between disruptive drug use and other drug problems is now established, and has been examined from two directions: prevalence of disruptive drug use if another problem existed and prevalence of another problem if disruptive drug use occurred.

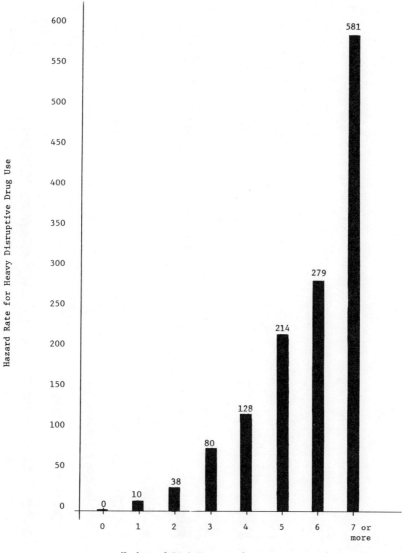

Figure 13.3   Bar Graph of the Number of Risk Factors Excluding Drug Use with the Hazard Rate for Heavy Disruptive Drug Use (11 or More Times of Use During the Past 6 Months).   A hazard rate of 100 indicates the total sample average.

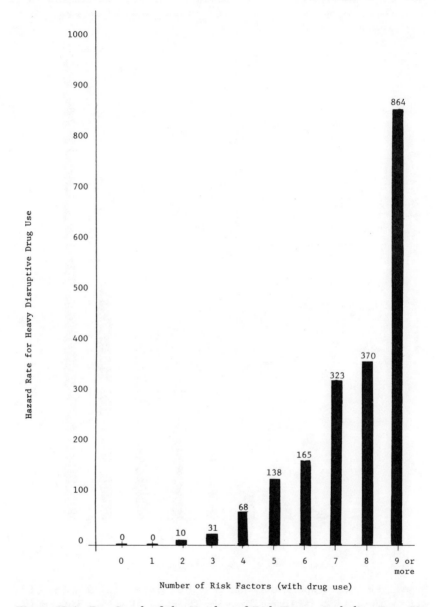

Figure 13.4   Bar Graph of the Number of Risk Factors Including Drug Use with the Hazard Rate for Heavy Disruptive Drug Use (11 or More Times of Use During the Past 6 Months).   A hazard rate of 100 indicates the total sample average.

These two directions provide two slightly different perspectives for the employer. First, an employer must know to what extent using drugs on the job may suggest that an employee has other problems with drugs. Analyses regarding this issue indicated that, compared to those who did not use drugs on the job, those who did were 3.1 times more likely to admit to having trouble with alcohol during the past four years; 3.9 times more likely to admit to having trouble with drugs in the past four years; 2.6 times more likely to have had an accident that was drug related in the past six months; 2.2 times more likely to have been arrested or convicted of driving while intoxicated during the past four years; 4.4 times more likely to have been arrested or convicted for selling or possessing drugs in the past four years; 2.3 times more likely to have attended an alcohol treatment program in the past four years; 12.8 times more likely to have sold any illegal drugs during the past six months; and 3.8 times more likely to have had a bad reaction to marijuana during the past six months.

These figures make it abundantly clear that someone who uses drugs at work is at substantially higher risk for a variety of drug-related problems, in particular selling drugs. Thus, if an employee is caught or identified as using drugs on the job, the person is also more than likely to have trouble with drugs in other contexts as well. In other words, disruptive drug use may be one symptom of a general syndrome of drug problems that must be confronted for successful rehabilitation. It must be kept in mind also that some of these other drug problems may occur at work as well, and compound the consequences of disruptive drug use. For instance, the higher rates of selling drugs and having drug-related accidents may reflect events on the worksite (e.g., Cohen, 1984; Lyles, 1984; Washton & Gold, 1987).

Second, an employer must know the likelihood of an applicant who has had other problems with drugs using drugs on the job. In this regard, the prevalence of disruptive drug use was examined for those who had and had not had other problems with drugs. Compared to those who have not had a particular drug problem, those who have had a particular drug problem were more likely to engage in disruptive drug use. In particular, they are 2.0 times more likely if they have had trouble with alcohol during the past four years; 2.2 times more likely if they have had drug problems in the past four years; 1.8 times more likely if they have had a drug-related accident in the past six months; 1.7 times more likely if they have been arrested or convicted for driving while intoxicated during the past four years; 2.2 times more likely if they have been arrested or convicted for selling or possession of drugs in the past four years; 1.6 times more likely if they have attended an alcohol treatment program in the past four years; 3.7 times more likely if they have sold any illegal drugs in the past six months; and 3.0 times more likely if they have experienced a negative reaction to marijuana in the past six months.

It is also clear from these analyses that if these events have not occurred, there is not a substantial reduction in the prevalence of disruptive drug use. The absence of these other drug problems does not reduce substantially the chances that an employee will use drugs on the job (e.g., Lings, Jensen, Christensen, & Moller, 1984; Rothberg & Chloupek, 1978), but the presence of these problems markedly increases the chances that an employee will use drugs on the job.

If this type of information were available for personnel screening, an employer could make a more informed decision on the likelihood of an employee's using drugs on the job. Unfortunately, such information is rarely available or admitted to by the applicant. For this reason, the employer might find the risk factor index useful. Moreover, if an applicant supplied information concerning other drug problems, the employer could easily incorporate it into the existing risk factor index, and by doing so increase its discriminating capability.

The two risk factor indices developed here demonstrated moderate efficiency at distinguishing the prevalence, frequency, and heavy use of drugs on the job or at school. Their greatest utility rests on the end points of the scales. Those with very few risk factors were quite unlikely to engage in disruptive drug use, whereas those with many risk factors were extremely likely to use drugs in the workplace. Unfortunately, approximately 50 percent of the sample falls in the middle range of risk factors, where the likelihood of disruptive drug use was no different from the sample average (i.e., no predictive utility).

The strongest associations between risk factors and disruptive drug use were found for the prevalence of any use (the use/nonuse distinction). From the employer's standpoint, this is perhaps the most important finding. Moderate associations were found for predicting frequency of disruptive drug use, and somewhat smaller associations were found for predicting heavy use of drugs at work or school.

The risk factor index with drug use was more powerful than the index without drug use. If it is possible to determine reliably whether an employee or applicant has used cannabis or cocaine during the past six months (or whatever period of time is appropriate for practical purposes), then this risk index scale could be used.

Cut points on continuous measures or scales should always be adjusted for the pool of applicants or employees being tested, since it is likely that they may vary from my sample of young adults. In addition, further research may identify other factors indicative of high risk for disruptive drug use and should be incorporated in the scales.

Finally, the indices developed here measure *only* the likelihood that a person will use drugs on the job, and offer no proof. Both high and low scores on the index only indicate probabilities and tendencies; they do not prove that drugs have or have not been used on the job. For instance, fully 10 percent of those receiving nine or more risk factors on the index with drug use had not used drugs on the job or at school during the past six months. Although fully 90 percent had engaged in disruptive drug use, the association is not perfect and errors and misclassifications certainly arise. Thus, I recommend that the index be used in an advisory context and not as the basis for final decisions. A particularly high score should be cause for concern and investigation. Those with very low scores will probably not use drugs on the job. Little can be said about those who score in the middle range; some will and some won't use drugs on the job.

Chapter 14

CONCLUSIONS

The problem of drug use in the workplace is a complex one that requires a calm and level-headed approach based upon the best available scientific and clinical evidence. It is a serious problem that can affect the employee, co-workers, the company, and society.

The current national hysteria over drug abuse has promoted irresponsible and unfounded paranoia about the extent and consequences of drug use on the job. Data are simply not currently available to support some of the inflammatory comments being presented in the popular press and professional journals. For instance, Lyles (1984) quoted a Drug Enforcement Administration official, who said, "Today, drug use at the workplace is as common as the coffee break." Lyles (1984) expanded this statement by declaring that "drug dealing is as common as the coffee break" (p. 46). Such assertions are misleading, and employers need to carefully examine such claims. Is every employee, at least twice a day (assuming two coffee breaks per day), either selling drugs at work or using drugs at work? Lyles' claim is clearly ridiculous, and totally unsupported by research. If the drugs of concern are caffeine or cigarettes, Lyles' claim may be valid. These are certainly substances of abuse that can undermine the health and productivity of a company, but they are not the drugs of concern.

The hysteria affects the general public as well. A recent study of a community sample of adults found that one-quarter of them believed that over 50 percent of all Americans have a drug abuse problem (Oskamp et al., 1987). Yet there is no scientific evidence to support this view.

According to the research presented in this book, less than one-third of young adults had used alcohol or an illicit drug while at work or school during the past six months. Most of the one-third had only done this once. Again, less than 13 percent of these young adults had sold any illicit drug during the past six months. These figures do indicate a serious problem, but one that is not as great as some would have us believe.

It is relatively easy to identify the false reports and horror stories, even when published by reputable journals. It is more difficult to ascertain the true extent of the problem of drug use in the workplace. Drug abuse is a problem, whether at work or in the home, and the employer must gauge the company response to the magnitude of the problem based on scientific research, not on outlandish claims and scare tactics. Overreaction can be just as destructive to a company as underreaction or no reaction. Overreaction can lead to morale problems, suspicion and distrust between workers, managers, supervisors, and others, hostility and paranoia, and lack of commitment to the job and its goals.

Employers have a social and legal responsibility to maintain a safe work environment; drug use on the job threatens this safety. Employers who hope to deal constructively with the problem of drug use on the job will seek reliable research to guide them in making decisions that affect the company and its personnel.

Limitations of the Findings

Even though this data set may be one of the most extensive sources currently available on the prevalence and correlates of disruptive drug use, it has several serious drawbacks. First, the sample is only moderately sized, and it is always better to have larger samples in order to yield the most reliable estimates. Second, the sample is limited to young adults, and patterns and correlates of disruptive drug use may be different at older ages. Third, the sample is geographically limited to the Los Angeles metropolitan area and certainly drug use patterns can differ by region of the country and nation in the world. Fourth, I was not able to identify specific occupations and thereby types of jobs that are plagued by disruptive drug use (although I did have several relevant work-related variables). Fifth, there were more women in the sample than men, which may have biased the findings toward women (although mean differences existed between men and women on their levels of disruptive drug use, tests that compared the correlates of disruptive drug use were not typically different for men and women). Sixth, the data were totally based on self-reports, leaving the validity of these responses somewhat in question (see the discussion of validity in chapter 2). Despite these drawbacks, some definite conclusions can be drawn.

Summary of the Findings

In chapter 1, I posed questions for each chapter, with the intent of focusing each chapter on a substantive issue. The question posed for chapter 2 concerned the characteristics of the sample and the types of measures and analyses used. The sample was a group of 739 young adults who were participants in an ongoing study of teenage and young adult drug use and development. Thus, data were also available from when they were adolescents. Most of the young adults lived in the Los Angeles County area; the group can be regarded as a community sample of young adults. Most were employed full or part time.

In chapter 3 I was concerned with the prevalence, extent, and types of disruptive drug use. Nearly one-third of the sample (31 percent) admitted to being drunk, stoned, or high on at least one psychoactive substance while at work or school during the past six months. Alcohol was the most prevalent class of substances used, and marijuana was the most prevalent individual substance used at work or school. Not a single person in the sample had used heroin in these contexts. Men engaged in disruptive alcohol use and disruptive cannabis use more prevalently than women. There was no sex difference on disruptive use of hard drugs. Those in part-time jobs, full-time jobs, and attending junior colleges reported the highest rates of disruptive use. Those in a university or the military reported the least disruptive drug use, with a notable exception for alcohol use in the military, which was particularly high.

In chapter 4 I addressed whether disruptive drug use was limited to a particular substance, or whether it was characterized by use of multiple drugs. Disruptive drug use was not limited to a single substance, but often entailed the use of different substances within one class (i.e., beer, wine, and liquor) and different substances across classes (i.e., beer and marijuana). Although some people only used one type of drug at work or school, others engaged in disruptive polydrug use. This indicates that for many workers exposure for using one substance may not capture the extent of the problem; these workers are more than likely using other drugs at the worksite.

In chapter 5 I examined the kinds of people who engage in disruptive drug use, based on background and demographic information. Those most likely to have engaged in disruptive drug use were male, either black or white, had few educational plans, had cohabited sometime in their life, had no children, and were not currently married. Higher income was related to greater disruptive use of cocaine and hard drugs. No differences were found for age (the range was too narrow), amount worked, and divorce history.

In chapter 6 I examined how disruptive drug use was related to using drugs in general, and found that general and disruptive drug use (reflecting high levels of polydrug use) were highly associated. Those who were heavily involved with drugs away from work were at high risk for using drugs at work. Heavy use of a specific drug away from work (in all contexts) was the strongest predictor of using the same drug on the job. Interestingly, even cigarettes were an important predictor of disruptive drug use. Further, using drugs at work typically occurred in a sequence of increasing drug involvement, after using an illicit drug (cannabis or cocaine) away from work. Men used drugs at work sooner in this sequence (after cannabis) than women (after cocaine).

In chapter 7 I examined how disruptive drug use was associated with other work-related factors or work conditions. In general, disruptive drug use was not highly associated with many work-related variables, including income, collecting public assistance, amount worked, and support for work problems. Disruptive drug use was most related to job instability (frequently being fired) and committing vandalism at work, and only slightly to job dissatisfaction. It appeared that disruptive drug use did not result from problems and unhappiness in the workplace.

In chapter 8 I explored a wide range of personality, emotional functioning, social support, and problems in life factors as correlates of disruptive drug use. In general, I found a variety of small effects that did not explain a great deal of the variance in disruptive drug use. Using drugs at work was only slightly related to relationship and family problems, or emotional distress. Disruptive drug use was most highly related to having drug and alcohol problems, lacking law abidance, being liberal, feeling powerless, and lacking injury hysteria (low fearfulness). In other words, disruptive drug use was not typically a result of life problems or general unhappiness (although a few small associations with these variables were found). Disruptive drug use was most related to being nonconforming, having low fearfulness, having trouble with an intimate relationship, acknowledging drug or alcohol problems, and feeling powerless.

In chapter 9 I examined how disruptive drug use was related to other types of deviant behavior. Disruptive drug use was strongly related to all types of deviant and criminal behavior and attitudes, including low social conformity, criminal behaviors, high sexual involvement, and selling drugs. It was particularly related to dealing drugs. Indeed, disruptive drug use was an indicator of a generally deviant lifestyle. These associations with disruptive drug use are the strongest ones found in all analyses presented here.

In chapter 10 I traced the stability and change of disruptive drug use from high school to young adulthood. Disruptive drug use was modestly to moderately stable over this four-year period, although less stable than general drug use (emphasizing the abuse or problem quality of the behavior). Even though the percentage of the sample engaging in any disruptive drug use was virtually the same at adolescence and young adulthood, disruptive cannabis use decreased over time (particularly for females) and disruptive hard drug use increased over the same period (particularly for males). There was a consistency in the use of specific substances at both times. The sex differences remained about the same at both periods. General cocaine use as a teenager was one of the best predictors of later disruptive drug use. These analyses confirm that disruptive drug use represents an aspect of the person that is manifested in different situations.

In chapter 11 I examined how a variety of personality features and life views as a teenager affected disruptive drug use over time. There were numerous within-time correlations with adolescent disruptive drug use. In terms of prediction, however, only a few significant variables emerged. Disruptive drug use as a young adult was increased by early low social conformity, low law abidance, prior disruptive drug use, general cocaine use, low illness sensitivity, unhappiness about the future, and introversion.

In chapter 12 I tested whether an addictive personality, or other motivation to use drugs, was related to later disruptive drug use. In general, there was only limited support for this hypothesis. Greater general motivation for cannabis use increased disruptive drug use, as well as general drug use. Two small effects, however, suggested that disruptive drug use was more a function of addiction motivations (needing the drug to get through the day) than social motivations (to fit in), which were most closely linked to general drug use.

In chapter 13 I examined how disruptive drug use was related to other problems with drugs, and developed risk factor indices for predicting disruptive drug use. Disruptive drug use was associated with having difficulty with drugs in many other areas of life than just at work. For instance, drug use at work was significantly associated with selling drugs and getting arrested for drug law violations. Two risk factor indices were developed and moderately predicted use, frequency, and heavy use of drugs at work or school. Eight percent of the sample used drugs heavily at work, as defined by being high on the job more than eleven times or more during the past six months.

Disruptive drug use was largely a function of the person rather than the environment, regardless of whether the environment is defined as work or home. The tendency to engage in disruptive drug use is an individual characteristic in a rebellious, nonconforming, deviant, and perhaps acting-out personality that was also evident in high school. In other words, disruptive drug use is not situationally generated; it is a manifestation of a general syndrome of problem behavior both related to and separate from drug use.

Disruptive drug use represents a type of drug abuse that carries with it several messages regarding deviance, rebelliousness, and irresponsibility. At least among these subjects, disruptive drug use was not largely an act of addiction in the traditional sense, but instead represented an inability to handle drugs in ordinary life. This in turn reflected low social conformity, which was manifested in other attitudes and behaviors.

Young adults who were disruptive drug users also used drugs as teenagers. Heavy use of drugs as a teenager has important consequences for a person's maturity and sense of responsibility later in life (Newcomb & Bentler, 1988a). Young people come to rely on drugs to handle stress and therefore do not learn other coping mechanisms. The teenager is expected to learn various coping skills, but this is also the age when drug use is initiated. If young adults who use drugs on the job or in the classroom follow the pattern, they will display a narrow range of coping skills. Enhancement and expansion of such skills may be an essential component for intervening with disruptive drug users.

It is likely that a distinction can be drawn between those who engage in disruptive alcohol use and those who engage in disruptive cannabis, cocaine, and hard drug use. The alcohol user was predicted the least successfully in virtually all of the analyses. Disruptive alcohol use may be less strongly tied to general deviance than is disruptive use of illicit drugs. If this distinction is valid, different approaches might be needed for reaching users of these two classes of drugs at work. Unfortunately, the characterization of the disruptive drug user applies most to illicit drugs and less for alcohol. Alcohol is certainly a major problem at the workplace, but there were fewer systematic associations with those who used alcohol on the job than with those who used illicit substances. Nevertheless, disruptive alcohol users may also lack effective coping skills.

Employers' Response

It is likely that drugs are being used on the worksite or in the classroom. Some employees and students, but probably not all, and only a very small percentage, are using drugs on a regular basis. How should this be handled?

Many articles have been written to suggest particular techniques for handling the drug-using employee; fewer have been written to address the student using drugs at school (e.g., Schwartz, 1984). Much of this material can be helpful, but the most important elements of a successful approach to drug use on the job or in the classroom are a comprehensive plan and total support from top-level management or administration. Without both of these, the program is doomed to failure or only limited success.

It is not the goal of this book to provide all the solutions to the problem of drug abuse in the workplace; my goal is to provide information so that effective programs can be created within a realistic context. One of the best comprehensive sources currently available is *Strategic Planning for Workplace Drug Abuse Programs*, written by T. E. Backer (1987) and published by the National Institute on Drug Abuse.

Backer (1987) stresses that the most effective way to confront drug use in the workplace is to make three commitments: (1) a clear and explicit drug policy from the leaders of the company; (2) personnel, financial, and community resources to handle the problem; and (3) a strategic plan that is fully integrated into the organizational structure. Backer (1987) identifies ten steps in implementing a drug abuse program in a company: (1) setting an organizational drug policy; (2) developing a written program design covering all aspects of operations, staffing, and financing of program components; (3) supervisory training on drug abuse; (4) identification (including drug testing) and outreach; (5) workplace security; (6) assessment and referral; (7) counseling and treatment; (8) follow-up; (9) record keeping and evaluation; and (10) prevention, and employee and family education. Backer (1987) provides detailed programs and policy statement suggestions.

The most critical aspect of any program is the commitment of the company to the project as an integral and ongoing component of the organization (e.g., Backer, Liberman, & Kuehnel, 1986). Lukewarm or mixed support undermines the effort from the start.

Administrative innovations in conjunction with other reforms can bring about wide-ranging changes in a company (e.g., Fennell, 1984).

Of course, the steps laid down by Backer (1987) are not easy and require a great deal of information and investment of time and personnel. There are technical problems in various aspects of the program. For instance, how should managers and supervisors handle drug-using workers, and which approaches work best (e.g., Beaumont & Allsop, 1984; Googins & Kurts, 1980; Heyman, 1976; Madonia, 1984; Trice & Beyer, 1984; Wright, 1983)? If identified and confronted, what should happen to the employee (e.g., Walsch & Hingson, 1985)? What about the legal issues of privacy and wrongful discharge (e.g., Knox & Fenley, 1985; Landis, 1986; Schachter & Geidt, 1985)? What is the role of unions in the corporate response to drug use on the job (e.g., Johnson, 1981; Putnam & Stout, 1982)? These are tough questions, with no simple answers. The problem of drug use in the workplace, however, will not go away and demands effective and vigorous intervention (e.g., McClellan, 1984; Smith, 1981).

Implications for Drug Testing

Many employers mistakenly see drug testing as the panacea to their drug problems. Unfortunately, this is far from the ideal solution for several reasons, mostly because of the technical, practical, and legal aspects of drug testing.

Although increasingly accurate, drug testing is not foolproof and both false positives and false negatives can be obtained (e.g., Cohen, 1986; Gampel & Zeese, 1986). When people's lives and careers can be destroyed by a measurement error in urinalysis, we must take a careful look at the process, for no test is perfectly accurate (e.g., MacKenzie, Cheng, & Haftel, 1987). A recent monograph edited by Hawks and Chiang (1986) for the National Institute on Drug Abuse reviewed many of the technical issues involved in drug testing: establishing a urinalysis program (Hawks, 1986), specimen collection and handling (Manno, 1986b), choosing a laboratory (Willette, 1986), and interpretation of test results (Manno, 1986a).

Even if technical problems of accuracy and reliability are solved, other major problems remain. First, alcohol is one of the most widely used drugs in the workplace, according to my study and others (Hawks, 1986). Drug-testing programs typically do not assess for alcohol use, which leaves this type of abuser undetected.

Nearly everyone uses alcohol (not necessarily at work), which would show up on a urinalysis and make the test useless (unless one could identify blood levels sufficiently high to guarantee intoxication and impairment on the job). This raises another concern: drug testing can only indicate recent use of a particular substance and not whether the drug was used on the job or whether the employee was actually high or stoned on the job (Hawks, 1986). In other words, a positive test for marijuana could not also indicate whether the drug had been used on the weekend in the privacy of the employee's home or at work (Ching & Hawks, 1986).

The final concern regards the legality of drug testing. There is probably less uproar regarding preemployment drug screening than random or probable cause drug testing of current employees (Engleking, 1986). Nevertheless, applicant screening can only weed out the heaviest users (or dumbest ones) who do not quit using drugs a week or two before the test. Screening does not guarantee that drugs won't be used in the future; in fact, research indicates that such testing efforts may not be cost effective (e.g., Lewy, 1983). The courts may prohibit the use of drug testing on a variety of legal grounds, such as invasion of privacy (both constitutional and general tort issues), employment discrimination, handicap discrimination, defamation, and wrongful discharge (e.g., Bompey, 1986; Kendall, 1986).

Some might say that even with these limitations, drug testing is better than nothing. Yes, it is better than nothing, but not better than prevention, education, and compassionate intervention. Drug testing is only a stopgap effort; the real change comes by changing the work environment and making it more responsive to the employee's needs. This requires greater managerial investment, which some companies choose not to make, turning nearsightedly to drug testing as a solution.

Even if every obstacle were surmounted, drug testing would still provide no guarantee that employees will not use drugs on the job. If drug testing of applicants were used, more than half the workforce might not get jobs. Well over one-half of all young adults have used marijuana sometime in their life, and well over one-third have used an illicit drug during the past year (NIDA, 1986, 1987). Nevertheless, all of these people are not going to be using drugs on the job. Again, drug testing is not used to identify alcohol users, who are a large segment of the population.

The most effective way for dealing with drug use on the job is, first, prevention, and then, if this fails, vigorous and compassionate intervention (Backer, 1987). Drug testing may seem to be an easy way out of the problem of employee drug abuse, but it is simply not a solution.

A Quick Look at Illicit Drug Users

Knowing that someone has used illicit drugs is not de facto evidence that the person has used drugs on the job, and to illustrate this I provide one last series of analyses. These analyses include most of the variables already presented from the young adult data, but only those subjects who reported any use of an illicit substance during the past six months (cannabis, cocaine, or hard drugs) are included. In other words, this sample includes those who could be identified by the *best* drug test, one that could detect use up to six months ago. The any use continuous measure of disruptive drug use was used as the criterion variable.

Of the total sample, 381 had used an illicit drug during the past six months (52 percent). Of these 381 young adults, 50 percent indicated that they had used a drug at work or school during the same period. Although this is higher than the general prevalence of disruptive drug use for the entire sample (31 percent), fully half of the illicit drug users did not use drugs at work or school. If an employer dismissed employees because of positive drug tests, 50 percent of those dismissed would be employees who did not use drugs on the job.

There were thirty-seven significant correlations between the frequency of any disruptive drug use scale and the young adult variables for this sample (see table 14.1). Two multiple regression analyses were run for these variables: one with all variables, and one with deviance items removed (i.e., drug use, trouble with drugs, criminal behavior, sexual activity).

Using all variables, those illicit drug users who engaged in disruptive drug use were black, were white, smoked a lot of cigarettes, smoked cannabis, used a lot of cocaine, had trouble with their job, engaged in vandalism at work, perceived low organizational support for work problems, were extroverted, had low injury hysteria, had low illness sensitivity, had poor relationships with parents, had good relationships with peers, sold drugs, felt lonely, and felt powerless. These variables were able to account for over 40 percent of the variance of disruptive drug use among these illicit drug users. Even the multiple regression equation without the deviance variables was able to account for over 30 percent of the variance in disruptive drug use for this sample.

The same analyses were run again, but this time with a selection

Table 14.1 Correlates and Multiple Regression Analyses of Disruptive Drug Use Given Illicit Drug Use ($n = 381$)

Variable	r	With Deviant Variables Beta	Without Deviant Variables Beta
sex (female)	-.15**	-.04	-.08
cigarettes	.18***	.11*	.15**
alcohol	.13**	.08	[a]
cannabis	.09*	.10*	[a]
cocaine	.29***	.22***	[a]
hard drugs	.09*	.07	[a]
nonprescription medication	.02	-.06	[a]
age	.02	.00	-.02
educational plans	-.01	.00	-.04
income	.12**	.04	.09
ever cohabited	.04	-.03	.03
high school graduate	.00	-.03	-.07
have children	-.04	.03	.02
collected welfare	-.04	-.03	-.06
collected food stamps	-.05	-.02	-.04
ever divorced	-.01	.02	.04
currently married	-.10*	-.08	-.07
black	.06	.16*	.16*
white	.06	.15*	.16*
Asian	-.06	.03	.02
unhappy with job	.01	.03	.07
trouble with job	.19***	.11*	.12*
amount worked	.07	.05	.04
full-time job	.07	.01	.03
vandalism at work	.13**	.12*	[a]
advice from family	.09*	-.02	.03
advice from friends	.13**	.08	.04
family support	-.03	-.01	.02
satisfaction with family support	-.08	.01	-.03
number of			
sexual partners	.13*	-.01	[a]
steady partners	.05	-.06	[a]
age first intercourse	-.16**	-.05	[a]
confrontational acts	.11*	.01	[a]
thefts	.20***	.06	[a]
property damage	.08	.04	[a]
sold drugs	.34***	.20***	[a]
trouble with drugs/alcohol	.20***	.01	[a]
trouble with drugs past 4 years	.16**		
trouble with alcohol past 4 years	.12**	.04	[a]
trouble with health	.03	.06	.05
unhappy with health	-.04	-.07	-.05
health problems past 4 years	-.04	-.02	-.05
friends' support	-.01	-.06	-.03
satisfaction with friends' support	-.03	.03	.03

organizational support	−.06	−.14**	−.10*
satisfaction with			
organizational support	−.01	.01	.08
ambition	.09*	−.03	−.05
attractiveness	.03	−.07	−.01
congeniality	−.11	.00	−.02
deliberateness	−.10*	−.03	−.05
diligence	−.01	.04	.03
extroversion	.14**	.11*	.12*
generosity	.04	−.08	−.04
invulnerability	.08	.01	.04
law abidance	−.22***	−.01	−.12*
leadership	.12**	.02	.05
liberalism	.09*	.04	.10*
objectivity	−.01	−.05	−.06
orderliness	.00	.03	.06
religiosity	.01	.05	.08
self-acceptance	−.04	−.07	−.09
headache prone	−.02	.07	.03
insomnia	.06	.03	.00
injury hysteria	−.15**	−.10*	−.11*
depression	.00	−.02	−.02
trust physicians	−.09*	−.06	−.05
trust medicine	−.09*	−.06	−.06
illness sensitivity	−.10*	−.11*	−.07
thought disorganization	.09*	.07	.11*
good relationship with:			
parents	−.15**	−.13*	−.11*
family	−.10*	−.02	−.02
adults	−.06	.04	.02
peers	.08	.14*	.12*
psychosomatic symptoms	.11*	.06	.10
unhappy with family	.05	.01	.07
poor relationship with family			
past 4 years	.13**	.07	.10
loneliness	.05	.15*	.15*
trouble in relationship	.12**	.04	.03
unhappy in relationship	.06	.01	.01
lonely in relationship	.02	.00	−.02
trouble handling feelings	.07	.05	.07
self-derogation	.04	.05	−.02
unhappy handling feelings	.00	−.01	.01
in control	−.02	−.01	−.01
feel powerful	−.08	−.16**	−.14*
personal control	−.02	−.02	−.09
inner resources	.13**	.08	.10
independent	.04	−.02	.00
respect for others	.08	.05	.04
Multiple Regression Summary			
R		.64	.56
R²		.41	.31
F-ratio		2.24***	1.78***

[a]Excluded from analyses.

*p < .05; **p < .01; ***p < .001.

of variables: the statistical program chose the best variables to account for the frequency of disruptive drug use (see table 14.2). Both equations were significant, demonstrating systematic differences between those who use drugs at work and those who use illicit drugs in the privacy of their own homes. Most of the findings are similar to those reported earlier and those just listed above. For the equation without deviance items, frequency of disruptive drug use was predicted by low law abidance, poor relationship with parents, trouble with work, higher income, being male, heavy use of cigarettes, feeling powerless, and belief in having many inner resources.

Finally, the same analyses without deviance items were run for men and women separately (see table 14.3). Sixty-two percent of the illicit-drug-using men had used a drug at work or school during the past six months. For men who have used illicit drugs, greater disruptive drug use was predicted from low self-acceptance, low trust in physicians, low illness sensitivity, having a full-time job, and heavy use of cigarettes. Interestingly, the self-acceptance and illness sensitivity effects for higher disruptive drug use are contrary to established sex differences on these scales (e.g., Newcomb & Bentler, 1987c; Stein, Newcomb, & Bentler, 1986b). Forty-six percent of the illicit-drug-using women engaged in disruptive drug use at least once during the past six months. For women who have used illicit drugs, greater disruptive drug use was predicted from low law abidance, low injury hysteria, more extroversion, less depression, having trouble with a job, more psychosomatic symptoms, and feeling powerless. Again, several of the variables related to higher levels of disruptive drug use are contrary to established sex differences on these scales. The variables are law abidance, injury hysteria, extroversion, and depression (Newcomb & Bentler, 1988b; Stein, Newcomb, & Bentler, 1986b). One hypothesis derived from these findings is that those who have disturbances or conflicts in their gender roles may be more likely to engage in disruptive drug use, even when they are illicit drug users. Thus, gender role conflicts or dysphoria may partially account for illicit drug users becoming disruptive drug users.

These analyses supply important information but they also demonstrate clearly that just knowing whether or not someone has used an illicit drug in the recent past (information available from drug testing) is simply not sufficient to predict who will use drugs on the job. Many people who use illicit drugs do not use drugs on the job and endanger a business. These differences are, however, systematic. If information such as that given in the tables could be linked to positive drug tests, greater predictive ability could be achieved. Where drug testing is not used or is not possible, the risk factors presented in the previous chapter could be particularly useful in identifying potentially problematic employees.

Implications for Prevention

Prevention and education about drug use in the workplace are the most efficient and cost-effective methods for creating a long-term drug-free worksite (e.g., Byars, 1983). Whereas most work-based drug programs focus on the rehabilitation and treatment of the current drug users, education and prevention can often solve problems before they become serious. Gardner (1982) has emphasized several steps for effective education within an organization. These include informing the workforce of the problem and its seriousness, altering the social climate in regard to alcohol and drugs, identifying problem people, eliminating "cover-up" behaviors (of both the employee and the supervisor), and instituting a clearly stated system for help. McClellan (1984) offers additional suggestions based on learning and reinforcement theory, such as designating key contact people in the organization and introducing short face-to-face presentations, reinforced with posters, leaflets, mailings, etc. Particular emphasis should be placed on the fact that it is a company problem that could potentially affect anyone and that everyone in the company, from the president on down, is concerned with dealing with it.

One primary objective is to change the work culture or environment to one that does not encourage, and in fact discourages, drug use on the job (Fine, Akabas, & Bellinger, 1982; Trice & Beyer, 1982; Waddell, 1986). Another objective is to provide nonthreatening assistance to the employee having problems. The work milieu should foster and reward sober job performance, and offer alternatives to drugs and drinking on the job, to meet whatever needs the drug use fulfills.

The analyses presented in this book suggest other considerations in the prevention and education efforts. Certain employees are at high risk for disruptive drug use and may warrant special attention. For instance, men are at greater risk than women, and men may therefore need to learn alternate ways of handling their stress or demonstrating their rebelliousness than getting high on the job. Adaptive options must be presented in an attractive manner to the employee. Among teenagers, alternative programs for the at-risk student are much more successful than socially oriented programs (Tobler, 1986).

Table 14.2   Stepwise Selection of the Best Predictors of Disruptive Drug Use Given Illicit Drug Use ($n = 381$)

With Deviant Variables		Without Deviant Variable	
Variable	Beta	Variable	Beta
cannabis	.11**	law abidance	-.17***
cocaine	.27***	good relationship with parents	-.12**
hard drugs	.11**	trouble with work	.16**
extroversion	.12**	income	.13**
injury hysteria	-.09*	sex (female)	-.09*
illness sensitivity	-.13**	cigarettes	.17***
good relationship with parents	-.11**	feel powerful	-.11*
trouble with work	.14***	inner resources	.13**
support from organization	-.12**		
black	.12**		
sold drugs	.17***		
feel powerful	-.13***		
inner resources	.13**		
Multiple Regression Summary			
R	.53		.42
R²	.28		.17
F-ratio	11.23***		8.69***

*$p < .05$; **$p < .01$; ***$p < .001$.

Table 14.3 **Stepwise Selection of the Best Predictors of Disruptive Drug Use Given Illicit Drug Use by Sex excluding Deviance Variables**

Men (N = 111)		Women (N = 270)	
Variable	*Beta*	*Variable*	*Beta*
self-acceptance	−.35***	law abidance	−.17***
trust physicians	−.18**	injury hysteria	−.19***
illness sensitivity	−.22**	extroversion	.12*
full-time job	.24**	depression	−.16**
cigarettes	.23**	trouble with job	.18***
		psychosomatic symptoms	.15**
		feel powerful	−.18**
	Multiple Regression Summary		
R	.53		.41
R²	.28		.17
F-ratio	8.21***		7.54***

*$p < .05$; **$p < .01$; ***$p < .001$.

I also found that disruptive drug use was greater among those who did not feel that there were places to which they could turn for help regarding work or employment problems. Community or within-company resources must be made available and easily accessible. Further, disruptive drug use was higher among those who felt powerless. Greater involvement and participation by employees in their work roles should increase their commitment and respect for their jobs.

In important ways, disruptive drug use implies a disrespect for the job and the company. It says that employees do not value their work sufficiently to perform it soberly. Part of this is a difficulty respecting any traditional values or norms, and represents a general rebellious attitude. The employer must undertake to enhance the value of the job, and the employee must make an investment in the work. Job rotations can provide a bigger picture through which employees come to appreciate the significance of their job. Work groups improve social support, provide technical and emotional assistance, and encourage greater accountability for personal behavior.

The last few suggestions may seem to go against the evidence of my research, since disruptive drug use is not strongly related to problems in the work environment. Nevertheless, even though the changes and modifications I am suggesting do not necessarily remediate an adverse environment, they are the best ways to reach the users and change their attitudes and outlook.

Finally, my results indicate that disruptive drug use is one facet of a lifestyle that is characterized by deviance, rebelliousness, and other drug problems. Disruptive drug use is not an isolated event or behavior, but rather a consistent and moderately predictable aspect of a problem lifestyle. Thus, for prevention efforts to be successful, the programs must address many aspects of deviance and irresponsible behavior. Only confronting disruptive drug abuse ignores the larger problem in which this behavior is embedded. This larger problem can include vandalism on the job, selling drugs, and other criminal behaviors that are detrimental for any business.

Employers can approach this issue in a comprehensive manner by creating a primary prevention program directed at enhancing healthy living. A major component of this program could focus directly on drug abuse in the workplace. Other components could focus on stress management, communications training, and identification with the company, all of which improve the quality of the employee's life, reduce medical expenses, increase worker satisfaction, and improve productivity.

Implications for Employee Assistance Programs

When primary prevention fails or is ineffective with particular people, secondary and tertiary prevention must be made available. These programs provide (or give referrals to other programs that provide) direct intervention with the problem employee. These programs may be therapy or counseling to deal with the troubled employee, along with working with the supervisor to modify the work environment (e.g., Asma, Hilker, Shevlin, & Golden, 1980). In addition, nondrug-using employees are also victims of the abuser and deserve attention (e.g., Clute, 1980), in order to create effective systematic and enduring changes in the attitudes of all employees and the health of the organization.

Alcoholism was one of the first major employee problems to hit modern industry (e.g., Masi, 1979). Industry's response was to create work-based occupational alcohol programs. More recently, these have expanded to include drug problems and other personal difficulties (e.g., DuPont & Basen, 1980). These broader approaches are typically called employee assistance programs (EAP). There is no question that these programs can be effective and provide significant cost savings to a business (e.g., Blum & Roman, 1985; Freedberg & Johnston, 1979; Korcok, 1983; Moberg, Krause, & Klein, 1982). It is beyond the scope of this book to review this literature (see reviews by Asma et al., 1980; DuPont & Basen,

1980; McClellan, 1984; Walker & Shain, 1983). Needless to say, there are methodological problems in assessing such programs. For instance, Kurtz, Googins, and Howard (1984) identified four measures for assessing the success of an occupational alcoholism program. These included: (1) change in drinking behavior; (2) record of work performance, indicated by absenteeism, disciplinary actions, accidents, sick and injured days used, turnover rate, and job efficiency; (3) cost effectiveness to the employer based on increased work performance; and (4) penetration rate, or the extent the program reaches its target population.

Even though compassion, acceptance, and vigorous intervention may be useful for the employee and the company (e.g., Black, 1984; Shirley, 1984), there may be some situations when these treatment ideals conflict with security needs and goals (e.g., Frank, 1983).

Results of the current study have important implications for the focus of EAPs. Much of what was previously discussed for prevention applies here as well, and is not extensively repeated. Of particular importance is the fact that disruptive drug use is only one aspect of a troubled and deviant lifestyle. Treating only the drug abuse does not solve the problem. Lifestyle changes must be made in order to prevent relapse. The broad nature of the problem must be directly confronted and alternative coping behaviors taught and reinforced. Particularly among drug-abusing men, there is a distrust of the medical profession, so a careful, nonthreatening approach must be taken. Nevertheless, the approach must be firm and direct. Disruptive drug use must be treated in the context of the behavior, which is embedded in a rebellious and nonconforming attitude and lifestyle.

The most critical conclusion drawn from the present analyses and relevant to EAPs is that disruptive drug use is not a function of the work or family environment of the employee. Rather, it is a function of the person, and reflects an enduring and persistent problem. This problem affects how employees value and respect their jobs, and deal with the other responsibilities of adult roles. And this must be kept in mind and confronted when treating those who use drugs on the job. Earlier environmental conditions may certainly have generated the deviant attitudes and behavior (probably during adolescence), but the present environment of the young adult seems largely unrelated to the use of drugs on the job. This is true at least in terms of unhappiness and frustration. This does not mean that certain aspects of the environment may have permitted or allowed the drug use to occur. For instance, those in jobs with little or no direct supervisory control are at greater risk

for disruptive drug use than those in jobs more carefully moni-
tored. On the other hand, engaging in disruptive drug use does
not assure a happy and problem-free life away from work, which
may synergistically compound the drug problem. That drug problems at work may not be related directly to problems in other
areas of life does not mean that these problems should be avoided
when counseling the employee.

My findings do not provide sufficiently detailed information
about how to structure the most effective EAP. They offer hints
and suggestions about specific areas and approaches, but the
treatment literature on drug abuse can offer more specific suggestions for counseling the drug-abusing employee.

Finally, even though more men than women engage in disruptive drug use, women are rapidly acquiring the habits of men as
they gain social and economic parity. Drug use patterns of men
and women are converging (e.g., Kaestner, Frank, Marel, &
Schmeidler, 1986), and special attention must be given in the
coming years to whether women are increasing their drug use on
the job as well. The special issue of drug use among women in the
workplace has started to receive more attention, quite justifiably
(e.g., Cahill, Volicer, & Neuburger, 1982; Vicary, Mansfield,
Cohn, Koch, & Young, 1985). For instance, norms governing
drinking behavior in business environments are less clearly defined for women than for men (Shore, 1986).

A Final Word

There is a significant and persistent problem of drug use in the
workplace and on campus. Alcohol and cannabis are the primary
drugs of abuse, with cocaine lagging behind but increasing in
prevalence. I have been able to identify specific patterns of disruptive drug use that are characteristic of this community sample of
young adults. Moreover these analyses have provided one of the
most detailed descriptions of drug use in the workplace from the
employee's perspective. The patterns I have found may not characterize disruptive drug use of current employees of older ages,
but they may be a portent of things to come as these young adults
grow older.

Drugs and drug use are now a fact of life, whether the drug be
cigarettes, caffeine, alcohol, prescribed medications, or illicit
drugs (i.e., cannabis, cocaine, and hard drugs). Disruptive drug
use represents an irresponsible use of drugs and cannot be tolerated. If we as a country are going to tolerate and even encourage

drug use, we must also systematically teach moderation and appropriateness of use to people at a very young age. Disruptive drug use is an example of a failure to teach values that has affected almost one-third of this sample. The young adults in this segment of the sample are not drug-crazed fiends or junkies, and most don't believe they have any problem with drugs or alcohol. Nevertheless, their priorities and attitudes have allowed them to use drugs in contexts that are obviously not appropriate. Greater responsibility and temperance toward ingestion of drugs must be taught at an earlier age than young adulthood.

Although there are many personal and individual reasons for using drugs, many of these are derived from cultural and societal norms (e.g., Zucker & Gomberg, 1986). These attitudes and values have permitted drugs to be used irresponsibly and must change if drugs are to be used appropriately. One critical task is to teach alternative coping behaviors and effective ways of living at young ages, so that drugs do not become a primary or sole method of solving problems. Education rather than criminal sanctions is the best method for internalizing responsible behaviors, such as a careful use of drugs. Similarly, cutting off the supply of one drug doesn't eliminate the need or desire for drugs (e.g., Waddell, 1986). There will always be alternate drugs to use for the person who wants them.

Finally, it is my hope that this research will be followed up by other studies, so that even greater detail about drug use in the workplace can be uncovered. My initial attempts and tentative answers need to be confirmed or denied by other studies.

REFERENCES

ADAMHA (Alcohol, Drug Abuse, and Mental Health Administration) (1987). *Scientific and technical guidelines for drug testing programs*. New York: Business Research Publications.

Aiken, G. J. M., & McCance, C. (1982). Alcohol consumption in offshore oil rig workers. *British Journal of Addiction, 77,* 305–310.

Alden, W. F. (1986). The scope of the drug problem: A national strategy. *Vital Speeches of the Day,* 751–756.

Allen, J., & Mazzuchi, J. (1985). Alcohol and drug abuse among American military personnel: Prevalence and policy implications. *Military Medicine, 150,* 250–255.

Aneshensel, C. S., & Huba, G. J. (1983). Depression, alcohol use, and smoking over one year: A four-wave longitudinal causal model. *Journal of Abnormal Psychology, 92,* 134–150.

Asma, F. E., Hilker, R. R. J., Shevlin, J. J., & Golden, R. G. (1980). Twenty-five years of rehabilitation of employees with drinking problems. *Journal of Occupational Medicine, 22,* 241–244.

Bachman, J. G., O'Malley, P. M., & Johnston, L. D. (1984). Drug use among young adults: The impacts of role status and social environment. *Journal of Personality and Social Psychology, 47,* 629–645.

Backer, T. E. (1987). *Strategic planning for workplace drug abuse problems*. Rockville, MD: National Institute on Drug Abuse.

Backer, T. E., Liberman, R. P., & Kuehnel, T. G. (1986). Dissemination and adoption of innovative psychosocial interventions. *Journal of Consulting and Clinical Psychology, 54,* 111–118.

Baltes, B. P., & Brim, O. G., Jr. (eds.) (1982). *Life-span development and behavior*. New York: Academic Press.

Baumrind, D. (1983). Specious causal attributions in the social sciences: The reformulated stepping-stone theory as exemplar. *Journal of Personality and Social Psychology, 45,* 1289–1298.

Beary, J. F., Mazzuchi, J. F., & Richie, S. I. (1983). Drug use in the military: An adolescent misbehavior problem. *Journal of Drug Education, 13,* 83–93.

Beaumont, P. B., & Allsop, S. J. (1984). An industrial alcohol policy: The

223

characteristics of worker success. *British Journal of Addiction, 79,* 315–318.

Beeman, D. R. (1985). Is the social drinker killing your company? *Business Horizons,* January–February, 54–58.

Belohlav, J. A., & Popp, P. O. (1983). Employee substance abuse: Epidemic of the eighties. *Business Horizons,* July–August, 29–34.

Bentler, P. M. (1980). Multivariate analysis with latent variables: Causal modeling. *Annual Review of Psychology, 31,* 419–456.

Bentler, P. M. (1983). Some contributions to efficient statistics in structural models: Specification and estimation of moment structures. *Psychometrika, 48,* 493–517.

Bentler, P. M. (1986a). Structural modeling: An historical perspective on growth and achievements. *Psychometrika, 51,* 35–51.

Bentler, P. M. (1986b). *Theory and implementation of EQS: A structural equations program.* Los Angeles: BMDP Statistical Software.

Bentler, P. M. (1987a). Latent variable structural models for separating specific from general effects. Prepared for Health Services Research Conference: Strengthening Causal Interpretations of Non-experimental Data, Tucson, April 1987.

Bentler, P. M. (1987b). Structural modeling and the scientific method: Comments on Freedman's critique. *Journal of Educational Statistics, 12,* 151–157.

Bentler, P. M., & Bonett, D. G. (1980). Significance tests and goodness of fit in the analysis of covariance structures. *Psychological Bulletin, 88,* 588–606.

Bentler, P. M., & Chou, C.-P. (1986). *Statistics for parameter expansion and construction in structural models.* Paper presented at the American Educational Research Association meeting, San Francisco, April 1986.

Bentler, P. M., & Newcomb, M. D. (1978). Longitudinal study of marital success and failure. *Journal of Consulting and Clinical Psychology, 46,* 1053–1070.

Bentler, P. M., & Newcomb, M. D. (1986). Personality, sexual behavior, and drug use revealed through latent variable methods. *Clinical Psychology Review, 6,* 363–385.

Bentler, P. M., & Newcomb, M. D. (in preparation). Some nonstandard approaches to structural modeling: Conditional covariance matrices and separation of general from specific effects.

Black, D. (1984). Out of control. *Canadian Business,* February, *32,* 34–35.

Blane, H. T., & Leonard, K. E. (eds.) (1987). *Psychological theories of drinking and alcoholism.* New York: Guilford.

Blatt, S. J., Quinlan, D. M., Chevron, E. S., McDonald, C., & Zuroff, D. (1982). Dependency and self-criticism: Psychological dimensions of depression. *Journal of Consulting and Clinical Psychology, 50*, 113–124.

Blum, T. C., & Roman, P. M. (1985). The social transformation of alcoholism intervention: Comparisons of job attitudes and performance of recovered alcoholics and non-alcoholics. *Journal of Health and Social Behavior, 26*, 365–378.

Bompey, S. H. (1986). Drugs in the workplace: From the batter's box to the boardroom. *Journal of Occupational Medicine, 28*, 825–832.

Braham, J. (1986). Cocaine creeps toward the top. *Industry Week*, October, 34–38.

Bray, R. M., et al. (1986). *DOD worldwide survey of alcohol and nonmedical drug use among military personnel*. Research Triangle Park, NC: Research Triangle Institute.

Brewster, J. M. (1986). Prevalence of alcohol and other drug problems among physicians. *Journal of the American Medical Association, 255*, 1913–1920.

Brook, J. S., Whiteman, M., Gordon, A. S., & Cohen, P. (1986). Dynamics of childhood and adolescent personality traits and adolescent drug use. *Developmental Psychology, 22*, 403–414.

Brown, S. A. (1985). Expectancies versus background in the prediction of college drinking patterns. *Journal of Consulting and Clinical Psychology, 53*, 123–130.

Brown, S. A., Goldman, N. S., Inn, A., & Anderson, L. R. (1980). Expectations of reinforcement from alcohol: Their domain and relation to drinking patterns. *Journal of Consulting and Clinical Psychology, 48*, 419–426.

Browne, M. W. (1984). Asymptotically distribution-free methods for the analysis of covariance structures. *British Journal of Mathematical and Statistical Psychology, 37*, 62–83.

Bry, B. H. (1983). Predicting drug abuse: Review and reformulation. *International Journal of the Addictions, 18*, 223–233.

Bry, B. H., McKeon, P., & Pandina, R. J. (1982). Extent of drug use as a function of number of risk factors. *Journal of Abnormal Psychology, 91*, 273–279.

Burmaster, D. R. (1985). Employee drug use creates losses but proper policies can control it. *Occupatonal Health and Safety*, December, 39–41.

Burt, M. R. (1982). Prevalence and consequences of alcohol use among U.S. military personnel, 1980. *Journal of Studies on Alcohol, 43*, 1097–1107.

Butler, M. C., Gunderson, E. K. E., & Bruni, J. R. (1981). Motivational determinants of illicit drug use: An assessment of underlying dimensions and their relationships to behavior. *International Journal of the Addictions, 16*, 243–252.

Byars, T. (1983). Educate to eradicate. *Security Management*, December, 32–34.

Cahill, M. H., Volicer, B. J., & Neuburger, E. (1982). Female referral to employees assistance programs: The impact of specialized intervention. *Drug and Alcohol Dependence, 10*, 223–233.

Carman, R. S. (1979). Motivations for drug use and problematic outcomes among rural junior high school students. *Addictive Behaviors, 4*, 91–93.

Castro, F. G., Newcomb, M. D., & Cadish, K. (1987). Lifestyle differences between young adult cocaine users and their nonuser peers. *Journal of Drug Education, 17*, 89–111.

Castro, J. (1986). Battling the enemy within. *Time*, March 17, 52–61.

Chassin, L. (1984). Adolescent substance use and abuse. *Advances in Child Behavioral Analysis and Therapy, 3*, 99–152.

Chiang, C. N., & Hawks, R. L. (1986). Implications of drug levels in body fluids: Basic concepts. In R. L. Hawks & C. N. Chiang (eds.), *Urine testing for drugs of abuse* (pp. 62–83). Rockville, MD: National Institute on Drug Abuse.

Christiansen, B. A., & Goldman, M. S. (1983). Alcohol-related expectancies versus demographic/background variables in the prediction of adolescent drinking. *Journal of Consulting and Clinical Psychology, 51*, 249–257.

Christiansen, B. A., Goldman, M. S., & Inn, A. (1982). Development of alcohol-related expectancies in adolescents: Separating pharmacological from social-learning influences. *Journal of Consulting and Clinical Psychology, 50*, 336–344.

Clarno, J. C. (1986). The impaired dentist: Recognition and treatment of the alcoholic and drug-dependent professional. *Dental Clinics of North America, 30*, s45–s52.

Clayton, R. R., & Ritter, C. (1985). The epidemiology of alcohol and drug abuse among adolescents. *Advances in Alcohol and Substance Abuse, 4*, 69–97.

Clayton, R. R., & Tuchfeld, B. S. (1982). The drug-crime debate: Obstacles in understanding the relationship. *Journal of Drug Issues, 12*, 153–165.

Clayton, R. R., Voss, H. L., Robbins, C., & Skinner, W. F. (1986). Gender differences in drug use: An epidemiological perspective. In B. A. Ray & M. C. Braude (eds.), *Women and drugs: A new era for research* (pp. 80–99). Rockville, MD: National Institute on Drug Abuse.

Clute, J. E. (1980). Aiding the "other victims" on the job. *Occupational Health and Safety*, February, 34–35, 38.

Cohen, S. (1984). Drugs in the workplace. *Journal of Clinical Psychiatry, 45*, 4–8.

Cohen, S. (1986). Drug urinalysis: Selected questions. *Drug Abuse and Alcoholism Newsletter, 15,* 10.

Cohen, S. (1987). Causes of the cocaine outbreak. In A. M. Washton & M. S. Gold (eds.), *Cocaine: A clinician's handbook* (pp. 3–9). New York: Guilford.

Consensus Summary (1986). *Interdisciplinary approaches to the problem of drug abuse in the workplace*. Rockville, MD: National Institute on Drug Abuse.

Conway, T. L., Ward, H. W., Vickers, R. R., & Rahe, R. H. (1981). Occupational stress and variation in cigarette, coffee, and alcohol consumption. *Journal of Health and Social Behavior, 22,* 155–165.

Cook, R., Walizer, D., & Mace, D. (1976). Illicit drug use in the Army: A social-organizational analysis. *Journal of Applied Psychology, 61,* 262–272.

Cosper, R. (1979). Drinking as conformity. *Journal of Studies on Alcohol, 40,* 868–891.

Cosper, R., & Hughes, F. (1982). So-called heavy drinking occupations. *Journal of Studies on Alcohol, 43,* 110–118.

Cronin-Stubbs, D., & Schaffner, J. W. (1985). Professional impairment: Strategies for managing the troubled nurse. *Nursing Administration Quarterly,* Spring, 44–54.

Cutter, H. S. G., & Fisher, J. C. (1980). Family experience and the motives for drinking. *International Journal of the Addictions, 15,* 339–358.

Donovan, D. M., & Marlatt, G. A. (1982). Reasons for drinking among DWI arrestees. *Addictive Behaviors, 7,* 423–426.

Donovan, J. E., & Jessor, R. (1983). Problem drinking and the dimensions of involvement with drugs: A Guttman scalogram analysis of adolescent drug use. *American Journal of Public Health, 73,* 543–552.

Donovan, J. E., & Jessor, R. (1985). Structure of problem behavior in adolescence and young adulthood. *Journal of Consulting and Clinical Psychology, 53,* 890–904.

Donovan, J. E., Jessor, R., & Jessor, L. (1983). Problem drinking in adolescence and young adulthood: A follow-up study. *Journal of Studies on Alcohol, 44,* 109–137.

DuPont, R. L. (1987). Cocaine in the workplace: The ticking time bomb. In A. M. Washton & M. S. Gold (eds.), *Cocaine: A clinician's handbook* (pp. 192–201). New York: Guilford.

DuPont, R. L., & Basen, M. M. (1980). Control of alcohol and drug abuse in industry: A literature review. *Public Health Reports, 95,* 137–148.

Engleking, P. R. (1986). About one-fourth of the Fortune 500 companies now screen applicants for drugs. *American Academy of Occupational Health Nursing, 34,* 417–419.

Estroff, T. W. (1987). Medical and biological consequences of cocaine abuse. In A. M. Washton & M. S. Gold (eds.), *Cocaine: A clinician's handbook* (pp. 23–32). New York: Guilford.

Fennell, M. L. (1984). Synergy, influence, and information in the adoption of administrative innovations. *Academy of Management Journal, 27*, 113–129.

Fillmore, K. M. (1984). Research as a handmaiden of policy: An appraisal of estimates of alcoholism and its cost in the workplace. *Journal of Public Health Policy*, March, 40–64.

Fimian, M. J., Zacherman, J., & McHardy, R. J. (1985). Substance abuse and teacher. *Journal of Drug Education, 15*, 139–155.

Fine, M., Akabas, S. H., & Bellinger, S. (1982). Cultures of drinking: A workplace perspective. *Social Work*, September, 436–440.

Frank, C. F. (1983). Where there's drug abuse. *Security Management*, September, 126–128.

Freedberg, E. J., & Johnston, W. E. (1979). Changes in feelings of job satisfaction among alcoholics induced by their employer to seek treatment. *Journal of Occupational Medicine, 21*, 549–552.

Freedman, D. A. (1987). As others see us: A case study in path analysis. *Journal of Educational Statistics, 12*, 101–128.

Freud, S. (1905). *Three essays on the theory of sexuality.* Standard Edition, Vol. 7 (1953). London: Hogarth.

Gampel, J. C., & Zeese, K. B. (1986). Are employers overdosing on drug testing? *Business and Society Review*, 34–38.

Gardner, A. W. (1982). Identifying and helping problem drinkers at work. *Journal of Social and Occupational Medicine, 32*, 171–179.

Gfroerer, J. (1985). Influence of privacy on self-reported drug use by youth. In B. A. Rouse, N. J. Kozel, & L. G. Richards (eds.), *Self-report methods of estimating drug use: Meeting current challenges to validity* (pp. 22–30). Rockville, MD: National Institute on Drug Abuse.

Glick, P. C., & Lin, S. (1986). More young adults are living with their parents: Who are they? *Journal of Marriage and the Family, 48*, 107–112.

Goffman, E. (1961). *Asylums: Essays on the social situation of mental patients and other inmates.* Garden City, NY: Anchor Books.

Gollob, H. F., & Reichardt, C. S. (1987). Taking account of time lags in causal models. *Child Development, 58*, 80–92.

Goodwin, D. W., Van Dusen, K. T., & Mednick, S. A. (eds.) (1984). *Longitudinal research in alcoholism.* Boston: Kluwer-Nijhoff.

Googins, B., & Kurtz, N. R. (1980). Factors inhibiting supervisory referrals to occupational alcoholism intervention programs. *Journal of Studies on Alcohol, 41*, 1196–1208.

Gordon, J. (1987). Drug testing as a productivity booster? *Training, 24*, 22–34.

Grinspoon, L., & Bakalar, J. B. (1976). *Cocaine: A drug and its social evolution*. New York: Basic Books.

Guinn, B. (1983). Job satisfaction, counterproductive behavior and circumstantial drug use among long-distance truckers. *Journal of Psychoactive Drugs, 15*, 185–188.

Gupta, N., & Beehr, T. A. (1979). Job stress and employee behaviors. *Organizational Behavior and Human Performance, 23*, 373–387.

Gupta, N., & Jenkins, G. D. (1984). Substance use as an employee response to the work environment. *Journal of Vocational Behavior, 24*, 84–93.

Haack, M. R., & Harford, T. C. (1984). Drinking patterns among student nurses. *International Journal of the Addictions, 19*, 577–583.

Hackman, J. R. & Lawler, E. E. (1971). Employee reactions to job characteristics. *Journal of Applied Psychology Monograph, 55*, 259–286.

Halikas, J. A., Weller, R. A., Morse, C. L., & Hoffman, R. G. (1984). Use of marijuana and other drugs among adult marijuana users: A longitudinal study. *Comprehensive Psychiatry, 25*, 63–70.

Harlow, L. L. (1985). *Behavior of some elliptical theory estimators with nonnormal data in a covariance structures framework: A Monte Carlo study*. Ph.D. dissertation, UCLA.

Harlow, L. L., Newcomb, M. D., & Bentler, P. M. (1986). Depression, self-derogation, substance use, and suicide ideation: Lack of purpose in life as a mediational factor. *Journal of Clinical Psychology, 42*, 5–21.

Harrell, A. V. (1985). Validation of self-report: The research record. In B. A. Rouse, N. J. Kozel, & L. G. Richards (eds.), *Self-report methods of estimating drug use: Meeting current challenges to validity* (pp. 12–21). Rockville, MD: National Institute on Drug Abuse.

Havighurst, R. J. (1952). *Developmental tasks and education*. New York: McKay.

Havighurst, R. J. (1972). *Developmental tasks and education* (3d ed.). New York: McKay.

Hawkins, M. R., Kruzich, D. J., & Smith, J. D. (1985). Prevalence of polydrug use among alcoholic soldiers. *American Journal of Drug and Alcohol Abuse, 11*, 27–35.

Hawks, R. L. (1986). Establishing a urinalysis program—prior considerations. In R. L. Hawks & C. N. Chiang (eds.), *Urine testing for drugs of abuse* (pp. 1–4). Rockville, MD: National Institute on Drug Abuse.

Hawks, R. L., & Chiang, C. N. (eds.) (1986). *Urine testing for drugs of abuse*. Rockville, MD: National Institute on Drug Abuse.

Hays, R. D., Widaman, K. F., DiMatteo, M. R., & Stacy, A. W. (1987). Structural equation models of current drug use: Are appropriate models so simple(x)? *Journal of Personality and Social Psychology, 52*, 134–144.

Herold, D. M., & Conlon, E. J. (1981). Work factors as potential causal agents of alcohol abuse. *Journal of Drug Issues, 11,* 337–356.

Heyman, M. M. (1976). Referral to alcoholism programs in industry. *Journal of Studies on Alcohol, 37,* 900–907.

Hirschi, T., & Selvin, H. (1973). *Principles of survey analysis.* New York: Free Press.

Hore, B. D., & Plant, M. A. (eds.) (1981). *Alcohol problems in employment.* London: Croom Helm.

Huba, G. J., & Bentler, P. M. (1982). A developmental theory of drug use: Derivation and assessment of a causal modeling approach. In B. P. Baltes & O. G. Brim, Jr. (eds.), *Life-span development and behavior,* Vol. 4 (pp. 147–203). New York: Academic Press.

Huba, G. J., & Bentler, P. M. (1983a). Causal models of the development of law abidance and its relationship to psychosocial factors and drug use. In W. S. Laufer & J. M. Day (eds.), *Personality theory, moral development, and criminal behavior* (pp. 165–215). Lexington, MA: Heath.

Huba, G. J., & Bentler, P. M. (1983b). Test of a drug use causal model using asymptotically distribution free methods. *Journal of Drug Education, 13,* 3–14.

Huba, G. J., & Bentler, P. M. (1984). Causal models of personality, peer culture characteristics, drug use, and criminal behaviors over a five-year span. In D. W. Goodwin, K. T. Van Dusen, & S. A. Mednick (eds.), *Longitudinal research in alcoholism* (pp. 73–94). Boston: Kluwer-Nijhoff.

Huba, G. J., & Harlow, L. L. (1983). Comparison of maximum likelihood, generalized least squares, ordinary least squares, and asymptotically distribution free parameter estimates in drug abuse latent variable causal models. *Journal of Drug Education, 13,* 387–404.

Huba, G. J., Newcomb, M. D., & Bentler, P. M. (1981). Comparison of canonical correlation and interbattery factor analysis on sensation seeking and drug use domains. *Applied Psychological Measurement, 5,* 291–306.

Huba, G. J., Newcomb, M. D., & Bentler, P. M. (1986). Adverse drug experiences and drug use behaviors: A one-year longitudinal study of adolescents. *Journal of Pediatric Psychology, 11,* 203–219.

Huba, G. J., Wingard, J. A., & Bentler, P. M. (1981). A comparison of two latent variable causal models for adolescent drug use. *Journal of Personality and Social Psychology, 40,* 180–193.

Hughes, J. P. W. (1975). Alcoholism in industry. *Medical Science Law, 15,* 22–27.

Jenkins, C. D. (1976a). Recent evidence supporting psychologic and social risk factors for coronary disease, part I. *New England Journal of Medicine, 294,* 987–994.

Jenkins, C. D. (1976b). Recent evidence supporting psychologic and social risk factors for coronary disease, part II. *New England Journal of Medicine, 294,* 1033–1038.

Jenkins, G. D. (1984). Substance use as an employee response to the work environment. *Journal of Vocational Behavior, 24,* 84–93.

Jessor, R., & Jessor, S. L. (1977). *Problem behavior and psychosocial development.* New York: Academic Press.

Jessor, R., & Jessor, S. L. (1978). Theory testing in longitudinal research on marijuana use. In D. B. Kandel (ed.), *Longitudinal research on drug use: Empirical findings and methodological issues* (pp. 41–71). Washington, DC: Hemisphere.

Johnson, L. (1981). Union responses to alcoholism. *Journal of Drug Issues, 11,* 263–277.

Johnston, L. D., & O'Malley, P. M. (1986). Why do the nation's students use drugs and alcohol? Self-reported reasons from nine national surveys. *Journal of Drug Issues, 16,* 29–66.

Johnston, L. D., O'Malley, P. M., & Bachman, J. G. (1987). *National trends in drug use and related factors among American high school students and young adults, 1975–1986.* Rockville, MD: National Institute on Drug Abuse.

Jones, C. L., & Battjes, R. J. (eds.) (1985). *Etiology of drug abuse: Implications for prevention.* Rockville, MD: National Institute on Drug Abuse.

Jöreskog, K. G., & Sörbom, D. (1985). *LISREL VI: User's guide.* Mooreville, IN: Scientific Software.

Kaestner, E., Frank, B., Marel, R., & Schmeidler, J. (1986). Substance use among females in New York State: Catching up with the males. *Advances in Alcohol and Substance Abuse, 5,* 29–49.

Kalant, O. J. (1980). Sex differences in alcohol and drug problems—some highlights. In O. J. Kalant (ed.), *Alcohol and drug problems in women: Research advances in alcohol and drug problems,* Vol. 5. New York: Plenum.

Kamali, K., & Steer, R. A. (1976). Polydrug use by high-school students: Involvement and correlates. *International Journal of the Addictions, 11,* 337–343.

Kandel, D. B. (1975). Stages in adolescent involvement in drug use. *Science, 190,* 912–914.

Kandel, D. B. (ed.) (1978). *Longitudinal research on drug use: Empirical findings and methodological issues.* Washington, DC: Hemisphere.

Kandel, D. B. (1980). Drug and drinking behavior among youth. *Annual Review of Sociology, 6,* 235–285.

Kandel, D. B. (1984). Marijuana users in young adulthood. *Archives of General Psychiatry, 41,* 200–209.

Kandel, D. B., Davies, M., Karus, D., & Yamaguchi, K. (1986). The consequences in young adulthood of adolescent drug involvement. *Archives of General Psychiatry, 43,* 746–754.

Kandel, D. B., & Faust, R. (1975). Sequence and stages in patterns of adolescent drug use. *Archives of General Psychiatry, 32,* 923–932.

Kandel, D. B., Kessler, R. C., & Margulies, R. Z. (1978). Antecedents of adolescent initiation into stages of drug use: A developmental analysis. In D. B. Kandel (ed.), *Longitudinal research on drug use: Empirical findings and methodological issues* (pp. 73–98). Washington, DC: Hemisphere.

Kandel D. B., & Logan, J. A. (1984). Periods of risk for initiation, stabilization, and decline in drug use from adolescence to early adulthood. *American Journal of Public Health, 74,* 660–666.

Kandel, D. B., Murphy, D., & Karus, D. (1985). Cocaine use in young adulthood: Patterns of use and psychosocial correlates. In N. J. Kozel & E. H. Adams (eds.), *Cocaine use in America: Epidemiologic and clinical perspectives* (pp. 76–110). Rockville, MD: National Institute on Drug Abuse.

Kaplan, H. B. (1975). Increase in self-rejection as an antecedent of deviant responses. *Journal of Youth and Adolescence, 4,* 438–458.

Kaplan, H. B. (1985). Testing a general theory of drug abuse and other deviant adaptations. *Journal of Drug Issues, 15,* 477–492.

Kaplan, H. B. (1986). *Social psychology self-referent behavior.* New York: Plenum.

Kendall, R. M. (1986). Drug testing: Societal safeguard or invasion of privacy? *Occupational Hazards,* August, 43–45.

Knox, J., & Fenley, A. (1985). Alcohol problems at work: Some medical and legal considerations. *Psychiatrists' Report, 14* (1), 32–35.

Korcok, M. (1983). Worksite anti-alcoholism saves jobs, money. *Medical News,* May, 2427–2433.

Kozel, N. J., & Adams, E. H. (eds.) (1985). *Cocaine use in America: Epidemiologic and clinical perspectives.* Rockville, MD: National Institute on Drug Abuse.

Kraus, J. F., Borhani, N. O., & Franti, C. F. (1980). Socioeconomic status, ethnicity, and risk of coronary disease. *American Journal of Epidemiology, 111,* 407–414.

Kurtz, N. R., Googins, B., & Howard, W. C. (1984). Measuring the success of occupational alcoholism programs. *Journal of Studies on Alcohol, 45,* 33–45.

Labouvie, E. W. (1986). The coping function of adolescent alcohol and drug use. In R. K. Silbereisen, K. Eyferth, & G. Rudinger (eds.), *Development as action in context: Problem behavior and normal youth development* (pp. 229–239). Berlin: Springer-Verlag.

Labouvie, E. W., & McGee, C. R. (1986). Relation of personality to alcohol and drug use in adolescence. *Journal of Consulting and Clinical Psychology, 54,* 289–293.

Landis, B. I. (1986). Discharging the drug dealer . . . and making it stick. *Security Management,* August, 68–70.

Lanphier, C. M., & McCauley, G. F. (1985). Prevalence and consequences of nonmedical use of drugs among Canadian forces personnel: 1982. *American Journal of Drug and Alcohol Abuse, 11,* 231–247.

Laufer, W. S., & Day, J. M. (eds.) (1983). *Personality theory, moral development, and criminal behavior.* Lexington, MA: Heath.

Lederer, J. F. (1985). Six unresolved safety problems. *Professional Safety,* July 21–25.

Lettieri, D. J. (1985). Drug abuse: A review of explanations and models of explanations. *Advances in Alcohol and Substance Abuse, 4,* 9–40.

Lettieri, D. J., Sayers, M., & Pearson, H. W. (eds.) (1980). *Theories on drug abuse: Selected contemporary perspectives.* Rockville, MD: National Institute on Drug Abuse.

Levenson, R. W., & Gottman, J. M. (1978). Toward the assessment of social competence. *Journal of Consulting and Clinical Psychology, 46,* 453–462.

Levy, S. I. (1973). A case study of drug-related criminal behavior in business and industry. In J. M. Sher (ed.), *Drug abuse in industry.* Springfield, IL: Thomas.

Levy, S. R., & Rasher, S. P. (1981). Relation of intensity and frequency of student drug use to reasons for use. *Journal of School Health,* May, 341–346.

Lewy, R. (1983). Preemployment qualitative urine toxicology screening. *Journal of Occupational Medicine, 25,* 579–580.

Lings, S., Jensen, J., Christensen, S., & Moller, J. T. (1984). Occupational accidents and alcohol. *International Archives of Occupational and Environmental Health, 53,* 321–329.

Lodge, J. H. (1983). Taking drugs on the job. *Time,* August, 52–60.

Loehlin, J. C. (1987) *Latent variable models: An introduction to factor, path, and structural analysis.* Hillsdale, NJ: Erlbaum.

Long, J. V. F., & Scherl, D. J. (1984). Developmental antecedents of compulsive drug use: A report on the literature. *Journal of Psychoactive Drugs, 16,* 169–182.

Lyles, R. I. (1984). Should the next drug bust be in your company? *Personnel Journal,* October, 46–49.

Lyons, T. F. (1971). Role clarity, need for clarity, satisfaction, tension, and withdrawal. *Organizational Behavior and Human Performance, 6,* 99–110.

Lyons, T. F. (1972). Turnover and absenteeism: A review of relationships and shared correlates. *Personnel Psychology, 25,* 271–281.

MacCallum, R. (1986). Specification searches in covariance structure analyses. *Psychological Bulletin, 100,* 107–120.

MacKenzie, R. G., Cheng, M., & Haftel, A. J. (1987). The clinical utility and evaluation of drug screening techniques. *Pediatric Clinics of North America, 34,* 423–436.

Maddahian, E., Newcomb, M. D., & Bentler, P. M. (1986). Adolescents' substance use: Impact of income, ethnicity, and availability. *Advances in Alcohol and Substance Abuse, 5,* 63–78.

Madonia, J. F. (1984). Managerial responses to alcohol and drug abuse among employees. *Personnel Administrator,* June, 134–139.

Mangione, T. W., & Quinn, R. P. (1975). Short note: Job satisfaction, counterproductive behavior, and drug use at work. *Journal of Applied Psychology, 60,* 114–116.

Manno, J. E. (1986a). Interpretation of urinalysis results. In R. L. Hawks & C. N. Chiang (eds.), *Urine testing for drugs of abuse* (pp. 54–61). Rockville, MD: National Institute on Drug Abuse.

Manno, J. E. (1986b). Specimen collection and handling. In R. L. Hawks & C. N. Chiang (eds.), *Urine testing for drugs of abuse* (pp. 24–29). Rockville, MD: National Institute on Drug Abuse.

Margulies, R. Z., Kessler, R. C., & Kandel, D. B. (1977). A longitudinal study of onset of drinking among high school students. *Journal of Studies on Alcohol, 38,* 897–912.

Markowitz, M. (1984). Alcohol misuse as a response to perceived power-lessness in the organization. *Journal of Studies on Alcohol, 45,* 225–227.

Marlatt, G. A., & Rohsenow, D. J. (1980). Cognitive processes in alcohol use: Expectancy and the balanced placebo design. In N. K. Mello (ed.), *Advances in substance abuse: Behavioral and biological research.* Greenwich, CN: JAI Press.

Masi, D. (1979). Combating alcoholism in the workplace. *Health and Social Work, 4,* 42–59.

McCarthy, W. J., & Newcomb, M. D. (1987). Cognitive and behavioral self-efficacy: Results of hierarchical confirmatory analyses of 24 scales of personal effectiveness. Under editorial review.

McClellan, K. (1984). Work-based drug programs. *Journal of Psychoactive Drugs, 16,* 285–303.

McDonnell, R., & Maynard, A. (1985). The costs of alcohol misuse. *British Journal of Addiction, 80,* 27–35.

Mello, N. K. (ed.) (1980). *Advances in substance abuse: Behavioral and biological research.* Greenwich, CN: JAI Press.

Milbourn, G., Jr. (1984). Alcoholism, drug abuse, job stress: What small business can do. *American Journal of Small Business, 8,* 36–48.

Miller, J. D., Cisin, I. H., Gardner-Keaton, H., Harrell, A. V., Wirtz, P. W., Abelson, H. I., & Fishburne, P. M. (1983). *National survey on drug abuse: Main findings 1982*. Rockville, MD: National Institute on Drug Abuse.

Mills, C. J., & Noyes, H. L. (1984). Patterns and correlates of initial and subsequent drug use among adolescents. *Journal of Consulting and Clinical Psychology, 52*, 231–243.

Moberg, D. P., Krause, W. K., & Klein, P. E. (1982). Posttreatment drinking behavior among inpatients from an industrial alcoholism program. *International Journal of the Addictions, 17*, 549–567.

Murry, D. M., & Perry, C. L. (1985). The prevention of adolescent drug abuse: Implications of etiological, developmental, behavioral, and environmental models. In C. L. Jones & R. J. Battjes (eds.), *Etiology of drug abuse: Implications for prevention* (pp. 236–256). Rockville, MD: National Institute on Drug Abuse.

Newcomb, M. D. (1984). Sexual behavior, responsiveness, and attitudes among women: A test of two theories. *Journal of Sex and Marital Therapy, 10*, 272–286.

Newcomb, M. D. (1986a). Cohabitation, marriage, and divorce among adolescents and young adults. *Journal of Social and Personal Relationships, 3*, 473–494.

Newcomb, M. D. (1986b). Nuclear attitudes and reactions: Associations with depression, drug use, and quality of life. *Journal of Personality and Social Psychology, 50*, 906–920.

Newcomb, M. D. (1987). Consequences of teenage drug use: The transition from adolescence to young adulthood. *Drugs and Society, 4*, 25–60.

Newcomb, M. D. (in press). Nuclear anxiety and psychosocial functioning among young adults. *Basic and Applied Social Psychology*.

Newcomb, M. D., & Bentler, P. M. (1985). The impact of high school substance use on choice of young adult living environment and career direction. *Journal of Drug Education, 15*, 253–261.

Newcomb, M. D., & Bentler, P. M. (1986a). Cocaine use among adolescents: Longitudinal associations with social context, psychopathology, and use of other substances. *Addictive Behaviors, 11*, 263–273.

Newcomb, M. D., & Bentler, P. M. (1986b). Cocaine use among young adults. *Advances in Alcohol and Substance Abuse, 6*, 73–96.

Newcomb, M. D., & Bentler, P. M. (1986c). Drug use, educational aspirations, and workforce involvement: The transition from adolescence to young adulthood. *American Journal of Community Psychology, 14*, 303–321.

Newcomb, M. D., & Bentler, P. M. (1986d). Frequency and sequence of drug use: A longitudinal study from early adolescence to young adulthood. *Journal of Drug Education, 16*, 101–120.

Newcomb, M. D., & Bentler, P. M. (1986e). Loneliness and social support: A confirmatory hierarchical analysis. *Personality and Social Psychology Bulletin, 12,* 520–535.

Newcomb, M. D., & Bentler, P. M. (1986f). Substance use and ethnicity: Differential impact of peer and adult model. *Journal of Psychology, 120,* 83–95.

Newcomb, M. D., & Bentler, P. M. (1987a). Changes in drug use from high school to young adulthood: Effects of living arrangement and current life pursuit. *Journal of Applied Developmental Psychology, 8,* 221–246.

Newcomb, M. D., & Bentler, P. M. (1987b). The impact of late adolescent substance use on young adult health status and utilization of health services: A structural-equation model over four years. *Social Science and Medicine, 24,* 71–82.

Newcomb, M. D., & Bentler, P. M. (1987c). Self-report methods of assessing health status and health service utilization: A hierarchical confirmatory analysis. *Multivariate Behavioral Research.*

Newcomb, M. D., & Bentler, P. M. (1988a). *Consequences of adolescent drug use: Impact on the lives of young adults.* Beverly Hills, CA: Sage.

Newcomb, M. D., & Bentler, P. M. (1988b). Impact of adolescent drug use and social support on problems of young adults: A longitudinal study. *Journal of Abnormal Psychology.*

Newcomb, M. D., & Bentler, P. M. (in press a). Antecedents and consequences of cocaine use: An eight-year study from early adolescence to young adulthood. In L. Robins (ed.), *Straight and devious pathways from childhood to adulthood.* Cambridge, MA: Cambridge Press.

Newcomb, M. D., & Bentler, P. M. (in press b). The impact of family context, deviant attitudes, and emotional distress on adolescent drug use: Longitudinal latent variable analyses of mothers and their children. *Journal of Research in Personality.*

Newcomb, M. D., Bentler, P. M., & Collins, C. (1986). Alcohol use and dissatisfaction with self and life: A longitudinal analysis of young adults. *Journal of Drug Issues, 16,* 479–494.

Newcomb, M. D., Bentler, P. M., & Fahy, B. (1987). Cocaine use and psychopathology: Associations among young adults. *International Journal of the Addictions, 22,* 1167–1188.

Newcomb, M. D., & Chou, C.-P. (1987). Social support among young adults: A multitrait-multimethod assessment of quantity and satisfaction within six life areas. Under editorial review.

Newcomb, M. D., Chou, C.-P., Bentler, P. M., & Huba, G. J. (in press). Cognitive motivations for drug use among adolescents: Longitudinal tests of gender differences and predictors of change in drug use. *Journal of Counseling Psychology.*

Newcomb, M. D., Fahy, B., & Skager, R. (in press). Reasons to avoid drug use among teenagers: Associations with actual drug use and implications for prevention among different demographic groups. *Journal of Alcohol and Drug Education*.

Newcomb, M. D., & Harlow, L. L. (1986). Life events and substance use among adolescents: Mediating effects of perceived loss of control and meaninglessness in life. *Journal of Personality and Social Psychology, 51*, 564–577.

Newcomb, M. D., Huba, G. J., & Bentler, P. M. (1981). A multidimensional assessment of stressful life events among adolescents: Derivation and correlates. *Journal of Health and Social Behavior, 22*, 400–415.

Newcomb, M. D., Huba, G. J., & Bentler, P. M. (1983). Mother's influence on the drug use of their children: Confirmatory tests of direct modeling and mediational theories. *Developmental Psychology, 19*, 714–726.

Newcomb, M. D., Huba, G. J., & Bentler, P. M. (1986). Life change events among adolescents: An empirical consideration of some methodological issues. *Journal of Nervous and Mental Disease, 174*, 280–289.

Newcomb, M. D., Maddahian, E., & Bentler, P. M. (1986). Risk factors for drug use among adolescents: Concurrent and longitudinal analyses. *American Journal of Public Health, 76*, 525–531.

Newcomb, M. D., Maddahian, E., Skager, R., & Bentler, P. M. (1987). Substance abuse and psychosocial risk factors among teenagers: Associations with sex, age, ethnicity, and type of school. *American Journal of Drug and Alcohol Abuse, 13*, 413–433.

Newcomb, M. D., McCarthy, W. J., & Bentler, P. M. (1987). Cigarette smoking, academic lifestyle, and self-efficacy: An eight-year study from early adolescence to young adulthood. Under editorial review.

Newman, F. H. (1983). Industry's new Achilles' heel. *Security Management*, December, 13–18.

NIDA (National Institute on Drug Abuse) (1986). *Capsules: Overview of the 1985 national household survey on drug abuse*. Rockville, MD: National Institute on Drug Abuse.

NIDA (National Institute on Drug Abuse) (1987). *National household survey on drug abuse: Population estimates 1985*. Rockville, MD: National Institute on Drug Abuse.

Nurco, D. N. (1985). A discussion of validity. In B. A. Rouse, N. J. Kozel, & L. G. Richards (eds.), *Self-report methods of estimating drug use: Meeting current challenges to validity* (pp. 4–11). Rockville, MD: National Institute on Drug Abuse.

O'Donnell, J. A., & Clayton, R. R. (1982). The stepping-stone hypothesis: Marijuana, heroin, and causality. *Chemical Dependencies: Behavioral and Biomedical Issues, 4*, 229–241.

Olkinuora, M. (1984). Alcoholism and occupation. *Scandinavian Journal of Work and Environmental Health, 10,* 511–515.

Olson, L. (1986). Corporate America's hidden cocaine crisis. *Working Woman,* March, 122–125, 128, 145.

Osgood, D. W. (1985). *The drug-crime connection and the generality and stability of deviance*. Paper presented at the Meetings of the American Society of Criminology.

Oskamp, S., DeRyke, S., Carlson, M., Kelsoe, P., McKeever, C., Murphy, G., Okada, M., Phillips, B., Shira, L., & Sobolew-Shubin, A. (1987). *Current attitudes toward drug testing under various circumstances*. Paper presented at the Western Psychological Association, Long Beach, CA, April 1987.

Palmer, P. V. (1983). The Air Canada programme for rehabilitation of the alcoholic employee/pilot. *Aviation, Space and Environmental Medicine,* July, 592–594.

Partridge, R. W., & Reed, M. C. (1980). Alcohol and drug problems in the workplace. *Journal of Psychedelic Drugs, 12,* 71–72.

Paton, S., Kessler, R. C., & Kandel, D. B. (1977). Depressive mood and illegal drug use: A longitudinal analysis. *Journal of Genetic Psychology, 131,* 267–289.

Pechacek, T. F., Murray, D. M., Luepker, R. V., Mittelmark, M. B., Johnson, C. A., & Shutz, J. M. (1984). Measurement of adolescent smoking behavior: Rationale and methods. *Journal of Behavioral Medicine, 7,* 123–140.

Pentz, M. A. (1985). Social competence and self-efficacy as determinants of substance use in adolescence. In S. Shiffman & T. A. Wills (eds.), *Coping and substance use* (pp. 117–142). Orlando, FL: Academic Press.

Plant, M. A. (1977). Alcoholism and occupation: A review. *British Journal of Addiction, 72,* 309–316.

Plant, M. A. (1978). Occupation and alcoholism: Cause or effect? A controlled study of recruits to the drink trade. *International Journal of the Addictions, 13,* 605–626.

Plant, M. A. (1979). Occupations, drinking patterns and alcohol-related problems: Conclusions from a follow-up study. *British Journal of Addiction, 74,* 267–273.

Plant, M. A. (1981). Risk factors in employment. In B. D. Hore & M. A. Plant (eds.), *Alcohol problems in employment*. London: Croom Helm.

Putnam, S. L., & Stout, R. L. (1982). Union-related correlates of employee referrals to an occupational alcoholism project in a health maintenance organization. *Journal of Occupational Medicine, 24,* 225–233.

Quayle, D. (1983). American productivity: The devastating effect of alcoholism and drug abuse. *American Psychologist, 38,* 454–458.

Ray, B. A., & Braude, M. C. (eds.) (1986). *Women and drugs: A new era for research*. Rockville, MD: National Institute on Drug Abuse.

Robins, L. (ed.) (in press). *Straight and devious pathways from childhood to adulthood*. Cambridge, MA: Cambridge Press.

Robins, L. N. (1984). The natural history of adolescent drug use. *American Journal of Public Health, 74*, 656–657.

Robins, L. N., & Przybeck, T. R. (1985). Age of onset of drug use as a factor in drug and other disorders. In C. L. Jones & R. L. Battjes (eds.), *Etiology of drug abuse: Implications for prevention* (pp. 178–192). Rockville, MD: National Institute on Drug Abuse.

Roman, P. M. (1981). Job characteristics and the identification of deviant drinking. *Journal of Drug Issues, 11*, 357–364.

Rothberg, J. M., & Chloupek, R. J. (1978). A longitudinal study of military performance subsequent to civilian drug use. *American Journal of Public Health, 68*, 743–747.

Rouse, B. A., Kozel, N. J., & Richards, L. G. (eds.) (1985). *Self-report methods of estimating drug use: Meeting current challenges to validity*. Rockville, MD: National Institute on Drug Abuse.

Russell, D., Peplau, L. A., & Cutrona, C. E. (1980). The revised UCLA loneliness scale: Concurrent and discriminant validity evidence. *Journal of Personality and Social Psychology, 39*, 472–480.

Sadava, S. W. (1985). Problem behavior theory and consumption and consequences of alcohol use. *Journal of Studies on Alcohol, 46*, 392–397.

Sadava, S. W. (1987). Interactional theories. In H. T. Blane & K. E. Leonard (eds.), *Psychological theories of drinking and alcoholism*. New York: Guilford.

Sadava, S. W., & Secord, M. J. (1984). *Problem drinking in context*. Paper presented at the International Congress of Psychology, Acapulco, Mexico, August 1984.

Sadava, S. W., & Thompson, M. M. (in press). Loneliness, social drinking, and vulnerability to alcohol problems. *Canadian Journal of Science*.

Sarason, B. R., Shearin, E. N., Pierce, G. R., & Sarason, I. G. (1987). Interrelations of social support measures. *Journal of Personality and Social Psychology, 52*, 813–832.

Satorra, A., & Bentler, P. M. (1987). Robustness properties of ML statistics in covariance structure analysis. Under editorial review.

Schachter, V., & Geidt, T. E. (1985). Cracking down on drugs. *Across the Board*, November, 28–37.

Schilling, M. E., & Carman, R. S. (1978). Internal-external control and motivations for alcohol use among high school students. *Psychological Reports, 42*, 1088–1090.

Schmidt, N., & Sermat, V. (1983). Measuring loneliness in different relationships. *Journal of Personality and Social Psychology, 44,* 1038–1047.

Schreier, J. W. (1987). *Substance abuse in organizations, 1971–1986: Realities, trends, reactions*. Milwaukee, WI: Far Cliffs Consulting.

Schwartz, S. (1984). A study of drug discipline policies in secondary schools. *Adolescence, 19,* 323–333.

Seeman, M., & Anderson, C. S. (1983). Alienation and alcohol: The role of work, mastery, and community in drinking behavior. *American Sociological Review, 48,* 60–77.

Segal, B. (1986). Intervention and prevention of drug-taking behavior: A need for divergent approaches. *International Journal of the Addictions, 21,* 165–173.

Segal, B., Huba, G. J., & Singer, J. (1980). Reasons for drug and alcohol use by college students. *International Journal of the Addictions, 15,* 489–498.

Sher, J. M. (ed.) (1973). *Drug abuse in industry*. Springfield, IL: Thomas.

Shiffman, S., & Wills, T. A. (eds.) (1985). *Coping and substance abuse*. Orlando, FL: Academic Press.

Shirley, C. E. (1984). Alcoholism and drug abuse in the workplace. *Office Administration and Automation*, November, 24–27, 90.

Shore, E. R. (1985). Alcohol consumption rates among managers and professionals. *Journal of Studies on Alcohol, 46,* 153–156.

Shore, E. R. (1986). Norms regarding drinking behavior in the business environment. *Journal of Social Psychology, 125,* 735–741.

Siegel, R. K. (1987). Cocaine smoking: Nature and extent of coca paste and cocaine free-base abuse. In A. M. Washton & M. S. Gold (eds.), *Cocaine: A clinician's handbook* (pp. 175–191). New York: Guilford.

Slattery, M., Alderson, M. R., & Bryant, J. S. (1986). The occupational risks of alcoholism. *International Journal of the Addictions, 21,* 929–936.

Smith, D. E., & Seymour, R. (1985). A clinical approach to the impaired health professional. *International Journal of the Addictions, 20,* 713–722.

Smith, G. M. (1980). Perceived effects of substance use: A general theory. In D. J. Lettieri, M. Sayers, & H. W. Pearson (eds.), *Theories on drug abuse: Selected contemporary perspectives* (pp. 50–58). Rockville, MD: National Institute on Drug Abuse.

Smith, G. M., & Fogg, C. P. (1978). Psychological predictors of early use, late use and non-use of marijuana among teenage students. In D. B. Kandel (ed.), *Longitudinal research on drug use: Empirical findings and methodological issues* (pp. 101–113). Washington, DC: Hemisphere.

Smith, R. (1981). Alcohol and work: A promising approach. *British Medical Journal, 283,* 1108–1110.

Steele, P. D. (1981). Labor perceptions of drug use and drug programs in the workplace. *Journal of Drug Issues, 11,* 279–292.

Stein, J. A., Newcomb, M. D., & Bentler, P. M. (1986a). The relationship of gender, social conformity, and substance use: A longitudinal study. *Bulletin of the Society of Psychologists in Addictive Behaviors, 5,* 125–138.

Stein, J. A., Newcomb, M. D., & Bentler, P. M. (1986b). Stability and change in personality: A longitudinal study from early adolescence to young adulthood. *Journal of Research in Personality, 20,* 276–291.

Stein, J. A., Newcomb, M. D., & Bentler, P. M. (1987a). An eight-year study of multiple influences on drug use and drug use consequences. *Journal of Personality and Social Psychology, 53,* 1094–1105.

Stein, J. A., Newcomb, M. D., & Bentler, P. M. (1987b). Personality and drug use: Reciprocal effects across four years. *Personality and Individual Differences, 8,* 419–430.

Stein, J. A., Newcomb, M. D., & Bentler, P. M. (in press). The structure of drug use behaviors and consequences among young adults: A multitrait-multimethod assessment of frequency, quantity, worksite, and problem substance use. *Journal of Applied Psychology.*

Stern, M. P., Haskel, W. L., Wood, P. D. S., Osann, K. E., King, A. B., & Farqubar, J. W. (1975). Affluence and cardiovascular risk factors in Mexican Americans and other whites in three northern California communities. *Journal of Chronic Disease, 28,* 623–636.

Sullivan, E. J. (1986). Cost savings of retaining chemically dependent nurses. *Nursing Economics, 4,* 179–182, 200.

Tanaka, J. S., & Huba, G. J. (1984). Confirmatory hierarchical factor analyses of psychological distress measures. *Journal of Personality and Social Psychology, 46,* 621–635.

Tennant, F. S., Detels, R., & Clark, V. (1975). Some childhood antecedents of drug and alcohol abuse. *American Journal of Epidemiology, 102,* 377–384.

Thorne, C. R., & DeBlassie, R. R. (1985). Adolescent substance abuse. *Adolescence, 20,* 335–347.

Tobler, N. S. (1986). Meta-analysis of 143 adolescent drug prevention programs: Quantitative outcome results of program participants compared to a control or comparison group. *Journal of Drug Issues, 16,* 537–568.

Traub, S. H. (1983). Characteristics of female college student drug use. *Journal of Drug Education, 13,* 177–186.

Trice, H. M., & Beyer, J. M. (1982). Social control in worksettings: Using the constructive confrontation strategy with problem-drinking employees. *Journal of Drug Issues, 12,* 21–49.

Trice, H. M., & Beyer, J. M. (1984). Work-related outcomes of the constructive-confrontation strategy in a job-based alcoholism program. *Journal of Studies on Alcohol, 45,* 393–404.

Vicary, J. R., & Lerner, J. V. (1983). Longitudinal perspectives on drug use: Analyses from the New York longitudinal study. *Journal of Drug Education, 13,* 279–285.

Vicary, J. R., Mansfield, P. K., Cohn, M. D., Koch, P. B., & Young, E. W. (1985). Substance use among women in the workplace. *Occupational Health Nursing,* October, 491–495.

Violanti, J., Marshall, J., & Howe, B. (1983). Police occupational demands, psychological distress and the coping function of alcohol. *Journal of Occupational Medicine, 25,* 455–458.

Waddell, B. (1986). Corporate response to the drug epidemic. *Business Forum,* Summer, 32.

Walker, K., & Shain, M. (1983). Employee assistance programming: In search of effective interventions for the problem-drinking employee. *British Journal of Addiction, 78,* 291–303.

Walsh, D. C., & Hingson, R. W. (1985). Where to refer employees for treatment of drinking problems. *Journal of Occupational Medicine, 27,* 745–752.

Washton, A. M., & Gold, M. S. (1984). Chronic cocaine abuse: Evidence for adverse effects on health and functioning. *Psychiatric Annals, 14,* 733–739.

Washton, A. M., & Gold, M. S. (1987). Recent trends in cocaine abuse as seen from the "800 COCAINE" Hotline. In A. M. Washton & M. S. Gold (eds.), *Cocaine: A clinician's handbook* (pp. 10–22). New York: Guilford.

Watson, J., Mattera, G., Morales, R., Kunitz, S. J., & Lynch, R. (1985). Alcohol use among migrant laborers in western New York. *Journal of Studies on Alcohol, 46,* 403–411.

Wetli, C. V. (1987). Fatal reactions to cocaine. In A. M. Washton & M. S. Gold (eds.), *Cocaine: A clinician's handbook* (pp. 33–54). New York: Guilford.

Willette, R. E. (1986). Choosing a laboratory. In R. L. Hawks & C. N. Chiang (eds.), *Urine testing for drugs of abuse* (pp. 13–19). Rockville, MD: National Institute on Drug Abuse.

Wingard, J. A., Huba, G. J., & Bentler, P. M. (1979). The relationship of personality structure to patterns of adolescent substance use. *Multivariate Behavioral Research, 14,* 131–143.

Wright, P. C. (1983). How managers should approach alcoholism and drug abuse in the work place. *Business Quarterly,* Winter, 53–56.

Yamaguchi, K., & Kandel, D. B. (1984). Patterns of drug use from adolescence to young adulthood: III. Predictors of progression. *American Journal of Public Health, 74,* 673–681.

Yamaguchi, K., & Kandel, D. B. (1985a). Dynamic relationships between premarital cohabitation and illicit drug use: An event history analysis of role selection and role socialization. *American Sociological Review, 50,* 530–546.

Yamaguchi, K., & Kandel, D. B. (1985b). On the resolution of role incompatibility: A life event history analysis of family roles and marijuana use. *American Journal of Sociology, 90,* 1284–1325.

Zucker, R. A., & Gomberg, E. S. L. (1986). Etiology of alcoholism reconsidered: The case for a biopsychosocial approach. *American Psychologist, 41,* 783–793.

INDEX